Praise for *Why Do They Act That Way?*

"Walsh focuses on how adolescent brain development and chemistry lead to troubling behaviors. He shows parents how to respond constructively to traits like risk taking, sullenness, and refusal to follow rules. An engaging narrative style and insight into adolescents' minds make Walsh's book enjoyable as well as informative."

—*Library Journal*

"Dr. Walsh is a teacher, scientist, therapist, and parent and all of these roles enable him to deliver a powerful, practical book on the teenage brain. Usually when I study the brain, my eyes cross and I fall asleep, but Walsh is a storyteller with the gifts of simplicity and clarity. This book is an easy read, but its message is fresh, nuanced, and important. I recommend it to all parents who ask themselves, 'Why do they act this way?'"

—Mary Pipher, PhD, author, *Reviving Ophelia*

"Teenagers . . . those baffling and scary creatures your adorable kids turned into, leaving you puzzled and angry all the time. Dave Walsh's weaving together of current understanding of the teenage brain with years of clinical experience with teens has produced a thoughtful, practical, and down-to-earth guide that enables parents to understand and deal well with their teenager. If you are struggling with your adolescent, or even anticipating your child's entrance into those crazy years, this book will show you why it all makes sense and how to help both you and your teen have the healthiest, sanest passage."

—Gail Saltz, MD, assistant professor of psychiatry,
New York Presbyterian Hospital; *Today Show* mental
health contributor; author of *Becoming Real*

"*Why Do They Act That Way?* is a comprehensive guide to the biology behind just about every adolescent behavior a parent or teacher might encounter. Drawing from his extensive clinical experience, Dr. Walsh walks the reader through many situations he has helped resolve through an understanding of how teen brains grow and develop. His gentle humor and friendly exploration of some personal parenting mishaps make this a highly readable and helpful book. You'll finish it feeling as if you've just had coffee with someone who is not only entertaining and enlightening but who knows exactly how it feels to be the mom or dad of a twenty-first-century teen."

—Cheryl Dellasega, PhD, author of *Surviving Ophelia, Girl Wars*
(with Charisse Nixon, PhD), and *Mean Girls Grown Up: Adult Women
Who Are Still Queen Bees, Middle Bees, and Afraid-to-Bees*

"The adolescent brain is NOT an oxymoron! Parents and teachers need to understand its critical developmental needs, and Dr. Walsh's clear, scientific, and humane counsel is just the ticket. I especially like his real-life stories and the chapter on helping kids manage the media."

—Jane M. Healy, PhD, educational psychologist and author of
Your Child's Growing Mind and *Failure to Connect*

Why Do They Act That Way?

A SURVIVAL GUIDE TO THE ADOLESCENT BRAIN FOR YOU AND YOUR TEEN

SECOND EDITION

David Walsh, PhD

With Erin Walsh, MA

ATRIA PAPERBACK

NEW YORK   LONDON   TORONTO   SYDNEY   NEW DELHI

ATRIA PAPERBACK
A Division of Simon & Schuster, Inc.
1230 Avenue of the Americas
New York, NY 10020

This Atria Paperback edition June 2014

ATRIA PAPERBACK and colophon are trademarks of Simon & Schuster, Inc.

For information about special discounts for bulk purchases, please contact Simon & Schuster Special Sales at 1-866-506-1949 or business@simonandschuster.com.

The Simon & Schuster Speakers Bureau can bring authors to your live event. For more information or to book an event contact the Simon & Schuster Speakers Bureau at 1-866-248-3049 or visit our website at www.simonspeakers.com.

Manufactured in the United States of America

10 9 8 7 6 5 4 3 2 1

Library of Congress Cataloging-in-Publication Data

Walsh, David Allen.
    Why do they act that way? : a survival guide to the adolescent brain for you and your teen / David Walsh, Ph.D; with Erin Walsh, M.A.—Second edition.
        pages cm
    Includes bibliographical references and index.
    1. Developmental psychobiology. 2. Developmental neurobiology. 3. Developmental psychology. 4. Adolescent psychology. I. Walsh, Erin, 1981– II. Title.
        QP363.5.W356 2014
        155.5—dc23   2013045413

ISBN 978-1-4767-5557-1
ISBN 978-0-7432-7482-1 (ebook)

To my wife, Monica, my partner
in parenting three adolescents

CONTENTS

Why Do They Act That Way?

Preface to the Second Edition

When I first wrote *Why Do They Act That Way? A Survival Guide to the Adolescent Brain for You and Your Teen*, now a decade ago, my goal was to translate cutting-edge brain science for parents of preteens and teens. My own experience as a parent, as well as my years of counseling, had convinced me that this chapter of the parenting adventure was often perplexing, frustrating, and scary. Over the years I had heard many versions of "I don't know what has gotten into him. He used to like doing things with the family and was actually interested in what I had to say. Now he doesn't want to be seen with us, thinks everything I say is stupid, and is often so grumpy it's hard to be around him."

My research in brain science convinced me that knowledge about the adolescent brain could make the journey a bit easier. My wife and I both knew that if we had this information when Dan, Brian, and Erin were adolescents, we would have worried less and been able to put the most stress-producing episodes into perspective. We also would have been less likely to take things personally. After all, it was a little hard to avoid taking umbrage when the voice on the other side of the slammed door mumbled, "What a jerk!"

The knowledge of what's going on inside our sons' and daughters' brains can bring some real comfort and reassurance. That's what Kelly from Chicago shared recently when she sent me a copy of this online review she had posted.

> With puberty in full swing for my son, I literally RAN to the library the other day and checked out an armful of books on how to successfully parent in this tumultuous time with dignity. (Admittedly, the dignity part was lacking these last weeks/months!) *Why Do They Act That Way?* was the only

book that I read from cover to cover. David Walsh keeps a perfect balance between the seriousness of firmly parenting teens and the light-heartedness of "this won't go perfectly and expect some bumps, hills, & mountains."

My empathy for adolescents increased when I began to truly understand the science behind brain development (or lack of in this case) that makes this a stage of impulsiveness, short-sightedness, testing authority, random bouts of anger or moodiness, and less common sense than he had at four. I feel really prepared to embrace my dear son with love and give him "roots" by setting realistic expectations and boundaries while still allowing him to "spread his wings" and become an individual.

The thank-yous I have received over the past ten years have been extremely gratifying. They have also motivated me to update the book. The explosion in neuroscientific discoveries has not slowed down. We are learning more each week about the miracle we all carry on top of our shoulders, and we continue to uncover more secrets about the adolescent brain. For instance, who knew a decade ago that physical exercise isn't just important for a healthy body but is critical for a well-functioning brain? Who knew that willpower comes in a limited supply and that its effectiveness wears out as teens resist impulses throughout the day? That's why it is unrealistic to let our teens keep their cell phones within reach at night and expect them *not* to respond to a two a.m. text. Answering that text is more a matter of willpower depletion than it is of open defiance. Speaking of texting, technology is another reason to update this book. When I wrote the first edition, Mark Zuckerberg hadn't yet started Facebook. Today it has more than one billion users, and most teens inhabit a social media site. No one had yet tweeted in 2003 but ten years later, in early 2013, more than twenty-four million tweets were sent in one day. Of course, this pales in comparison to the six billion daily texts. Your kids are likely to carry smartphones in their pockets that are more powerful than the computers that sat on our desks when the first edition of *Why Do They Act That*

Way? was published. And half of them can use those phones to text blindfolded! So I've revised the chapter on adolescents and media.

The new scientific information isn't just interesting. It changes some of our parenting strategies. For one example among many, we know a lot more now about the effects of bullying on the brain, and we also have better information about which prevention strategies work and which well-intentioned ones actually make things worse for the victims.

Hopefully this updated edition will equip parents even better for the daunting but exhilarating adventure of guiding our kids through adolescence with a minimum of serious bumps and bruises. I often joke that I wrote *Why Do They Act That Way?* to get revenge on Dan, Brian, and Erin. Now they're all parents themselves—and very good ones, I'm proud to say. Although my grandkids are still preschoolers, I hope that this updated book will be a resource for them as well.

ONE

Making Sense of Adolescence

Our youth now love luxury. They have bad manners, con-
tempt for authority; they show disrespect for their elders
and love chatter in place of exercise; they no longer rise
when elders enter the room; they contradict their parents,
chatter before company; gobble up their food and tyran-
nize their teachers.

—SOCRATES, FIFTH CENTURY BC

Probably the best way to describe adolescence is to say that it
begins at puberty and ends . . . sometime. That may sound silly
and unscientific, but it's the most accurate definition of *adolescence*
that I've come across. This definition is vague precisely because adolescence is an in-between stage determined not so much by what it
is but by what it is not. Adolescence is not childhood, and it is not
adulthood; it is the period in between those two stages. And because
today's kids get through childhood faster than kids did in the past,
their transition to adulthood now seems to be taking longer than
ever before.

The gap between teens and adults seems to be growing, too.
Three teenagers I spoke with told me that adults move away from
them on the bus when they get on. "Why do you think they do
that?" I asked.

"Because they're afraid of us," offered one boy.

His friend disagreed. "I think it's because they don't like us."

The proverbial generation gap is fast becoming a chasm. It's not easy being an adolescent. Just consider some of the things they face.

- They have to handle sexually maturing bodies that give rise to strong urges.
- They have to try to figure out and manage volatile and powerful emotions.
- They have to fit into a complex social network.
- They have to deal with immense peer pressure.
- They have to deal with wildly changing moods.
- They have to decide how they are going to respond to the temptation of tobacco, alcohol, and drugs.
- They have to figure out what their values are going to be.
- They have to renegotiate relationships with their parents.
- They have to get through school.
- They have to figure out how to get enough sleep.
- They have to begin to plan their future.
- They have to figure out how to keep the computers, tablets, and cell phones they love from crowding out everything else.

This list can get a lot longer. Any way you look at it, adolescents have a lot of balls in the air, and because they can't always handle their juggling acts with the utmost grace, the people around them—especially their parents—bear the brunt of teens' frustration. Over the years, I've come to understand that the adolescent years are the most difficult for parents and their teens.

Several years ago I received a call from a friend. "Do you have time for a cup of coffee?" he asked.

"Sure, when would you like to get together?"

"Right now?" was his instant reply.

Thirty minutes later we were sitting down in a neighborhood coffee shop. With tears in his eyes, Steve unloaded the worry, sadness, and anger he was feeling about his fourteen-year-old son, Kevin. A particularly nasty argument over a curfew had erupted earlier in the evening, capping several days of simmering conflict. "I called you because I'm at my wit's end. I don't understand what's happening, and I don't know if we'll be able to get through whatever comes next."

I have known Kevin since he was born. He grew up a bright, energetic, happy kid who loved doing things with his mom and dad. He was friendly, cooperative, talkative, and always game for some adventure. As I drank my coffee, Steve described Kevin's personality transformation. Almost overnight, Steve explained, Kevin had gone from happy to sullen, from talkative to quiet, from easygoing to hostile.

"Now it seems like everything turns into an argument. The chip on his shoulder is huge."

His eyes dropped to his coffee cup, where he was fiddling with a spoon. Finally he said, in a shaky voice, "This is so hard. I don't know what to do."

Adults from Socrates to my friend Steve have been perplexed and challenged by adolescents for thousands of years. Even the most mild-mannered kids pose difficulties for their parents, from needing to stock the pantry to meet their growth spurts to figuring out what to do when they sleep until noon. For the adults living and working with the adolescents who take a more volatile course to adulthood, the situations that arise—texting all night, dangerous accidents, teen drinking, drug use, and run-ins with the police, to name a few—can inspire hair-pulling anger and head-shaking bewilderment. Adults talk about each new generation of adolescents as evidence that the world is falling apart.

When you think about it, the rift between adults and adolescents is strange because every adult was once an adolescent. Everyone who has made it to adulthood remembers (if he or she wants to remember) how hard it can be to deal with the peer pressure, the physical changes of puberty, and worries about the future—who you are and what to do with your life—that are so characteristic of adolescence. You probably recall your own confusion and discovery, excitement and frustration, happiness and heartbreak during your teen years, but you and other adults are still no doubt surprised by each new generation of adolescents. They seem lazier, angrier, less capable of thinking through the consequences of their actions, and more willing to drive the adults in their lives insane.

"I would never have done that when I was her age," we parents think. Maybe you wouldn't have, but a few of your friends probably *did*. Insolence and door slamming are not new inventions. The world is not getting worse; it's staying exactly the same. Adults and adolescents have always had their difficulties getting along with one another.

Adults have so much trouble with kids on their way to adulthood because adolescents are such a bundle of paradoxes. On the one hand, they are fun, idealistic, energetic, altruistic, and enthusiastic. They are excited by new things and often willing to try new activities. They are curious about the world and eager to interact with new people. They may have serious, informed, adult conversations with you, but they are also prone to angry outbursts, defiant acts, foolish risk taking, and inexplicable plummets into despair. They can become fire-breathing dragons in the blink of an eye just because you said something about their hair. They can stay out until late at night without warning and lie about where they've been. One moment you can feel connected and comfortable with your teen, and the next you may wonder who replaced your child with a demon. Just when you think you've got an adolescent pegged—he's too timid, he's too aggressive, he's just right—he'll prove you wrong. Knowing what a teen will do next is like knowing the sound of one hand clapping. It's impossible. Most confusing of all, they do all of these things in the course of a single year, week, or even day.

Because of the challenging nature of adolescence, many parents and teachers find it easy to think the worst about teenagers. Years ago, when my son Brian was in high school, he and several of his friends were in the alley behind their friend Mark's house playing basketball, horsing around, acting rowdy, and generally having a great time. They were all nice kids, although some of them looked a little rough around the edges. As they played basketball one of Mark's neighbors, Alice, noticed them. The whole block probably noticed they were there, with all the noise they were making, but Alice had just realized her wallet was missing, and she knew whom to blame.

It happened like this. Mark's father, Jerry, was in the house reading the paper after work when the phone rang. It was Alice.

"Your son and his friends stole my wallet," she said.

"They stole your wallet?" Jerry said. "What do you mean, Alice?"

"I just came in the back door with my groceries, and then I went upstairs for a moment. When I came back down I noticed I'd left the door unlocked and my wallet was gone. I remember setting it on the kitchen table when I came in the door. One of them stole it."

Jerry was taken aback. To his knowledge these guys hadn't caused any serious trouble before. Had she seen one of them take it? No, she said, but it was there one moment and not the next. They had stolen it. What's more, she said, she was calling Phil, another neighbor who worked for the police department, and she was going to get him involved. Then she hung up.

Jerry went out back to talk to the boys. He told them about Alice's call and asked to hear their side of the story. Boiled down, their side was that Alice was crazy, they'd been playing ball the whole time, they weren't thieves, and none of them had taken the wallet. They were angry at the insinuation that they had stolen and indignant that Jerry might believe the story. He assured them he didn't think any of them would do such a thing, and went back inside to call Phil.

"They say they didn't take it, Phil. I believe them," Jerry said.

"Well, let me talk to Alice again," he said. "Maybe there's something she forgot to tell us." Jerry hung up and tried to go back to the paper, but he was too worked up, so he paced around the house, checking the back window to make sure the boys were still out there.

A few minutes later the phone rang again. It was Phil. Alice had just received a call from the grocery store. She'd left her wallet on the checkout counter. When Jerry went out back to tell the boys they'd been exonerated, they were relieved to hear that the wallet had been found but still smarting from the accusation that they'd taken it.

Alice was wrong to jump to conclusions about Brian and his friends, but it's hard to blame her for suspecting a rowdy group of adolescent boys. The concerns that adults have about adolescents are not without basis. The news media are filled with reports about youth crime, gangs, teenage pregnancy, alcohol and drugs, and other unsavory adolescent pastimes. The good things kids do rarely make the news.

Adolescence is a lot like the terrible twos, when children also get volatile, impulsive, unpredictable, and try adults' patience. The mood swings, the temper tantrums, the infatuation with the word *no,* the foolish risks—sound a lot like adolescence? Of course, there are a couple big differences. First, adolescents are bigger, stronger, and smarter than two-year-olds. This means they're harder to deal with. Second, the stakes are much higher for adolescents. The trouble they get into can be a lot more serious than screaming in a restaurant or falling off a couch. The push and pull of this time of life can fray anyone's nerves, regardless of age, and may cause even the most mild-mannered adults to think occasional dark thoughts about adolescents.

The purpose of this book is to prevent and cure those dark thoughts and to help you see more clearly what your teenager is going through. Adolescent behavior is linked to big changes going on in the brain, and once you know what these are, you can help your kid navigate the common dangers and challenges in his or her life. You *can* keep your own sanity and composure in the face of teenage emotional and behavioral upheavals.

The Parent Survival Kit: Appreciating Adolescents

To help you get started, in many chapters you will find a "Parent Survival Kit." It contains the knowledge, attitudes, and skills you need for the adventure of raising teenagers. The more items you find you already have in the survival kit, the better prepared you'll be to cope with your kids' teen years. A well-stocked kit will also help you maintain perspective, balance, and peace of mind, and you'll be better able to help your adolescent son or daughter survive the many conflicts and contradictions he or she will face.

The Parent Survival Kit asks a set of questions to help you assess how well prepared you are in that category. The more you answer yes, the better equipped you will be. If you don't answer yes very often, you'll find out later in the chapter how to get to yes.

Here's the first set of questions to help you evaluate yourself in the first survival category: understanding and liking adolescents.

PARENT SURVIVAL KIT

Appreciating Adolescents

Yes No

☐ ☐ 1. I like to meet and talk with adolescents.

☐ ☐ 2. I look forward to spending time with my kids.

☐ ☐ 3. I understand that some turmoil during adolescence is normal.

☐ ☐ 4. I know I need to be flexible and patient when my child is a teenager.

☐ ☐ 5. I understand that adolescents face many challenges.

☐ ☐ 6. It's not easy being a teenager today.

☐ ☐ 7. I'm confident that I can be a good parent for my teenager.

If you found yourself agreeing with the statements in the survival kit, you already have the empathy that is a key attribute for parenting teenagers. If you found yourself answering no to some items, that answer may change by the time you finish this book. If you return to these questions after reading the following pages, which explain why adolescents act the way they do, you may find yourself saying yes. I think you'll find yourself developing appreciation and understanding of your teen, which will help you see how you can be flexible and patient in your reactions to adolescents.

I actually like adolescents. I always have. Maybe it's because I've been lucky enough to spend tens of thousands of hours with them. I was a high school teacher for ten years, and a coach of both boys' and girls' sports for more than twenty. I coached basketball, track, and cross-country at the high school level, and I coached baseball, soccer, and softball at the youth level. When my own kids' park board teams couldn't find a coach, I was often recruited to fill in. Sometimes I coached sports I didn't completely understand. I remember asking my son's summer soccer team, "Okay, one more time. What is *offsides*?" The kids I coached were full of energy and life, ambition and hope. They played hard and mostly well with one another, supporting and encouraging fellow teammates.

I've also worked as a high school counselor and, after I received my doctorate, as a psychologist. For more than twenty years I directed inpatient and outpatient mental health and chemical dependency services for children and adolescents at Fairview Health Services in Minneapolis. For twelve years I was the founder, president, and main spokesman for the National Institute on Media and the Family. More recently I founded Mind Positive Parenting. In all these roles, I have had contact with thousands of kids, teachers, and parents every year.

I'm also the father of three children who made it through adolescence and into adulthood. Some of the lessons I learned helping my own three kids through adolescence were the result of trial and error, which this book, I hope, will help you avoid, but you may need to make some mistakes before you get things on the right track with your own kids. Sometimes you may even need to give your kids tough medicine—because you love them.

I have worked with all types of adolescents in all sorts of settings. I've spent time with straight-A students headed for the best colleges and with altruistic, dedicated kids involved in service projects. I've also been the counselor of kids sentenced to serve time after they made a mistake or ran into some bad luck—troubled and court-ordered kids who were up to their ears in drugs, crime, and violence. And, of course, I've worked with tons of kids who were somewhere in the middle.

One of the toughest students at the school where I worked was a girl named Mary, who had committed a series of offenses including truancy, drinking at a school-sponsored dance, and arguments with teachers. Her accumulated transgressions put her at risk of expulsion. In April of her junior year she was told that to stay in school, she had to meet with the school counselor every week. I was that counselor, and though I met with Mary weekly, I got nowhere with her for almost two months. Despite my best efforts, she was stonily silent or barely tolerant in her answers to my questions. June rolled around and toward the end of our final meeting I figured I had nothing to lose and risked telling her my real thoughts about her instead of trying to get her to open up.

"Do you know what I think is going on, Mary?" I asked.

"What do you think is going on?" she replied, bored.

"I think that beneath all the tough stuff, you're really hurting and scared. Scared that no one cares about you. You keep everyone at bay with your tough act because if no one can get close, you can't get hurt." By then I'd learned it's always the toughest kids who are hurting the most.

She sneered, unimpressed. Our time was up and she left my office without looking back. I thought, "I lost on this one." The school year ended, summer came and went, and the new school year began. Since I was no longer part of Mary's sentence I wasn't having my weekly meetings with her. I always went out of my way to greet her in the hallway, and underneath her tough exterior she actually seemed pleased that I did. It was in October that she came by my office. She stood there for a moment in the doorway. She clearly had something on her mind, so I invited her in and closed the door.

"I've been thinking about what you said last year," she said. "Maybe you're right."

That was the beginning of our first real conversation. Over the following weeks Mary told me her story. Her mother had died when she was only eight. Worse, she was convinced her father could not care less about her. I had met her father once during parent conferences. He was a very successful businessman and had seemed like a friendly, decent guy. I thought some counseling with Mary and her dad could really help the situation. She reluctantly agreed to come to a meeting if I would schedule it with her dad. I reached Mary's father on the phone that night and he seemed open and friendly. Of course he could make it.

"Mary isn't in any trouble, is she?"

I assured him that was not the case. We scheduled a time for an afternoon later in the week. The meeting was set for after-school hours so Mary wouldn't have to worry about being embarrassed by someone seeing her father meeting with the school counselor.

On the afternoon of the meeting she was in my office fifteen minutes early, as nervous as a cat. As the hour arrived she started to shake her head and speak her thoughts out loud.

"He's not coming," she said. "He's not going to make it."

I assured her that her father had told me he would be there.

"No. I know him. He's not going to show."

Sadly, she was right. He didn't show. And as the minutes passed, Mary's tough shell began to reappear. The vulnerable girl I'd been talking with for the last few weeks was being replaced by the distant one I'd sat with in silence the previous spring.

When I finally caught up with her father by phone that night, he was as affable as ever, and apologized profusely. "I am so sorry. I got caught in a meeting and it completely slipped my mind. For sure, we will reschedule." I told him how disappointed Mary had been. He said he would talk with her and call me with a good time to have the meeting. I stressed that I thought it was very important that he and Mary meet with me.

He never came in for the appointment, despite my repeated requests.

Mary was right about her father, and I think I was right about her. Her father's neglect had taught her that she had to shut out everyone in order to protect herself. Mary's father was probably unaware of how much he was hurting his daughter and that many of her behavior problems were caused, in part, by the fact that he wouldn't pay attention to her. Mary and I met intermittently during her senior year and we had some good conversations, but, as far as I know, the important talk with her dad never happened. That's too bad, because a better relationship with her father would have made adolescence a lot easier for Mary. Hers didn't have to be as hard for her as it was.

News About the Teen Brain

In this book I offer a number of ways to help adolescents, particularly by setting up new, better ways of listening to them and communicating with them. Throughout I stress three principles of parenting—connection, guidance, and love. Mary's problems, her father, and her behavior were neon signs that spelled trouble, but adolescents aren't always so easy to read. Until recently, we had no idea why adolescents sometimes act the way they do. We still can't explain everything, but thanks to the latest discoveries in neuroscience, we can explain adolescence better than ever before. The findings of brain research help us understand adolescent behavior. Seemingly unrelated behaviors, like sleeping late, constant texting, acting territorial, bursting into tears for no reason, and taking risks, make much more sense when you know what's happening inside the adolescent brain. Better yet, this new understanding of the adolescent brain can help us see how to be more helpful to the teens in our lives.

I have been sharing this groundbreaking research with parents and professionals in seminars and conversations. Every single time I begin to explain the adolescent brain, teachers are empowered by this new information and parents are relieved and hopeful. Most importantly, everyone gains a new understanding and empathy for adolescents.

Stories about real adolescents illustrate how the science of the brain works in everyday scenarios, how it comes to life in common situations that you're likely to recognize. Having a scientific perspective on the biological challenges of adolescence will help you interact more objectively with your child, maintain your cool, and offer guidance that can improve his or her life. As a parent or teacher, when you finally know what is really happening inside and outside teen brains, you will be able to do a better job of helping them get through this in-between stage. You'll be able to help them survive . . . and thrive.

I have made my share of mistakes with adolescents, as any of my kids and students would be happy to tell you, so, please, view the suggestions I make in this book through the lens of your own knowledge of your own kids and your experience caring for them. What is helpful for one adolescent may not necessarily be helpful for another. Trying to help teenagers is a process of experimenting with solutions. You need to figure out for yourself what works and what doesn't.

When my older son complained about my parenting decisions I often joked with him, "I'm sorry, but you're the first one. I'm still learning on the job." What I thought I had learned from my experience with him didn't always help with my other son, however, because the two of them have such different personalities and temperaments. And then, just when I thought maybe I had parenting down, along came my daughter. Parenting each kid was an adventure. Most of the adventure was fun, but some of it was frustrating and scary. I hope that my suggestions will help you take advantage of the fun and reduce the frustration and fright. If nothing else, gaining an understanding of how adolescent brain development makes teens act the way they do will help you devise strategies for helping your kids.

My friend Steve was one of the first people with whom I shared the new understanding of the adolescent brain that I present in this book. Having seen his son Kevin frequently during the previous six months, I knew that he was growing a lot, about an inch every month. I explained to Steve that the dramatic changes on the outside were being matched by equally dramatic changes in Kevin's brain. "My bet is that parts of his brain are doing somersaults. I think he's as confused as you are. So before you pack him up for boarding school or lock him in a room with a shrink, take a step back and get some perspective on what's going on." Steve and I talked about some strategies.

Not too long ago, I asked Steve how things were going with Kevin.

Steve smiled. "We still have our rough days, but things are so much better. You know, Dave, all parents should know what's going on in the adolescent brain. It's still no cakewalk with Kevin, but knowing what he's going through really helps."

No Longer a Child but Not Yet an Adult

Adolescence is one of the most challenging periods for parents like Steve because so much is in flux. Compare a photograph of a girl taken when she is in eighth grade with another taken at her high school graduation. In many instances you would be hard pressed to tell it was the same kid. Besides obvious changes in hairstyles and clothing, dramatic physical changes occur in a short amount of time during adolescence. Maybe she's taller, maybe she's thinner, or maybe her body has gone from a girl's to a woman's. The shape of her nose could even have changed. In four years adults generally just look a little older, but teens are transformed into what appear to be entirely new people.

Growth spurts and the changes that puberty causes are the most obvious physical differences between children and adolescents. A boy or girl enters adolescence as a child and leaves an adult. The transition from childhood to maturity is nothing short of a metamorphosis. Just as a caterpillar becomes a butterfly by living for a while cramped into a cocoon, kids must go through the awkwardness of adolescence to become fully grown up.

Because the teenage years are an in-between stage, it's sometimes awkward and difficult to know how to treat adolescents. They are no longer children, but they are also not yet adults. Many of them have trouble being in this in-between stage. The rules, the roles, and the roads to travel are either indistinct or too various to count. The in-between stage leaves everyone guessing what is appropriate and what is healthy.

Today the in-between stage may be more difficult than ever. Research shows that adolescence is getting longer. Adolescence begins with the physiological event of puberty, which is occurring earlier and earlier. In the nineteenth century the first signs of puberty were seen in an average kid at the age of seventeen. Today the average age is twelve. Different theories attempt to explain why puberty is starting earlier than it used to. One is that children now have better nutrition: a well-nourished body is better able to begin puberty than a malnourished one. Although thankfully there are not as many malnourished children as there used to be, more children are overweight than ever before. Research has also suggested that children who are overweight are more likely to start puberty earlier. Another theory is that food additives, processed foods, and growth hormones fed to animals that we eat may speed maturation. And one theory more contends that the many sexual images that children see on TV and in the movies stimulate the production of sex hormones, which tell the child's body that it is time to begin to develop sexually.

Because we do not have conclusive proof one way or another, it is not possible to say what causes the early onset of puberty. One of these theories may be correct, or some combination of them, or something else entirely. Whatever the explanation, puberty is starting earlier.

While puberty is the easy physiological marker for the beginning of adolescence, the end of adolescence is fuzzier. It is difficult to nail down biologically but can be defined socially as the taking on of an adult role in society. The end of adolescence is also coming later in life.

In previous generations, completing grade school or high school was the end of formal education. At that point most young people got a job to help support their family or started their own household. In today's highly complex, technological society, most young people need a postsecondary education or further training. As a result, many are not taking on adult roles, steady jobs, or real responsibilities until they are as old as twenty-five.

In the past, adolescence began around age thirteen and ended around age seventeen. Today adolescence can last a full fifteen years. Managing an in-between stage is challenging enough for four years, but having to navigate this awkward phase for more than a decade is really difficult. By the time most people reach adulthood, they've spent more than half their lives as adolescents.

The Physical Changes in the Teen Brain

Let's return for a moment to my example of the photographs over time of the girl. Between eighth grade and high school graduation, a teen undergoes visible external changes matched by biological changes on the inside, particularly in the brain. For a long time, the adolescent brain was believed to be very similar to an adult brain—a finished product. The body continued to change through adolescence, but the brain seemed fully grown, because the adolescent brain is actually the same size as an adult's. A newborn baby's brain is only about three-quarters of a pound and triples in size by his first birthday. Then it grows to three pounds by the time a child goes to kindergarten. It's easy to imagine that big changes are under way in the brain of a small child because the organ itself is growing so dramatically, but knowing that the adolescent brain is physically equal to an adult brain, scientists believed until recently that it had finished its development.

Swiss psychologist Jean Piaget, generally regarded as the founder of developmental psychology, has also influenced most views of the adolescent brain. Piaget identified the stages of cognitive development and dubbed the "last" stage of development—from eleven years to sixteen years, when a child learns to think abstractly—"formal operational thinking." Such thinking included using complex systems of symbols, like algebra, and understanding concepts such as morality and justice. Because adolescents can do these things, psychologists assumed that teens basically had adult brains that simply needed more experience to become fully mature.

Anyone who has ever argued with fifteen-year-olds knows they can think logically and abstractly. They can come up with extremely ingenious, complex, logical arguments for why you must give them a ride to a friend's house at ten o'clock at night. Piaget's picture of the adolescent's brain power wasn't wrong, but it was incomplete, because he was only concerned with the ability to reason. Complex reasoning is an extremely important function of the adult brain, but it is only one of many things that the brain does.

Scientists now know that the adolescent brain is not a finished product but a work in progress. Even though the teen brain does not alter in size or shape, a truly astounding amount of growth is still under way. In recent decades new technology has enabled scientists to peer inside living, working brains without damaging them, using MRI (magnetic resonance imaging) scans, PET (positron emission tomography) scans, fMRI (functional magnetic resonance imaging) scans, and SPECT (single photon emission computerized tomography). With these powerful machines, scientists can even watch specific brain cells in action. In the following chapters you'll learn more about adolescents than anyone knew just fifteen years ago.

Knowing why kids act as they do isn't quite enough, though, if you're dealing with anger, rebelliousness, or rudeness. I'll give you some strategies for coping with and even changing these challenging aspects of teen behavior. The fact is that teens sometimes have a tough time getting along with themselves, let alone with their parents and family.

When I was a high school counselor, I also taught one or two classes each semester, and, with daily contact, I got to know my students quite well. Some would often visit my counseling office just for a chat, sometimes to sort some things out, and other times to get help working through some really tough issues—like arguing, divorcing, or alcoholic parents; domestic violence; or even sexual abuse.

Tim was a student who dropped in periodically to sort things out. As he grew to trust me, our conversations about sports or classes evolved into deeper discussions, and Tim became more forthright about some of the confusion he was feeling—confident and happy some days, hypersensitive on others. On the fragile days Tim would get very upset when teased by his friends. He never let on to his buddies that their jokes bothered him, but he often descended into a funk for hours or days after being the butt of some passing wisecrack. Other times, he found himself getting angry over little things and going from feeling great to feeling down, all in the space of an hour, seemingly for no reason.

Tim was also confused by the dramatic change in his relationship with his parents. Close to both his mother and father since he was little, he felt fortunate his family didn't have the tougher problems of many of his friends. But that was changing, too. Tim felt irritated by many of the things his parents said, even resenting his father's cheerful "Good morning" at breakfast. Sometimes he found himself making snide or mean comments to his parents; later he would feel guilty. Although Tim's friends told him how lucky he was to have such nice parents, he felt simultaneously proud of and embarrassed by them.

One day in a class discussion I gave the students the following question: "If someone gave you a million dollars, what would be the first thing you would do with it?"

Tim was the first to answer: "I would give my parents a new house and then send them on a vacation to anywhere they wanted to go. They work so hard and never do anything for themselves."

After class I mentioned to Tim how surprised I was with his answer, given our earlier conversation in my office. His response was that he had surprised himself with his answer.

At parent conferences a week later, Jan and Charles, Tim's parents, stopped by to talk about Tim's progress in my class. I told them their son was doing fine. They were relieved because communication with him had been difficult and Tim wasn't sharing much about his classes. Before they left I told them about the discussion in class the week before. When I shared that Tim had immediately responded that he would buy them a new house and would pay for them to have the vacation of their dreams, Jan's eyes filled with tears.

"Did he really say that?" she asked.

"He did. You know, he really loves you two a lot."

"Boy, do I need to hear that right now. I feel like our relationship with him is completely disintegrating. We have so many arguments and he seems to be so angry with us all the time."

"Sometimes adolescents have to push you away for a while so they can figure out who they are," I responded. "But your relationship with Tim is going to survive. The thing to remember is that all of this is as confusing to Tim as it is to you."

Even when teens are difficult, it's important to remember that your kids are still your kids. Because Tim had been such a sweet kid, the teenage rudeness and anger came as quite a shock to his parents and they were disheartened. This happens in many families. The whole family gets along great when the kids are young, but when the going gets tough in the teenage years, one or both of the parents is demoralized, and asks,

"How could my child have become so rude, angry, and rebellious?" or "Maybe the connection I thought we had was just a figment of my imagination. What did I do wrong?"

It is completely natural to have these thoughts while parenting a volatile adolescent, especially if the change in your child is unexpected and dramatic. Even if just getting along is a challenge, however, you can't afford to stop parenting. Don't give up. If you continue to give your teens the connection, guidance, and love they need, even when you have trouble believing they're related to you, then you both will get through this time. It may take a few days, months, or years, but you'll find that your actions will make a difference. Eventually, you'll reestablish a loving relationship with your teen or adult child. It does take persistence and consistency in your messages and behavior, however.

Disillusionment is not the only mental trap for parents. Other parents may dread their child's adolescent years with so much foreboding and pessimism that their fears become a self-fulfilling prophecy. Parenting teenagers can be a tough job, but shepherding our children from youth to adulthood is not all drudgery. Frankly, the teenage years offer some of the most rewarding and exciting moments in a parent's life. To assume that our children will transform into unrecognizable creatures as soon as they hit puberty is to do them an enormous disservice. They are the same people they have always been, and they still need their parents to expect the best of them. At a time when a kid feels uncomfortable in his own skin, the last thing he needs is for his unconditional support—his parents—to treat him like an alien.

As a parent of a teen, don't be surprised if the road gets bumpy. On the other hand, don't look for trouble around every bend. As with so many other things, parenting an adolescent is a matter of balance.

Striking That Parental Balance

In the coming chapters I often rely on generalizations to describe adolescents. Your preteen or teen, however, is unique, with his or her own temperament and individual circumstances. Each teen will grow and change in his or her own way. So as you read the stories, examples, and scientific information in this book, you'll have to decide if and how they apply to the adolescent you know.

Emotional ups and downs, conflict, and communication problems are common during adolescence, but you don't want to respond to every difficult situation, conflict, or change with "They'll grow out of it." You need to decide when to intervene in order to help your adolescent make his or her way to adulthood. While your child will most likely experience a normal adolescence, you do need to be on the lookout for extreme problems. In the course of this book I will elaborate on some mental health issues. Problems like severe depression, drug or alcohol abuse, and eating disorders often have warning signs. Don't ignore them. The behavior of some adolescents can be so challenging—even if they don't have a serious psychological condition—that it can overwhelm a parent's skills and resources. Although rebelliousness and anger are common among adolescents, if these characteristics escalate into violent outbursts, cruelty toward siblings, extreme disrespect, and utter defiance, you need to seek professional help for your child. A good counselor can help you sort out the normal from the serious, facilitate better communication, and suggest practical strategies to get things back on track. You might first look for help at your child's school. Teachers, counselors, and school social workers understand adolescents, and since they know your son or daughter, they may have some very good insights. They may also know which local professionals would be the best fit for your family. If you seek help from a counselor, look for good chemistry between you and between the counselor and your child. This is key, so don't hesitate to interview more than one or to seek a second opinion.

What Is Your Parenting Style?

All of us have a style of parenting that includes different beliefs, attitudes, strategies, and tactics. Children don't arrive in the world with an owner's manual, so we have to decide quickly how we are going to respond to the thousands of different situations and challenges we face. To make things even more complicated, we need to keep adapting our style as our kids mature. For example, a ten-minute time-out for misbehavior makes sense for a five-year-old but is inappropriate for a teenager.

Among the influences that shape our style, none is more important than our own experiences as children. I was conducting a counseling session with fifteen-year-old Bill and his mother. After listing all Bill's shortcomings Connie leaned back and sighed, "It doesn't make any difference how often I hit him, he just doesn't change." At first I thought she was joking, but the look on her face convinced me she was serious. When I asked her to tell me more about how she dealt with Bill when he misbehaved, it became clear that slapping and hitting him were her mainstays of discipline. This method was misguided for a lot of reasons, not the least of which was the fact that Bill was nine inches taller and seventy-five pounds heavier than she.

I asked her if she thought hitting Bill was a good idea. "No, not really," she replied. "It worked when he was little, but he's gotten so big I can't even hurt the big lunk anymore!" When I asked her how she came to rely on hitting Bill for discipline, she responded without hesitation. "That's the way my father raised me. All of us kids would get a whack whenever we'd step out of line or mouth off. When Bill's father left us before he was a year old, I realized it was all up to me. I can remember my dad telling me to make sure Bill always knew who was in charge. He explained how spanking was a good teacher. I've always been able to keep Bill in line until the last couple of years. Now he won't listen to me, and he's getting into all kinds of trouble."

Like so many of us, Connie adopted the parenting style she grew up with. She may not have liked it as a child, but it was familiar to her. We all have a tendency to resort to the familiar, especially when we are under stress. I know that I have surprised myself on occasion by repeating things my parents said or did.

We will examine the topic of parenting styles further in chapter 4 and see how different styles work with teens. The first step, however, is to become aware of your own style and the forces that helped shape it. Here are some questions to help you do that (think back to your relationship with your parents when you were a teenager):

- Do you think your parents enjoyed being with you and your siblings and friends when you were a teen?
- How much time did your parents spend with you?
- Did your parents take an interest in what you were doing in and out of school?

- Were your parents easy to talk to?
- Would you describe your relationship with your parents as warm, cold, or something in between?
- Did your parents give you some space and independence?
- Did your parents usually agree when it came to rules and discipline?
- Did your parents share parenting responsibilities?
- How did your parents handle discipline?
- Did either of your parents use physical punishment?
- Were your parents lax, strict, or somewhere in between?
- Was it okay to make mistakes in your family?
- Were the rules clear when you were a teenager?
- How were disagreements handled between you and your parents?
- What was your curfew when you were a teenager?
- Did your parents ever call you names or put you down?
- Did your parents listen to you?
- What did you argue about most with your parents when you were a teen?
  - Grades
  - Money
  - Curfew
  - Dress
  - Friends
  - Alcohol or drugs
  - Chores
  - Religion
  - Disrespect
  - Music

Now go back over these same questions, but pretend you are your own son or daughter. How do your kid's answers compare with your own?

What did you learn?

- How is your parenting style like your parents'?
- How is your parenting style different from your parents'?

- What parts of your parents' style would you like to keep?
- What parts of your parents' style would you like to change?

Use these questions to examine your own parenting style. I'm sure you'll discover that you have some parts of your style that you want to keep, other parts that you want to modify, and still others that you might want to scrap. To change, you will need to do the following:

1. Become aware of what you need to change.
2. Consciously choose how you want to act.
3. Repeat it until it becomes comfortable.

Now pause and think about these two questions, with which I will conclude most chapters.

- What do I want to continue?
- What do I want to change?

Dos and Don'ts

These Dos and Don'ts are suggestions—good starting points for developing an effective style for parenting adolescents.

DO

✓ Stay in touch with your adolescent's teachers. Attend parent conferences and school events to keep communication open.
✓ Compare notes with other parents.
✓ Get to know your son's or daughter's friends and their parents.
✓ Learn as much as you can about adolescent growth and development to gain a realistic perspective on your child's behavior.
✓ Refresh your memory of your own adolescence. It does wonders for understanding your kids.

DON'T

✗ Don't panic if things get rocky with your preteens or teens. They may be having trouble; it doesn't mean they're going off the deep end. If you pay attention, you should be able to tell if the situation is getting serious.

✗ While tolerance and patience are essential, don't become a doormat for disrespectful behavior.

✗ Don't ignore warning signs of potentially serious problems, such as depression, alcohol or drug abuse, eating disorders, or extreme and persistent anger.

What do I want to continue?

_____

_____

_____

What do I want to change?

_____

_____

_____

TWO

A Guided Tour of Their Brains

On a bitterly cold January evening at a suburban middle school, I was to present a parent workshop called "Understanding Your Adolescent." Not expecting a large turnout on such a frigid evening, I hoped enough people would gather for a small group discussion. Surprisingly, the first parents arrived twenty minutes ahead of time and others kept streaming in until there were three hundred people filling all the cafeteria tables. Still wanting to make the evening interactive, I started with these questions: "What brought you out on such a cold night? What are you hoping to learn?"

The group needed no coaxing. The first response came from the back of the room. "I need to know how to survive," a woman shouted. The room erupted in laughter and many heads nodded in agreement. "Why are they so moody?" asked another woman. A man near the front asked, "What's the deal with raging hormones?" In a split second another man at the same table inquired, "What the heck is a hormone anyway?"

I decided to change my presentation on the spot, from exploring psychological issues to something more helpful—explaining the adolescent brain: how it's different from a child's and an adult's brain, and how its growth and development affect mood and behavior, among other things.

Brain Basics

Since our purpose is to understand how the adolescent brain develops, we will focus only on the brain parts and functions that play a major role in that story. First we'll examine brain cells, also called neurons, the building blocks of the brain. Next we'll turn to the structures of the brain to get an overview of its various parts and how those parts work together. We'll talk about hormones and neurotransmitters, the chemicals in the brain that communicate with the brain's different parts and that send messages between the brain and the body.

When talking about the brain here and in the chapters that follow, I'll stick to a widely accepted set of conventions. For example, I'll use the term *brain* when describing the organ itself and *mind* when describing what the brain does. The brain is the hardware. The mind is the software. Of course, this metaphor gets complicated right away because in the case of the human brain the software—the mind—can actually affect the makeup of the hardware and vice versa.

The brain, essentially, is an electrical system. Its neurons are specially suited to conduct electrical signals. All neurons share a common structure: each one has a cell body with a long cable or axon extending from it. Electrical impulses travel down the axons to branches, or dendrites, where they pass out of the cell through the branches, jump across a tiny gap, and enter the branches of neighboring neurons. At any time your brain is generating the equivalent of about twenty-five watts of electricity—enough to power a lightbulb.

A baby arrives in the world with about 100 billion neurons, each of which has an average of ten thousand branches. One hundred billion neurons with ten thousand branches each make the possible number of connections about one quadrillion. It is impossible to calculate the number of different ways to configure a quadrillion connections. We cannot even calculate how many possible songs could be composed by arranging in different combinations and different sequences the eighty-eight keys on a piano keyboard.

Francis Crick, the co-discoverer of the DNA molecule, thinks that the possible number of neural configurations in just one brain exceeds the number of atoms in the known universe.

When a baby is born, only about 17 percent of his neurons are linked. In the weeks, months, years, and *decades* that follow, all the rest of those billions of neurons get wired together. Two forces drive the wiring of the brain: genetics and experience. Genes provide the materials and rough blueprint needed to build a human being. Instructions encoded in our DNA determine which neurons connect with others and when. This wiring process driven by genetics is a kind of hard-wiring, complemented by the soft-wiring shaped by life experiences.

Take language, for example. Babies come into the world with the genetic ability to make sounds. A newborn's noises give us proof that he has survived childbirth and his lungs are working. His ability to vocalize is an example of hard-wiring, but which of the world's sixty-five hundred languages he learns to speak is shaped by the experiences he will have—by the customized soft-wiring.

For most of the last century, scientists debated whether genetics and natural inheritance or nurture and experience were more important in gaining skills, in learning quickly, and in succeeding in life. Recently it has become clear that in nearly all cases nature *and* nurture affect the brain's ability to interact with and respond to the environment.

The crucial role of experience in the brain is summed up in a favorite phrase of neuroscientists, "The neurons that fire together wire together." The more they fire together—pass on an electrical charge from one cell to another—the stronger the connections between the neurons become. This process continues throughout our lives and is, of course, at work during every moment of an adolescent's life. When a high school student is trying to remember a new Spanish word, she'd be well advised to write it out, say it out loud, and use it with her friends. Eventually she will remember it. By firing repeatedly, the neurons that do the work of thinking about that word make the connection strong enough to hold; they wire the new Spanish term into her brain.

I was talking with a group of teenagers and asked how many of them liked sports. I asked one of the girls whose hand was raised what her favorite sport was. "Tennis," was her quick reply.

"Do you remember what it was like when you first started playing tennis?" I asked.

She thought for a moment, smiled, and said, "I could barely hit the ball."

"Well, how's your tennis game now?" I asked.

"I'm pretty good. I'm on the varsity tennis team," she replied.

"How did you get from not being able to hit the ball to the varsity?" I asked.

"Well, I practiced," she responded.

"Of course," I said. "Do you know that makes you a brilliant neuroscientist. Practice translates the principle 'The neurons that fire together wire together.' Remember this mantra," I added. "*Whatever the brain does a lot of is what the brain gets good at.*" After a few seconds I added, "Whether it's tennis, math, texting, or video games: Whatever the brain does a lot of is what the brain gets good at."

For every one neuron there are about ten glial cells. Neurons wouldn't work properly without the support of the glial cells, which play three important roles: they transport needed nutrients to the neurons, dispose of dead neurons, and provide the raw material for the myelin—or insulation—of the neurons. Myelination is one of five important processes that we will learn about later in this chapter.

Some Important Brain Structures

The natural development of different brain structures is an important source of behavior change in adolescents. Neuroscientist Paul MacLean describes the human brain as being composed of three distinct brains all wired together to function as one—the triune brain.

The first of the three brains is the brain stem, the innermost part of the brain, sometimes referred to as our reptilian brain. It is responsible for unconscious physiological functions like breathing and heartbeat as well as involuntary responses. Moving your hand away from a hot pan on the stove when you burn your finger is an example of the brain stem at work. In short, the brain stem is responsible for many of the functions that keep us alive.

The second brain system is called the limbic brain. The word *limbic* comes from the Latin word *limbus*, meaning "ring." The limbic brain, which physically "rings" the brain stem, is the seat of emotion. It will figure prominently in our discussion of the adolescent brain. A lot of teen impulsiveness and anger are the result of limbic fireworks.

A few relevant structures within the limbic system are these:

- A small almond-shaped structure called the amygdala. The word comes directly from the Greek word for "almond." This little nut-shaped collection of brain cells is the seat of fear and anger and a main player in the adolescent brain. When someone surprises you by jumping out from behind a corner, your immediate response, fear, is governed by the amygdala. It's also responsible for the hair-trigger anger we see in our teenagers when we tell them they can't stay out till midnight with their friends.
- The hippocampus (named after the Greek word for "seahorse" because of its distinctive shape) plays a key role in encoding new memories. Someone with damage to his hippocampus might be able to tell you the date and location of every major battle in the Civil War but be unable to recall what happened five minutes ago. An adolescent's hippocampus can be even more damaged by drinking and drug use than an adult's.
- The hypothalamus is the master control center for the body's endocrine, or hormone, system, which we'll discuss in more detail in chapter 4. The hypothalamus plays a key role in triggering the "raging hormones" that have been long associated with adolescents. It is also involved in sexual orientation, sex drive, and sexual behavior.
- The ventral striatal (VS) circuit is involved in motivation. Recent research shows that an underactive VS in the adolescent brain may be the reason that many teens seem to lack drive. Teen "laziness" appears to be brain based.

The third brain system is the cortex, a name derived from the Latin for "tree bark," which is what the brain's layers and folds resemble. The cortex is what most of us mean when we use the word *brain*: it contains the gray matter that gives us conscious thought and reason; it is the seat of "higher" brain functions like calculating, planning, and language. These higher functions take up a lot of space: the cortex is 80 percent of all brain mass in humans. You might say humans are cortex heavy.

The cortex is vast, but we'll examine just the prefrontal cortex because it is so key to understanding adolescents. The prefrontal cortex, or PFC for short, is the part of the brain just behind the bone of your forehead. It plays the role of the brain's executive or CEO and is responsible for planning ahead, considering consequences, and managing emotional impulses. It is also called the brain's conscience.

Executive Function

We'll talk more about the prefrontal cortex for two reasons. First, it's a major construction site in the teen brain. Second, it's the part of the brain responsible for executive function. In 1985 there were five professional articles on executive function. By 2005 there were more than five hundred. Why the explosion in interest? We now understand that executive function is foundational for school success and life competence. There is also concern there is a serious decline in the critical skills needed for a healthy executive function.

Executive function includes a host of mental skills that determine how we learn, as opposed to what we learn. The behaviors include concentrating, screening out distractions, persisting in the face of frustration, calming down, assessing risk, and managing emotional impulses and behavior. Think of executive function as the brain's "air traffic controller." Just as the controller needs to keep track of, manage, and coordinate dozens of airplane takeoffs and landings on multiple runways in changing conditions, so also must the brain's executive function, located in the PFC, coordinate input from multiple brain circuits and systems. There are three parts of executive function:

- Working memory. Shorter even than short-term memory, working memory lasts only seconds or minutes. Working memory is where we "think." For instance, when reading a paragraph working memory enables you to remember what you read at the start. It helps us hold information while linking it to longer term memories, so we understand what we read.
- Inhibitory controls. These are the brain's filter and brake controls, enabling us to screen out distractions, manage impulses, and resist temptations.
- Mental flexibility. This is the brain's gear transmission allowing us to think outside the box, adjust to changes, and adapt to new information.

Left and Right Brains

The brain has two sides. The left hemisphere is where the analytical work gets done, from calculating to speaking, writing, and reading. The right brain is the headquarters for visual processing as well as more abstract thinking. The more intuitive half of the brain, the right, is more active when you are listening to music or daydreaming—imagining a beautiful sunset, for instance, or other visual images.

Clearly, we need and use both the left and the right sides of the brain. While the left brain is busy separating out the parts that constitute the whole—analyzing—the right brain is engaged in synthesis. It would be very difficult to function normally without either hemisphere. Nearly all actions we perform involve the left and right brains in combination. A dense network of neurons, the corpus callosum, connects the two hemispheres and facilitates communication between them.

The Brain's Chemistry Set

Hormones and neurotransmitters are two groups of chemicals that play roles in how the brain works. Our bodies produce more than sixty hormones in glands located throughout the body. Their job is to bring messages to various organs both inside and outside the brain. The technical name for the hormone system is endocrine, and since the brain is the master control center the entire network is often referred to as the neuroendocrine system.

Testosterone, estrogen, and progesterone are three hormones that take center stage in the adolescent brain, so we'll learn more about in chapter 4. At last count scientists have identified sixty-seven hormones, and they are essential to everyday life. Part of the brain, the hypothalamus, serves as the master control for the endocrine system, telling the glands when to ramp up production of hormones and which ones the body needs.

Neurotransmitters form the second group of brain chemicals. They are located in the microscopic gap between the branches of two connecting neurons—also known as a synapse, the Greek word for "gap." There is a stew of more than a hundred different chemicals, collectively known as neurotransmitters, swimming around in a synapse. Their job is to transmit the electrical charge from the neuron across the gap. Neurotransmitters, like dopamine and serotonin, are also nicknamed "molecules of emotion" because they play such critical roles in our emotional life.

Five Important Brain Processes

Knowing the structure of the brain and how all these parts and systems work together to perform complex functions at lightning speed will help you understand why adolescents are so impulsive, for one thing. But first we have to look at the stages of brain development, which involves several important processes.

These five processes, or pillars, can be described as

- use it or lose it,
- blossoming and pruning,
- the window of opportunity,
- the window of sensitivity,
- myelination (insulation of nerve cells).

As with a muscle, the brain needs to be exercised to develop. Neurons that fire most frequently become wired into the brain's electrical networks. The ones that don't get used wither away. The use-it-or-lose-it process is the corollary to the idea that the "neurons that fire together wire together." If you don't use certain neurons, they don't get wired into the networks and, as a result, they are expendable.

From the 1950s through the '70s, scientists David Hubel and Torsten Wiesel conducted a series of experiments that demonstrated the use-it-or-lose-it process and eventually earned them the 1981 Nobel Prize in Physiology or Medicine. In one of the early experiments, Hubel and Wiesel used newborn kittens and sutured their eyelids shut. The kittens were well cared for in every other way, received adequate nourishment, loving contact with their mother, and playtime with their brothers and sisters. At the end of three months the scientists removed the sutures from the kittens' eyelids. Even though the kittens' eyes were intact, they were blind and remained blind for the rest of their lives. Because the brain cells that would have been dedicated to vision had not been used, they had either withered away or become dedicated to some other useful function by the time the kittens could open their eyes.

The use-it-or-lose-it phenomenon, as present in humans as it is for kittens, comes into play in children's and teens' brains. For example, one circuit that develops in the adolescent brain enables teens to manage strong emotional impulses. The more we encourage adolescents to think before they speak or act, the stronger those connections become. True to the use-it-or-lose-it principle, teens who are never held accountable for taking charge of their impulses have difficulty developing that crucial skill.

This process ties in to the next pillar of brain development, the blossoming and pruning of brain cell branches, which accounts for the brain's growth spurts.

Our brains develop in fits and starts, not in an even, uniform way. The brain is modular in design, meaning particular brain circuits and structures govern specific brain functions. Cordoned off into different regions of the brain, every brain function seems to have its own timetable. As a child grows, certain brain structures associated with particular functions have periods of intense activity and development, while others remain relatively quiet. Then the quiet structures awaken and begin to develop rapidly, while previously active structures hit the end of their growth spurts. In the midst of a growth spurt, the brain's various structures are like a room full of preschoolers trying to take a nap; while two in one corner drift to sleep, three in another will act up. When those three go to sleep, others will wake up and fuss.

Neuroscientist Marian Diamond of the University of California, Berkeley figured out what these growth spurts are. At the onset of a growth spurt, the area of the brain ready for intense growth starts to overproduce dendrites, the branches at the end of the brain cells. During a growth spurt, these branches go through hypergrowth. As a result, the number of branches that grow greatly exceeds the number that will survive. This process is known as blossoming.

After this overproduction of dendrites, life experience and the use-it-or-lose-it process take over. Experience causes certain neurons to fire and, as they fire, the branch connections bridging one cell to another get stronger. The branches that don't fire begin to shrink, wither, and, eventually, disappear. This process is called pruning. Experience, therefore, prunes or sculpts the circuits of the brain.

The periods of blossoming and pruning are critical in brain development. Experiences during these periods, more than any other time, physically shape the brain's neural networks and have a huge impact on how the brain gets wired. Take, for example, Albert Einstein's advice about child rearing: "If you want your children to be brilliant, read them fairy tales. If you want them to be more brilliant, read them more fairy tales." As a three-year-old listens to a fairy tale, her brain is in the process of blossoming and pruning; she is developing the neural connections of imagination. While an adult might enjoy a fairy tale, it is not going to build his neural networks because the blossoming and pruning of those circuits happened many years earlier.

Consistent with the brain's modular design, these developmental processes occur at certain times and, if neurons are not wired together during these windows of opportunity, then the branches of these cells will start to be pruned away. As with a piece of underripe fruit, if you buy it green, you can let it sit for a couple of days to get ripe. But if you let it sit too long, it will spoil. You have a window of opportunity for eating the fruit. If you miss that opportunity, you end up with a moldy mush. When a window in the brain closes, you lose that opportunity.

That's what happened to Hubel and Wiesel's kittens. The window of opportunity to wire together the circuits for vision was open wide during their early months, but because the kittens' eyes were sewn shut, the neurons started to wither and die. By the time they were allowed to open their eyes, the window was already shut. The neurons originally dedicated for vision were no longer available.

The human brain develops in the same way. For example, one of the first hearing circuits that gets wired in a baby's brain is technically called phonemic awareness, the ability to distinguish different sounds. As a baby hears a *b* sound and an *r* sound, for instance, the circuits in the auditory cortex (the hearing center of the brain) wire together in response to these phonemes. With repetition—neurons firing together and wiring together—particular circuits fire in response to different sounds and enable the baby to recognize specific phonemes. Research shows that the window of opportunity for phonemic awareness is open widest in the first three years of life. It doesn't shut completely after that, but it is never again so wide open. This window of opportunity explains why one of the strongest predictors of a child's reading ability in school is the amount of one-to-one conversation between caregiver and child in the first three years of life. The ability to differentiate sounds is the first crucial step on the path that later will lead to the ability to associate sounds with letters. Kids who don't learn to distinguish sounds during that time usually have trouble learning to read later on. On the other hand, those kids who have lots of opportunity to wire together the circuits associated with different sounds have an advantage when it is time to learn to read. Reading's first lessons don't happen in school: they happen in the crib during that important window of opportunity.

Beneficial experiences enable the brain to wire the appropriate circuits during the blossoming and pruning periods of different brain modules. Experience determines which neural connections survive and which wither away. Adverse experiences during the blossoming and pruning periods have a greater negative impact than they might otherwise have, because when bad things happen, the brain is especially vulnerable to them, and can be more easily hurt. The same window, open for opportunities to wire the brain for a normal, healthy life, is open for whatever happens, good or bad. The flip side of the window of opportunity is the window of sensitivity.

Here's an example of sensitivity at work. A series of ear infections for a two-year-old baby, if severe and frequent enough, can interfere with the wiring that will enable the baby to differentiate sounds. His hearing may be impaired permanently. The window of sensitivity for the wiring of the auditory cortex is open wide, which makes it particularly susceptible to interference. An adult's auditory cortex is already wired. A few ear infections, as long as they heal eventually, won't impair his ability to distinguish the word *tad* from the word *dad*. A two-year-old's auditory cortex, however, is still under construction. Ear infections during the window of sensitivity may put him in danger of missing out on the prime time for learning sounds.

Many experts believe that, partly due to the window of sensitivity, people who are abused as children sometimes have severe emotional problems later in life. It makes sense. Whatever happens while the window is open wires the brain. Even if what happens is harmful, the window can't screen it out. Think of it this way: a heavy rainstorm usually doesn't damage a finished house; but it can ruin an addition that is being constructed if the room has only half a roof. This also explains why heavy alcohol use can be so damaging to the adolescent brain. The window of sensitivity to alcohol is open wide and the brain is more susceptible to alcohol's damaging effects because a teenager's brain is under construction.

The fifth pillar of brain development is myelination. Often referred to as white matter, myelin is a white fatty substance that covers the main cable of the neuron, the axon. Myelin acts as insulation for the neurons' axons. As the brain develops, neurons acquire a good, thick coating of the substance in a process called myelination. Axons that are not insulated with myelin are more prone to electrical interference from other cells than are fully myelinated cells; also, without this coating of myelin the electrical signals traveling along the axon can't move as quickly. In fact an electrical charge travels one hundred times faster on a myelinated neuron than on one without the myelin protection.

Loss of balance and motor coordination are just two of the problems that result from the disintegration of the myelin. Multiple sclerosis (MS), for instance, causes the deterioration of the myelin sheath and the resulting inefficient firing of brain cells. Because they don't have their protective insulation, the brain cells can't relay electrical signals properly. A natural effect of the lack of myelination is also seen in little babies. An infant flails his limbs, without much control over them, because so many of his neurons are still not myelinated. The neurons in the brain do not yet effectively communicate messages to each other or to the body. As a baby's neurons become myelinated, his movements become less jerky and more coordinated.

Until recently, researchers believed that all five of these key developmental processes were completed by the time a boy or girl reached puberty. The blossoming and pruning spurts in the brain were believed to finish by age ten and myelination by seven. A major finding in brain science, however, revealed that all five of these vital processes continue well into adolescence. In fact, key brain areas undergo their blossoming and pruning periods *only* during adolescence. Further, the corpus callosum, which connects the right and left hemispheres, is still undergoing major construction from childhood into adolescence. The myelination process in certain parts of the teen brain actually *increases* by 100 percent from the beginning of adolescence to the end. One of the circuits involved in emotional regulation, for example, is still being myelinated during adolescence, which accounts for the lightning-quick flashes of anger when you, for example, tell an adolescent she has to get off the computer so other people in the family can use it.

Adolescents' developmental windows relate to the wiring of impulse control, relationships, and communication. That's why we need to pay attention when an adolescent spends hours playing violent video games while his window of opportunity to develop healthy relationships is open wide. It also makes sense to encourage adolescents to get involved with service projects and volunteer opportunities while major brain circuits related to social relationships are blossoming and pruning.

The Parent Survival Kit: Adolescent Brain Basics

The following statements in the Parent Survival Kit will help you determine how much you have already learned about the workings of the brain.

————————————————————————— PARENT SURVIVAL KIT

Adolescent Brain Basics

Yes No

☐ ☐ 1. Experience plays a major role in the actual wiring of the brain.

☐ ☐ 2. The brain is more vulnerable during growth spurts.

☐ ☐ 3. The part of the brain called the limbic system is the center of emotion.

☐ ☐ 4. The hypothalamus is the master control center for teen hormonal changes.

☐ ☐ 5. The prefrontal cortex is the seat of executive function, responsible for planning ahead and managing emotions.

☐ ☐ 6. Brain circuits need to be used in order to develop.

☐ ☐ 7. The adolescent brain is still "under construction."

☐ ☐ 8. Important windows of opportunity and sensitivity remain open during adolescence.

———————————————————————————————————

The new discoveries about the adolescent brain have huge implications for parents, teachers, and other professionals involved with adolescents. Now we can get more specific about what's going on inside the teenage brain and you can really figure out why they act that way and what you can do about it.

THREE

Why Adolescents Are Impulsive

As a high school counselor and later a psychologist, I've had the privilege of knowing hundreds of families from all kinds of backgrounds. Because I get along with teens and have experience working with them, over the years teachers, clergy, and pediatricians frequently have referred me to families with teenagers needing help. After working with these families for a few years, I developed a reputation for being especially helpful with adolescents whose problems went beyond the normal ups and downs of family life. Sometimes a series of guided sessions where parents and adolescents could learn how to communicate better went a long way toward solving the problems. Other times teens needed more elaborate solutions, such as individual psychotherapy, the establishing of behavioral contracts that they would adhere to, or on occasion coordination with a physician for medication. Almost without exception my experiences working with families have been rewarding and enlightening, and I enjoy catching up with the adults my adolescent students or clients have become.

Ellie, the second oldest of a family of four, was a sophomore in high school when she began to get into trouble. Ellie was the first to give her mom and dad a run for their money. Her parents, Jack and Meg, were at a loss about what to do. The issues started off small, but quickly grew. Eventually the constant arguments, some truancy episodes, and run-ins with teachers brought things to a head. Ellie's high school principal recommended that her parents get in touch with me.

The fireworks started in the first session. Meg's frustration was evident as she blurted, "I'm tired of being Ellie's maid. She never does anything to help around the house." In a nanosecond Ellie was at the edge of her chair. "Oh yeah? Then who do you think took out the garbage last night?" Then Ellie looked at me and said, "She's always on my back." I could see Meg was ready with a rebuttal, so I quickly interrupted: "So, I guess communication is on the list of things to work on."

For that session and several others Jack, Meg, and Ellie explored better ways to communicate. For instance, I insisted that they stay focused on one issue at a time. Starting with the conflict involving chores, I asked Meg what she would like to see change. "I want Ellie to help out around the house." I told Meg that I knew in general what she wanted, but that her statement was too vague. I explained that misunderstandings would be inevitable unless she was specific. She and Jack agreed that they would list what "helping out" meant before the next session.

Then I turned to Ellie. "And what would you like to see different?" Ellie didn't need any time to think it over. "I want the two of them to get off my back."

"I can understand why you would want that, Ellie. Now what can you do differently to make that happen?"

"They need to stop being so crabby," was Ellie's answer. I was firm but friendly in my response. "Ellie, you didn't answer my question. I asked what *you* could change to get your parents off your back. The only thing you can really influence is your own behavior. You can't control their crabbiness."

We continued in that vein for five or six sessions. Jack and Meg got a lot better at being direct and specific about expectations. They also minimized the arguments by setting and enforcing consequences when Ellie did not comply with their requests. To Ellie's credit, she started taking more responsibility once she found out her parents were going to enforce consequences rather than nag. The three of them used the same skills to tackle other sources of friction, such as violating curfew and skipping classes. Progress came quickly, and within three months, the family had finished therapy.

Over the years I bumped into Jack now and then at the grocery store, so I knew that Ellie had finished high school near the top of her class, graduated from college, and become a high school teacher. I loved the irony: the girl who had been a holy terror for her teachers had chosen to become one herself. She is a very good teacher. Maybe her teenage struggles gave her an important insight into the lives of her students. Whatever the case, Ellie turned out to be a fine young woman and her parents never needed my help on her behalf again.

But that wasn't the end of my professional relationship with Jack and Meg. Eight years after I helped them with Ellie, I got a call from Jack.

"Can Meg and I come in to see you?"

"Sure. What's up? How's Ellie?"

"Oh, Ellie's fine. She's really happy teaching. Actually, she's engaged to be married. That's not why I'm calling, though. We want to talk to you about something else."

Later that week they were back in my office describing the difficulties they were having with their youngest child, fourteen-year-old Jerrid, whom I had not met. But I remembered Jack and Meg telling me he was the easiest of children to parent. The past six months had changed that. Like his sister before him, Jerrid seemed to get into one scrape after another. The latest involved an ugly shouting match between him and his gym teacher that resulted in a suspension. I went through some of my usual checklist. Any signs of alcohol or drug use? None. Any change in friends? No, he still hangs out with the same kids. Any big academic problems at school? Nope.

I smiled at Jack and Meg. "Sounds to me like a case of Phineas Gage syndrome," and I told them the story of one of the most famous figures in brain science.

Phineas Gage wasn't a scientist but a regular guy who happened to be in the wrong place at the wrong time. Nonetheless, he gave scientists an incredible window into the workings of the brain.

In late summer of 1848 Phineas Gage was the foreman of a railroad construction crew laying tracks in rural Vermont. By all accounts Gage was the kind of fellow anyone would like—honest, reliable, hardworking, smart, and respectful. His bosses were grateful for his loyalty and work ethic. The men on his work crew admired his kindness and integrity. On September 13, 1848, as Gage was tamping down a dynamite charge in preparation for blasting, the dynamite exploded and launched a thirteen-pound, four-and-a-half-foot tamping rod like a missile. Gage had no time to duck. The rod went straight through his head, entering just below his left cheekbone and coming out of the top of his head, landing thirty yards behind him.

Amazingly, the blast did not kill Gage, nor did he lose consciousness. Although the front part of the left side of his brain was instantly destroyed, he kept his eyes open and remained lucid throughout the event and its aftermath. According to eyewitness accounts, he was alert, "in full possession of his reason, and free from pain."

Gage's co-workers rushed him by cart to the nearest town where a young physician named Martyn Harlow had his practice. Over the following weeks, Harlow oversaw his treatment, and thanks to the excellent care and Gage's good health, the railroad foreman survived his dreadful accident. Within two months Phineas was well enough to return to his job at the Rutland and Burlington Railroad. But he soon lost his job with the railroad—and not because he couldn't do the work. The railroad let him go because, as his friends said, "Gage was no longer Gage."

In place of the responsible, affable Phineas Gage, whom everyone had loved, was a belligerent, cursing, dishonest schemer. No one could explain it, but even though Gage had physically survived, the man with the wonderful personality had died.

Gage lived for almost twelve years after that fateful September day in 1848, bouncing from job to job and place to place for over a decade. Finally, destitute and without notice, he died in 1860 in San Francisco.

Seven years after Phineas's death, his former physician persuaded the unfortunate railroad worker's family to exhume the body and send the skull to Dr. Harlow for study along with the cursed tamping rod. Eventually, the skull and tamping iron made their way to Harvard University, where they remain on display at the Warren Anatomical Museum to this day.

Every student of brain science learns about Phineas Gage, whose case demonstrated the link between the brain's frontal lobes and behavior. In his 1867 study, Harlow concluded that the transformation of Gage's personality was caused by the extensive damage to his frontal lobes. "The equilibrium . . . between his intellectual faculties and animal propensities seems to have been destroyed," Harlow wrote. In 1994, the University of Iowa's Hanna and Antonio Damasio, two of the world's leading neuroscientists, finally confirmed Harlow's judgment of what had happened to Gage using computer modeling and neural-imaging techniques. Gage's personality transformation was caused by damage to the prefrontal cortex. As CEO of the brain, the prefrontal cortex regulates how the rest of the body and other parts of the brain function. It is the decision maker, the planner that weighs the options that other parts of the brain present to it. The PFC is also one of the adolescent brain's major construction sites.

Dr. Jay Giedd, a neuroscientist at the National Institutes of Health in Bethesda, Maryland, is a pioneer in the use of the latest MRI scanning technology to unlock the secrets of the brain—including the prefrontal cortex. Because brain-scanning equipment is so expensive and because earlier technology was so invasive, most early brain scans were done for clinical reasons—to diagnose people with serious brain problems like epilepsy, tumors, and other problems needing help. Giedd, one of the first people to start scanning the brains of normal adolescents, has been doing so for more than twenty years. His nonclinical brain scans were critical in proving that the adolescent brain is not a finished product but a work in progress, in the midst of dynamic change.

Giedd discovered that the blossoming and pruning process in the brain is not completed in early childhood. One phase of blossoming and pruning winds down when children are still very young (in the terrible twos), but a second wave corresponds with adolescence. The blossoming—an overproduction of brain cell branches—peaks in the prefrontal cortex at around the ages of eleven or twelve. Just as puberty is getting under way, teen brains are furiously producing dendrites in the PFC. Then, the pruning process, whereby unused neuron branches wither and die, continues throughout adolescence. In short, the PFC (and all that it manages) changes throughout adolescence. Many teens show signs of the Phineas Gage syndrome, a dramatic change in personality, even though they don't lose their prefrontal cortex the way Phineas Gage did.

Because the PFC is the executive center of the brain, its job is to think ahead to consequences and to control impulses that shoot out of other regions of the brain. Because it is still developing during adolescence, however, teens do not have the impulse control of adults. Even if a kid comes into adolescence with a personality like the young Gage—hardworking, friendly, reliable, and kind—at one point or another he or she will probably turn into the gruff, irresponsible, unpleasant Gage. For example, if an adolescent is really frustrated with other people, he may not stifle the urge to say just what he's feeling about them at that moment—an impulse even adults have from time to time. An adult prefrontal cortex would say, "I'd better watch what I say," but an adolescent's PFC can short-circuit and he or she may mouth off, sometimes leading to unpleasant consequences.

To show what I mean, let me tell you my story of a Phineas Gage syndrome survivor. When my son Brian and his friends were teens, they got into big trouble for mouthing off at school one day. Their high school had an "open campus" for lunch, which meant that kids could leave the building for forty-five minutes and were expected to be back for their next class. The school's neighbors never had been thrilled with all of the teenagers wandering around in the middle of the day, but, for the most part, it was a good policy. The students almost always behaved themselves, got some sunshine, and blew off some steam.

One day, Brian, his friend Rudy, and a few others were heading out for lunch. Crossing the street from the school grounds, they noticed an approaching police car. Somehow they all had the same impulse to cross the street as slowly as possible. As they leisurely shuffled across, the squad car pulled up and was forced to stop and wait. The officer driving the squad car got out and told them they should stay out of the street when cars were coming. Depending on whose version you believe, he may have even called them "jerks."

The prudent thing would have been to keep their mouths shut at that point. That's what the boys' prefrontal cortexes should have told them to do. Instead, they proceeded to give the policeman a lecture on "pedestrian rights." Rudy topped it off by suggesting that maybe the cop was the one being the jerk. Soon Rudy the Lip was under arrest in the back of the cruiser, and the rest of the boys were in trouble with the assistant principal.

The boys' emotions were no different from other people's. The difference is that they felt the need to express themselves verbally because their impulse control center wasn't doing its job. Because their PFCs weren't fully wired, they didn't keep their thoughts and feelings to themselves as most of us would have had the good sense to do.

I'm reminded of a Calvin and Hobbes cartoon when I hear about mouthy kids. Calvin says something inappropriate, which prompts his mother to give him a time-out. In the final panel, Calvin is sitting in the corner saying to himself, "My trouble is my lips move when I think." Yet Calvin with a fully wired PFC would make for a pretty boring comic strip.

After I'd told Meg and Jack about the growth spurt of the teen's prefrontal cortex, Jack said, "I could handle a little more boredom these days. Jerrid's erratic behavior is making life a little too interesting." He paused for a moment. "Still . . . it's nice to know it really isn't all his fault he's giving us so much trouble."

Meg interjected. "Does that mean we should just wait this stage out and he'll be better when his brain is fully wired?"

Many parents struggle with this question, but I would say the answer is no. Even though it is not the teen's fault that his brain isn't fully under his control, it's his responsibility to get it under control. And it's your responsibility as a parent to help him. You can't simply dismiss his behavior or let it go. Even though he will probably settle back into his old pleasant personality eventually, you can't and shouldn't let him run wild until that happens. The experiences a teen has will have a big bearing on how he eventually learns to manage his own emotions and impulses. While his PFC is being pruned, you as a parent need to provide the guidance and structure that he will eventually internalize.

Just as Meg and Jack had done years before with Ellie, they needed to set clear expectations and consequences for Jerrid. Sit down with your child; be direct and specific about how you expect him or her to behave and what will happen if your expectations are not met. Enforce the consequences of any violation of the ground rules. These guidelines can help a teen learn to keep a lid on his impulses even when he doesn't want to. They may not always control their impulses enough to follow the rules, but they'll know when they've broken one.

It is crucial to let a teen know exactly what the consequences will be if he doesn't comply. Don't communicate the consequences as threats. Just let him know in a matter-of-fact way what will happen and that the consequences will be his own choices. Make sure you follow through on the consequences, or he will quickly figure out that he doesn't really have to observe the rules.

When you do have to lay down the law, don't get dragged into power struggles and screaming matches. They don't do any good. You have to keep your cool even if your kid doesn't. Finally, maintain a sense of humor and go out of your way to let him know you love him *and* like him. It's easy to get caught up in his abrasive personality at a time like this, so you have to make an effort to tell him you love him *and* that you still think he is a likable person.

When I relayed this to Meg and Jack, he replied, "I know you're right, but Jerrid has a way of pushing my buttons. I know I'm getting into way too many power struggles."

"I think it's because you and Jerrid are so much alike," said Meg. "You were so much better than me at avoiding power struggles with Ellie. Now with Jerrid it's just the reverse."

Jack turned to me and said, "Meg's right. So what should I do?"

Here's a three-step process to follow when things are getting heated with your teen:

1. When it's time for you to enforce a consequence, take a minute and visualize how you want to handle it. Picture yourself as calm and firm.
2. Tell him that it was his choice that is causing the consequence. Don't expect him to take this message calmly. He may try

to talk his way out of it or may want to argue. Don't join the argument.

3. If you feel your blood pressure rising, take a deep breath and remember this advice: *When you feel like taking the wind out of his sails, it is a better idea to take your sails out of his wind.*

At the end of our session Jack and Meg seemed relieved to have a new perspective on Jerrid and his behavior. As Jack said, "I can really relate to Phineas Gage's bosses. No wonder they fired him. I've felt like firing Jerrid from our family on more than one occasion during the past few months. I'll try to remember that saying about taking my sails out of his wind."

The Parent Survival Kit: Limits and Consequences

Dealing with impulsive behavior is one of the biggest challenges for parents. Outbursts and misbehavior can come to seem normal, but setting firm limits and consequences is essential. Teenagers need structure from parents while their "brain's supervisor," the prefrontal cortex, is under construction. You have to become their external brain for a while. Use this kit to assess your approach to putting boundaries around your teen's behavior.

PARENT SURVIVAL KIT

Limits and Consequences

Yes No

☐ ☐   1. My spouse and I agree on how to parent our teen.

☐ ☐   2. My spouse and I share parenting responsibilities.

☐ ☐   3. Our family rules are clear and consistent.

☐ ☐   4. I carry through and enforce consequences when necessary.

☐ ☐   5. I am able to negotiate with my teenager.

☐ ☐   6. I am consistent with limits and consequences.

☐ ☐   7. I am able to avoid power struggles with my adolescent.

☐ ☐   8. I don't "sweat the small stuff."

Don't be surprised or discouraged if you answered with more noes than you would like. For parents of teens, getting from no to yes is a process that requires a lot of attention and patience.

Dealing with the Extremes

Most parents of adolescents have challenges similar to Jack and Meg's. Some, however, have much more serious behavior to contend with. That was the case with Craig and Melinda. Their son, Troy, had always been a challenge. Even as a preschooler he had been exceptionally difficult to handle—throwing frequent tantrums, fighting with other children, and pushing hard against every limit Craig and Melinda set. During elementary school they had frequent parent conferences about Troy's poor grades and misbehavior.

Craig and Melinda had worked very hard to help their son over the years, attending seminars on "spirited children," reading all the popular parenting books, and having Troy evaluated by the best doctors and psychologists in the area. When he was in the sixth grade they took Troy to a child psychiatrist who diagnosed him with a condition called conduct disorder–childhood onset. After meeting with the psychiatrist Craig and Melinda had a diagnosis but little else. The only explanation for Troy's behavior that came close to making sense was that it was caused by some sort of inherited trait. Melinda's older brother had a long history of serious behavior problems and had spent time in prison for assault. When Craig asked the psychiatrist what he recommended, the reply was, "Keep doing what you're doing and pray he grows out of it."

Troy didn't grow out of it. The problems became more serious when he was a teenager: truancy, fighting, vandalism, and constant arguments at home about rules. Troy already had a police record and a juvenile probation officer by the time their pastor referred the family to me. I had read the case file and I knew that there was no history of abuse, neglect, chemical dependency, or family violence. Craig and Mary were good parents dealing with a very difficult teen. For our first meeting they met with me alone. Twenty minutes into the session Melinda asked a familiar question, "What did we do wrong?"

My answer was quick and direct. "Nothing! We're not going there. There are some therapists who always see the parents as the culprits. As far as I can tell, the two of you have been doing everything possible to be good parents." I could see the relief on their faces. I continued, "We're not going to look back. We may never discover the reason for Troy's problems. Even if we did, it wouldn't change what has to happen now. I recommend that we focus on the future, set realistic goals, and work on specific behaviors."

A strategy we used to help Troy get his behavior under control was behavioral contracting. The contracts are written agreements that spell out in easy-to-understand language the behavior that is expected and the consequences for breaking the contract. Parents and their teen sign the contract and then post it in a visible location in the home—say, on the family bulletin board in the kitchen, on the refrigerator, or next to the family computer. I encouraged Craig and Melinda to be realistic in their goals. "You can't turn everything around at once. A ten-page contract won't work. Pick the most important issue and start there." They quickly agreed that their biggest worry was his violent outbursts at home. Melinda admitted that she was afraid Troy would hurt her during one of his outbursts. The next task was to identify realistic consequences that they could enforce. "We will involve Troy in negotiating the contract, but you need to decide in advance what the possible consequences will be," I explained. Craig said that he was worried that his son would just defy any consequences. "Then we need to build that possibility into the contract," I replied. "How do we do that?" Craig asked. I explained to Craig and Melinda that they needed to be willing to up the ante with Troy to make the contract enforceable and to get his attention. I suggested communicating with his probation officer and the police to get their support and searching for a relative or friend who would be willing to take Troy in for a while. I think Melinda was shocked. "Are you serious, Dr. Walsh?"

"Yes, I am. It doesn't make sense to start a behavioral contract with consequences you don't think you can enforce. Troy will test that right away and if there's no backup, then you reinforce his defiance. Besides, it's unlikely you will have to resort to extremes if Troy knows you're serious."

Here is a copy of the behavioral contract Craig and Melinda negotiated with their son.

Behavioral Contract: Violence

1. This contract is entered into between Troy and his parents, Craig and Melinda, on _____ (date).

2. Whereas I agree that our home should be free of violence, and

Whereas I commit myself to resolve differences without violence,

Therefore I agree that I will express my anger in an appropriate way.

> I will refrain from screaming obscenities in the house.
> I will refrain from throwing items in anger.
> I will refrain from intentionally breaking any items.
> I will not strike or threaten to strike.
> I will not in any other way injure or threaten to injure anyone in my family.

3. I understand and accept that any failure to uphold this contract will result in my parents immediately contacting my probation officer or immediately contacting the police at their discretion.

I have read, understand, and accept the terms of this contract.

Troy _____

Craig _____

Melinda _____

Troy came to the next session with his parents. I explained to him that having a behavioral contract about violence was nonnegotiable. We wanted him to be involved in laying out the terms of the contract, but that the final decision on consequences for noncompliance rested with his parents. Troy thought the whole thing was ridiculous, but Craig and Melinda held their ground. Troy eventually signed the contract. A month later Troy became angry and broke a window during an argument with Melinda. She called the police, who responded quickly, removed Troy from the house, and talked with him in the squad car for fifteen minutes. They told him that if there was another complaint, they would arrest him. That was the only time Melinda needed to call the police.

In the months that followed, Craig and Melinda formed a number of contracts with Troy, covering topics like curfew, truancy, and drug use. Troy understood that his parents were committed to removing him from their home if he defied the consequences of the contracts. Craig's brother in another state agreed to take Troy in if necessary.

Troy's road through adolescence was very rocky, with more discipline problems at school and a few more scrapes with the police during his high school years. When Troy quit high school during his senior year, Craig and Melinda made a contract with him about getting a job and paying rent. Troy eventually got his GED, moved out, and got a job in the construction industry. Craig and Melinda had to adjust their expectations and hopes for Troy, but they are grateful that he is gainfully employed and law abiding. They also now have a stable, pleasant relationship with him.

Few adolescents are as challenging as Troy. Most teens will, however, test the patience of their parents as their prefrontal cortexes mature. All teens need parents who will provide the structure and support to help them as they develop adult restraint. Obviously you can adapt the behavioral contract according to the problem you're having with your teen. You'll need to do some planning in advance so that you know that you and your spouse or partner can enforce whatever consequences you plan to put in the contract. You should do this kind of advance planning with your spouse even when you are laying simpler ground rules for how you expect your teen to behave. You want your teen to understand the cause-and-effect nature of his actions on his life in the family so that he's able to function in the real world. The behavior contract is simply a stricter measure of his behavior than ground rules, and with greater consequences.

Here are some baselines for providing a supportive behavioral framework for your teen.

DO

- ✓ Set clear rules and expectations for behavior. For example, instead of saying, "Be nicer to your brother," say "You cannot hit your brother, call him names, or use put-downs."
- ✓ Have the conversations about expectations and consequences when things are calm and everyone can think clearly. For example, if your daughter comes in an hour after curfew and you are very upset, let her know that you are angry, and that you will talk with her in the morning. You will be better able to handle the necessary discipline when you are less agitated. Of course, you must make sure that you follow up as promised.
- ✓ Spell out consequences for noncompliance. Consequences for adolescents usually involve the loss of privileges. For example, "If you cannot limit your video games to one hour a night, then you will not be allowed to play video games for one week."
- ✓ Have your son or daughter state out loud his or her understanding of both the rules and the consequences. This both clears up any ambiguity and helps adolescents take responsibility. Write them down, if needed.
- ✓ Choose consequences that fit and make sure you can live with them. For example, instead of saying "You're grounded for the next month for taking the car after I told you not to," say "You're grounded for the weekend and you may not use the car for two weeks."
- ✓ Follow through on consequences.
- ✓ If your adolescents start yelling during an important discussion about rules, don't try to out-shout them. Say, "We don't seem to be able to have a discussion about this right now. When you're ready to discuss this without yelling, we'll talk." Then make sure to come back and finish the talk. They should not be allowed to go on to their next activity until the discussion has been completed.

DON'T

- ✗ Don't be surprised when adolescents get surly.
- ✗ Don't harass an adolescent about every little thing. Pick and choose issues that matter.
- ✗ Don't get dragged into power struggles. Calmly state your expectations and consequences and let your teen know that you expect that he will comply, but if he chooses not to, then he will have to accept the consequences.
- ✗ Don't make consequences into threats.
- ✗ Don't let your emotions get out of control when your son or daughter starts yelling. Take a deep breath and count to ten. Take a break if you need to.
- ✗ Don't let your adolescent get his or her way by yelling and threatening or by further objectionable behavior. That can reinforce a dangerous pattern.

What do I want to continue?

_____

_____

_____

What do I want to change?

_____

_____

_____

FOUR

Risky Business: Helping Teens
Put on the Brakes

Smart kids do stupid things. It's a simple fact of life. No one makes it through the teenage years unscathed. Even the meekest, smartest, most obedient, and sensible teenager will, at one point or another, find himself or herself facing the angry, disbelieving face of an adult who shouts, "What were you thinking?!"

All sorts of kids take foolish risks. It happens often enough that most people think of teenage risk taking as a part of growing up. But sometimes we're caught off guard. When good kids—the honor students, the class presidents, the kids who play sports, hold down after-school jobs, and follow the rules—get themselves into dangerous or destructive situations, we often don't know what to make of it. What *were* they thinking? And what could we have done to try to prevent it and what can we do to try to keep it from happening again?

Sometimes these risky behaviors drive a wedge between adults and teenagers. No one, including the teenager, can explain why she did it. To the adult trying to make sense of the situation, it may seem like the teenager is lying. The adult believes there must be a reason she took the foolish risk, because even a child should have been able to foresee the dangerous consequences. It's almost like the urge to act suppressed every other thought, even the one that should have said or in fact was saying, "You know, this doesn't seem like such a good idea." But that just doesn't make sense to an adult, who might think, "There must be something else going on here, she's hiding something from me." Because you didn't realize she might do something this risky, you're left wondering how well you know her; you no longer fully trust her.

I'll give you an example. When my son Dan was a high school junior, he and his friend Gaelen were waiting for the bus to take them to cross-country ski practice. Dan and Gaelen were smart kids. Good students and varsity athletes, they were well liked by their peers and respectful with adults. As they waited, they were breaking in a new Hacky Sack, a harmless, round beanbag designed to be kicked lightly with teammates. Because the new sack was tightly packed, it was hard to control, and so their efforts to loosen it through game play soon turned to stomping on it and throwing it at a brick wall. Then Dan got a bright idea. He'd driven the family car to school that day. Why not back over the bag a few times and use the weight of the car to loosen it up? Gaelen agreed that this seemed like a great idea. Worst-case scenario, they'd pop the sack open but be able to sew it back up after removing some of the beans, right? This was such a stroke of genius they ran right over to the car in the school parking lot and set to work. Gaelen would sit in the driver's seat, manipulating the gas and brake pedals and Dan would direct him from behind the car. The driver's-side door would remain open so that Gaelen could see and hear Dan. Gaelen would back up at most a couple of feet over the bag, stop the car, and then they would both examine the sack.

At the inner-city school these boys attended, the lot was packed with cars, jammed into cramped spots with the winter's plowed snowbanks encroaching on all sides. So intent were Gaelen and Dan on their brilliant plan, they didn't stop to think about the car next to them. And so, driver's door wide open, Gaelen stepped on the gas, backed up . . . and unleashed a sickening scraping sound that instantaneously drained the blood from their faces. They had wedged the door against the adjacent car, and bent the door back on its hinges. Luckily, the other car was unhurt. Unluckily, the Hacky Sack was still too tight.

The two boys missed practice that day. They drove slowly around town, the driver's door clutched to the car with Dan's left hand, trying to figure out a way to fix the car so that I wouldn't find out. After an auto repair shop owner told them it would require eight hundred dollars and days in the shop, they knew they had no choice but to confess.

The first words out of my mouth were "What were you thinking?"

Later, Gaelen said he realized what was happening but felt paralyzed. He couldn't move his foot to the brake. The other car was obviously too close. What had they been thinking? Years later, they still can't explain it. For some reason it was a lot easier to step on the gas pedal than it was to step on the brakes.

We shouldn't be too surprised if teenagers make some foolish mistakes. It's the parents' job to convert the mistakes into learning opportunities by making sure that our kids deal with the consequences. So Dan and Gaelen had to pay for the repairs themselves. Many of the stupid things that smart kids do end up as that incident did for Dan and Gaelen. It was foolish and a tad dangerous, but no one was hurt. They never had a good explanation for why it happened, but after they'd worked off the cost of fixing the car door, everything was okay. Sometimes, however, kids face harsher consequences for their reckless actions.

Some years ago Northbrook, Illinois, an affluent northern suburb of Chicago known for its white-collar citizens, large single-family homes, low crime rate, and reputable school system, was the site of an ugly, violent hazing incident. At a time when many kids in this country pass through metal detectors on the way into school to prevent violence, a quiet suburb like Northbrook seemed to offer safety and a good education, but the victims and perpetrators were students at the suburb's Glenbrook North High School. And, rather unusual for accounts of violent hazing, the victims were junior girls, and the perpetrating seniors were girls, too.

In hazing that spun wildly out of control, the victims were smeared with mud, garbage, pig entrails, and human feces. Some of them were kicked and beaten until they lost consciousness. One young woman was hospitalized with a head injury and possible brain damage. Others were treated at emergency rooms.

The hazing, in which graduating seniors initiated members of the next class with a series of humiliating activities, had been a tradition for years. Somehow, it went awry that spring. The story seemed so strange that reporters followed it for weeks and reported a series of suspensions, expulsions, criminal charges, and lawsuits. When it came time for graduation, more than thirty girls were prevented from walking with their peers at commencement. That's when reporters made the shocking discovery that some of the expelled girls were the top students in the class. These were girls with bright futures, college-bound from one of the best school districts in the country. For some reason they'd jeopardized their futures, nearly killed several of their fellow students, and participated in angry, reckless, despicable acts. Once again adults had the same question: What were they thinking?

Quickness to Anger

The risky behavior that emerges in the adolescent years can be a huge source of worry for adults. Even trustworthy kids wind up doing a few stupid things, and most parents really do lose sleep over their teens' potential to take foolish risks, especially when they're waiting up for a teen out late with friends. This adolescent inability to check their foolhardy impulses becomes a worse problem when coupled with a teen's quickness to anger, another tendency that seems to come suddenly out of nowhere.

Quickness to anger coupled with poor impulse control often results in rudeness and verbal abuse. Sometimes the stakes get higher. I was in ninth grade the first time I saw two angry kids get violently out of control. Smitty and Frank, both nice guys who rarely got into trouble, were playing touch football with a bunch of us after school. Quite a few of us were out on the field fooling around. At some point, one of the boys said something that the other thought was insulting and both started shouting. In seconds the shouting had escalated into a fight.

Smitty took a swing at Frank, who crumpled to the ground, his jaw badly broken. Smitty had also snapped two of his knuckles at the base of the fingers. In less than half a minute the situation had gone from a questionable insult to serious injuries, just because the two boys couldn't control their anger. None of us, Smitty and Frank included, could explain why it had happened.

To this day, fifty years later, Smitty cannot fully extend the two fingers he broke in ninth grade. Punching Frank permanently damaged his knuckles. Though the incident took place half a century ago, he is reminded of his sudden out-of-character burst of anger every day. Smitty used this experience to teach his own children the foolishness of lashing out and the importance of anger management, saying to his kids while holding up his permanently disfigured hand, "Look where being the macho tough guy got me."

Parents aren't likely to find many answers in the events that lead up to an outburst, because the cause probably was internal. We ask the wrong question when we wonder what smart adolescents are thinking when they do stupid things. A better question is "What's going on inside their brains?" Quickness to anger and a tendency to take risks both have their roots in the internal changes taking place inside adolescents. And both make a lot more sense when you understand the adolescent brain.

Hormones

Because the prefrontal cortex's wiring is still incomplete, the adolescent PFC can't always distinguish between a good decision and a bad one, no matter how intelligent the kid is. The ongoing wiring of the PFC helps explain why smart kids do dumb things and are quick to express anger, but it is only part of the equation. At the same time that adolescents are having trouble stifling impulses, they are being barraged with an unprecedented onslaught of powerful urges, lightning-quick mood changes, and confusing new feelings. For an explanation of these phenomena, we need to turn to a subject long associated with the adolescent years and often used to explain erratic behavior in teens: hormones.

A typical example: A mother, father, teenage daughter, and younger son are sitting down for a nice family dinner. The mother turns to her daughter and says, "Honey, tell your father what happened in school today."

Suddenly furious, the daughter shouts at her mother, "Mom! Just because I told you about that doesn't mean I wanted to tell Dad! And I'm not your trained parrot to speak whenever you want me to!

Why don't you tell him if you want him to know so badly! God, I hate this family!" Then she shoves back her chair, storms upstairs to her room, and slams the door.

The mother is horrified. Her daughter had seemed to be in such a good mood. "What did I do?" she asks. "Why did she scream at me?"

The son rolls his eyes. The father mutters, "Hormones," as he lifts his fork to his mouth.

Hormones actually are behind a wide range of erratic adolescent behaviors. As we saw in chapter 2 our bodies, through the endocrine system, manufacture chemical messengers, called hormones, in a dozen different glands that help regulate body function, interpret incoming data, and direct responses. Together the endocrine system and the brain and nervous system are called the neuroendocrine system

Here is an example of the neuroendocrine system at work. You're walking down your block alone at night, when suddenly a dark figure appears out of the shadows just ahead. Nerve impulses from your eyes travel to your brain, and your brain immediately sets to work alerting the body to the danger. Nearly instantaneously your brain sends signals to the adrenal glands located way down by your kidneys, and these glands begin pumping out a hormone you've probably heard of before, adrenaline. The surge of adrenaline initiates changes throughout your body: Your heart begins pounding. Your blood pressure increases. A surge of glucose courses through your body, giving you instant energy. Your metabolism races. Blood flows to your muscles, so you can act quickly. In short, you get an adrenaline rush. This is a classic example of the fight-or-flight response, a survival instinct. A second later you realize the shadow is just your neighbor and your cortex realizes you're not in danger, but because of the survival instinct unleashed by adrenaline, it may take a couple minutes for your body to return to normal. Even though it turned out to be nothing, your neuroendocrine system has used hormones to ensure your survival just in case. And it all happened in a fraction of a second.

Scientists have identified more than sixty different types of human hormones. They are essential to everyday life, and they are at play every moment of our lives, every year of our life. So if hormones regulate all sorts of bodily functions for all ages of people, why would we blame hormones for the teenage daughter's sudden outburst? We need to head back to the brain for the answer.

Part of the brain, the hypothalamus, serves as the master control for the endocrine system, telling the glands when to ramp up production of hormones and which ones the body needs. At the beginning of puberty, the hypothalamus sends a message (by hormone) to the pituitary gland to increase production of certain hormones throughout the body. Which hormones the pituitary produces depends on the child's sex, but for boys and girls this new order for additional hormones initiates all sorts of changes. We do not know what exactly triggers the hypothalamus, but whatever it is convinces the hypothalamus that the body is ready to become an adult and that it is time to produce growth hormones. Besides all of the other changes in puberty, the average girl will grow ten inches in the adolescent years, while the average boy will grow eleven inches.

To get a good understanding of the adolescent brain, we'll focus on the three main growth hormones: testosterone, estrogen, and progesterone. Each of them is present in both boys and girls in early childhood, but their concentrations in the two sexes change dramatically with puberty.

For boys the main growth hormone is testosterone, which triggers the big physical changes like dramatic growth spurts and sudden voice changes. Adolescent boys can have five to seven surges of testosterone every day (triggered by a message from the hypothalamus to the pituitary gland, of course) during the course of puberty. By the end of adolescence they can have 1,000 percent the amount of testosterone in their bodies that they had before puberty, and twenty times more than girls have at the same age. That's a lot of a powerful chemical surging through boys' bodies.

Testosterone doesn't just affect the body; it affects the brain, too. Specifically, testosterone has a powerful effect on the amygdala, the fight-or-flight center of the brain and the seat of fear and aggression. The amygdala also has receptors for testosterone, so, in the midst of puberty, especially during a hormonal surge, the amygdala is regularly overstimulated. As a result, boys become emotional powder kegs. While testosterone does all sorts of good things, it is also likely to trigger surges of anger, aggression, sexual interest, dominance, and territoriality. And because testosterone is geared toward quick tension release, adolescent boys are prone to follow any impulse that might release stress.

The everyday changes in a young teen's behavior are dramatic. Going into an eight-year-old boy's room is no big deal, but if you tread on a square inch of carpet in the room of a fourteen-year-old boy, you're likely to hear some version of "Get out of my room!" That territoriality comes from testosterone's influence on the amygdala.

For girls, there are two important growth hormones: estrogen and progesterone. Actually, estrogen is a family of different hormones, but for our purposes we'll consider it as one hormone. Just as testosterone triggers the physical changes in boys, estrogen is responsible for the changes in girls: the development of breasts, widening of the pelvis, the onset of menses, and all the other physical changes. Estrogen affects the brain as well.

Whereas the amygdala has a lot of docking stations for testosterone, it's the hippocampus—the memory center—where estrogen molecules find an abundance of welcoming ports. This connection may give girls some advantage when it comes to academic tasks requiring memory.

Neurotransmitters

Besides affecting the body's organs and parts of the brain, estrogen and progesterone also have a powerful influence over neurotransmitters. These brain chemicals travel between one neuron's dendrites to another's. Neurotransmitter molecules are like flying keys that shoot across the tiny gaps between neurons and lock into the next brain cell, carrying the impulse from one cell to another. The main neurotransmitters that are active in the adolescent brain are norepinephrine, dopamine, and serotonin. All three have a big influence on mood.

Norepinephrine is the energizer neurotransmitter. It prepares the body for its fight-or-flight response. It also has an important role in storing things in memory. Thanks to norepinephrine, anything that might be good to remember for future survival gets stored in memory. Like dopamine and serotonin, norepinephrine levels affect mood as they rise and fall.

Dopamine is the feel-good neurotransmitter. When you're feeling on top of the world, your dopamine is flowing. Human beings are attracted to things that increase levels of dopamine. One of the reasons that drugs and alcohol can become addictive is that they create surges of dopamine in the brain.

Serotonin is the neurotransmitter that stabilizes moods. In proper amounts it helps us feel relaxed and confident. A lack of serotonin can make us depressed or aggressive. Antidepressant drugs such as Prozac and Xanax increase levels of serotonin. Recent research also shows that chocolate increases the levels of dopamine and serotonin, which may explain why some people crave it.

Throughout puberty and into adulthood, estrogen and progesterone are in balance with each other in the female body. But the balance between them fluctuates throughout a woman's menstrual cycle. As the level of one hormone shifts, so does the level of the other. Because these hormones also have a particularly powerful influence over norepinephrine, dopamine, and serotonin, fluctuating hormonal levels can lead to dramatic, sudden mood swings. These swings can be as baffling to the girl who experiences them as they are to her family. Besides mood shifts, estrogen also influences reactions to stress, sex drive, and appetite.

A girl can be laughing uproariously on the phone with her friends, seeming to be happier than she's ever been. Fifteen minutes later she can be sobbing in despair over a difficult geometry problem. In the span of a few minutes she can go from the top of the world to the bottom of the basement. The shifting of estrogen and progesterone levels keeps a cocktail of neurotransmitters in flux in her body. Happiness from a good conversation and frustration from a hard math problem are emotions anyone would feel, but because neurotransmitters amplify moods, a seemingly small detail can blow an emotional reaction way out of proportion.

We can help girls deal with these emotional fluctuations by explaining the brain chemistry that makes their moods go haywire. This knowledge won't stop the emotional roller coaster, but some perspective will make it a bit easier to manage the ups and downs. In addition it is important for girls to get regular exercise. While important at any age, research shows that exercise during adolescence reduces depression, anxiety, and other emotional distress.

We'll further explore the differences in girls' brains and boys' brains in a later chapter, but for now we'll focus on a key similarity: in both sexes, hormonal fluctuation puts adolescents at the mercy of extreme impulses that they are not always capable of controlling. For boys, this impulsive behavior can be aggressive and angry. For girls, it can show up as amplification of a wide range of emotions. For many boys and girls, the intensity of their feelings—of the impulses firing in their brains, whether angry, sad, sexual, or territorial—is often surprising. Many of them have not felt such strong impulses during childhood.

Adolescence is a heck of a time for the impulse control center—the prefrontal cortex—to be under construction. Just when adolescents need it most, the PFC's ability to act rationally and think through problems and challenges breaks down. Even though the teen PFC is much closer to being mature, it's no match for overwhelming hormone-driven impulses.

Imagine a car with a brand-new, high-powered engine surging with high-octane fuel. When you press lightly on the gas pedal, the car shoots ahead. It takes almost nothing to accelerate, but this same fast car has brakes that were designed for a bicycle; they barely slow the car. Better brakes won't arrive for a few years. It's not a good match. If the car has a long way to go before it needs to stop, it'll probably be fine, but if it accelerates quickly and needs to stop suddenly, look out. You've got a hair-trigger gas pedal and the matching brakes are on back order.

Adolescent brains get the gas before the brakes. Puberty gives adolescents a body that looks like an adult's and a brain that is prone to wild fluctuations and powerful surges. The brain's gas pedal is ready for a NASCAR-paced adulthood. But because the PFC is not up to snuff, the brain's got the brakes of a Model T.

Companies like State Farm Auto Insurance understand this paradox perfectly. For a long list of reasons, seventeen-year-olds should be better drivers than sixty-year-olds. They've got better reflexes. They've got better eyesight. They've probably even got better spatial reasoning. And yet their auto insurance rates are double a sixty-year-old man's. Why? State Farm may not know brain science, but they understand statistics, and accident statistics prove that kids take a lot of risks. They've got impulses firing left and right and they don't have adequate impulse control. It's the gas-before-brakes phenomenon, and who understands the risks of quick acceleration with no power to stop better than an auto insurance company? So teenagers have to pay (although many parents are the ones really footing the bill) twice as much for the privilege of driving because they're twice as likely to do foolish things.

The Parent Survival Kit: Putting on the Brakes

We can't expect adolescents to always think ahead and act rationally. Impulsiveness and risk taking come with the adolescent territory. So parents have to function as the brakes until the teen brain installs its own set. Use this kit to see how you rate when it comes to helping adolescents put on the brakes.

PARENT SURVIVAL KIT

Putting on the Brakes

Yes No

☐ ☐   1. My child tends to act before he or she thinks.

☐ ☐   2. Hormones trigger flashes of anger and moodiness in my child.

☐ ☐   3. I have instituted some ways that I can act as the surrogate prefrontal cortex for my teen.

☐ ☐   4. I can generally stay calm even when my teen can't.

☐ ☐   5. I model respectful behavior in the way I treat my adolescent son or daughter.

☐ ☐   6. My teen and I have a common definition of respectful behavior.

☐ ☐   7. I know where my kids are, who they're with, and what they're doing.

Certain actions are more effective than others for helping teens brake. In chapter 1 you reflected on your own parenting style and how your family of origin influenced it. Now we will examine if that style works the best for the teenage years.

Parenting Styles

While each of us has our own unique way of parenting, our styles fall into three main categories: permissive, authoritarian, and structured. Which best describes your style?

PERMISSIVE	AUTHORITARIAN	STRUCTURED
Few rules	Rigid rules	Firm rules
Few consequences	Strict enforcement	Firm enforcement
Endless negotiation	No negotiation	Limited negotiation
Limited or erratic leadership	Autocratic leadership	Stable leadership
Emphasis on individuality	Emphasis on conformity	Balance
All opinions are equal.	Only parent's opinions count.	Opinions are respected.

Structured parenting is the most effective style to help adolescents put on the brakes. A permissive style does not provide sufficient structure and an authoritarian style either invites power struggles with teens or does not allow them the practice they need in negotiation and self-discipline. A parent using a structured style will cut adolescents slack, so that every transgression doesn't turn into a battle, but is able to draw a line when it comes to unacceptable behavior. Here's the story of two parents who had to develop a more structured style to deal with their two sons.

Patricia and Aaron prided themselves on being open-minded parents who wanted to trust their children and allow them freedom to express themselves. When their two sons were young, discipline was very lax. They would nag the boys to comply with requests but seldom imposed any consequences for misbehavior. On the rare occasions that Patricia or Aaron would attempt to discipline their sons, the boys would just argue and whine until they got their way.

Brothers Eric and Justin argued and fought a great deal when they were young. As they got older, the fights became more serious. Patricia grew concerned when Eric, by then an adolescent, inflicted large bruises on Justin. She tried to enlist Aaron's help in addressing the growing problem, but he responded that they were just boys and there was nothing to worry about. As the family atmosphere became more chaotic, Aaron often retreated to his home office, leaving Patricia to act as referee.

Events came to a head one day when Eric, fourteen, and Justin, eleven, were home alone after school. Justin had borrowed one of Eric's video games and loaned it to a friend without asking. Eric found out and told Justin he wanted the game back right away. Justin told him, essentially, to bug off. Eric became enraged, so Justin ran to his bedroom and locked the door. Chasing his brother, Eric kicked and pounded on the door until it broke open. Then he beat Justin mercilessly.

By the time Patricia arrived home the house was quiet. She called for the two boys, but there was no response. Her heart sank as she walked toward the bedrooms and saw the battered door on Justin's room. Rushing into the room, she found Justin bloodied and bruised, silently crying in his bed.

"Justin, what happened? Are you all right?"

"That %$*# tried to kill me," Justin moaned.

Before taking Justin to the emergency room, Patricia tracked down Eric at a friend's house and ordered him home. Then she called Aaron on his cell phone and told him to come home immediately because there was an emergency. When Patricia and Justin returned home with the ER's diagnosis of a broken nose, Aaron was in his office and Eric was in his room playing a video game. Patricia insisted that they all sit down and talk about what happened. The conversation got nowhere. When Eric and Justin started to argue, Aaron again retreated to his office. The next day Patricia sought advice from the employee assistance counselor at her company. The counselor referred her to me.

My first meeting with Patricia and Aaron didn't include their sons. Patricia did most of the talking. She described the constant fighting between the boys, complained about Aaron's lack of involvement, and said she was worried the family was falling apart. Aaron said he didn't think it was that serious. He thought the fighting was normal sibling friction. He summed up his opinion: "They'll eventually work it out."

I asked them to describe their parenting style and what had happened when the boys were younger. Then I turned to Aaron and asked him if he wanted to know what I thought. He said he did, so I was very direct.

"This is serious. Your boys are out of control and it is your responsibility as parents to establish order."

Before there was time for any debate, I gave them a piece of paper and asked them to list the characteristics they wanted Eric and Justin to have when they were twenty-five years old. "You need to both agree on the list," I added. I left for a cup of coffee and returned a couple of minutes later. Their list was similar to that of most parents: honest, respectful, responsible, happy, successful, well educated.

"How are you going to help your sons get from here to there? They're not going to get there on their own. Kids only develop those desirable traits with structure, guidance, involvement, discipline, and love. Based on what you have told me today, I can say love is not at question here. The two of you obviously love your kids. The rest of the list needs work, however."

The hour was almost up, and Patricia asked if they should bring the boys to the next session.

"I don't think so, Patricia. If you are willing to come back, I think the three of us need to work together for a while."

They did come back, and during the following weeks we covered a lot of territory. Aaron's father had been a very harsh authoritarian, and Aaron wanted to make sure he didn't repeat that pattern. He came to understand that there is a middle ground between his permissive style and his father's autocratic manner. Aaron also realized that his refusal to discipline his sons was not based on principle but rather on his extreme discomfort with conflict.

Patricia and Aaron had their hands full with Eric and Justin in large part because they had never held their boys accountable in any consistent way. Then, when Eric hit adolescence, there was no history of appropriate discipline to fall back on.

The parents felt overwhelmed by the chaos in their family, so I encouraged them to start with one or two of the most pressing problems. They both agreed with me that the violent fights and kicking and breaking things had to stop. I had them spell out their expectations clearly on a piece of paper, which they taped onto the refrigerator. They also agreed on consequences for violations and they pledged to back each other up. Patricia extracted a commitment from Aaron that he wouldn't disappear when things got tense. I reinforced Patricia's point. "Aaron, your sons need to know you won't back down. Don't yell or scream. Keep your cool, but be very clear that you and Patricia are in charge and that violent, disrespectful behavior is going to stop."

After several sessions I suggested that it was time to have the boys join us in counseling. I divided the session into two sections. During the first forty-five minutes of the hour both parents talked with their sons, and I played a minor background role as observer. Then we spent the last fifteen minutes debriefing without the boys in the room. I shared some reactions and offered some suggestions, and Patricia and Aaron made very quick progress. Here's how the third session with the boys went.

Patricia and Aaron had printed out a clear plan for change.

THE RESPECT PLAN

GOAL: We will treat one another with greater respect in our family.

THE BEHAVIORS

1. No hitting

2. No name-calling

3. No swearing [they listed the words they wanted stopped]

4. No throwing things

REWARDS: When you accumulate five days, during which you both have met the goals for respect, then you (Eric and Justin) can each choose a reasonably priced reward, e.g., movie, trip to pizza parlor, skiing, etc.

CONSEQUENCES: If there is hitting, name-calling, swearing, or throwing things, there will be no television or video games for the following two days.

When the session began, Aaron looked directly at the boys and said, "We have to learn to treat each other with more respect. Your mother and I have put together a list of the behaviors that must change." Patricia took over and told the boys how the plan would work and asked for their input on rewards. Then she finished by saying, "We want you to learn how to be respectful. I promise you that your father and I will follow through on both the rewards and the consequences." Aaron added one more comment. "Boys, I think that I have let you down by retreating to my office and not taking charge when I should have. I will change that. Your mother and I are together on this."

Patricia and Aaron followed through with their plan. There was no magic, but little by little they asserted their parental authority and the family chaos subsided. In effect, they had to learn how to become the brakes for their adolescent sons' supercharged amygdalas. Eric's rage was out of control in large part because he'd never been taught to keep it in check, so it led him to do things that he wouldn't have done if he'd been acting rationally. Both Eric and Justin had fully functional gas pedals, but their brakes hadn't been installed yet.

The combination of a developing prefrontal cortex and raging hormones presents some of the biggest challenges in parenting. While we need to expect and tolerate some trying behavior from our teenage sons and daughters, we also need to provide the structure and discipline they need to keep their behavior from becoming destructive to the family, themselves, and others.

DO

- ✓ Adjust expectations about adolescent behavior in light of their brain changes. It is normal for adolescents to act without thinking of the consequences, to react impulsively, and to display raw emotions and mood swings.
- ✓ Examine your parenting style to determine if it is permissive, authoritarian, or structured.
- ✓ Follow the structured parenting approach, which emphasizes clear limits and enforcement of consequences in a caring and respectful manner.
- ✓ Practice a lot of patience. It often helps to remember your own adolescent years. Another way is to take deep breaths and count to ten.
- ✓ Get support from other parents and friends. Comparing stories lessens the burden.
- ✓ Loosen but don't let go. For example, even though the curfews will get later as teens grow older, they should still have them.
- ✓ Know where your kids are and what they are doing. If you suspect they are lying about their whereabouts, let them know you will be checking up, and then do so.
- ✓ Maintain and enforce standards of behavior. Respect and decency needn't disappear just because teens are having a brain growth spurt.

DON'T

- ✗ Don't tolerate abusive or disrespectful behavior. Stop any conversation if your teen starts to swear at you or threaten you. Make it clear that all privileges are suspended until you can finish the conversation without that behavior.
- ✗ Don't lose your temper if and when your adolescent son or daughter does.

✗ Don't get caught in the trap of destructive verbal battles.
✗ Don't make mountains out of molehills. There are plenty of important issues to pay attention to.

What do I want to continue?

_____

_____

_____

What do I want to change?

_____

_____

_____

FIVE

What We Have Here Is a Failure to Communicate

One Friday night Erin, my sixteen-year-old daughter, borrowed the car. Having just received her driver's license, she was in stiff competition with her two older brothers for use of the family vehicle, but this night she had finally won the car lottery. I handed her the keys and she walked out the door. It was her first weekend night out with the car and she was very excited. I was, truth be told, a little nervous, but just before her curfew expired, my wife, Monica, and I heard the familiar sound of tires on the driveway through our bedroom window. I listened as the back door opened and closed and footsteps shuffled up the stairs and into the bathroom. After the noises of tooth brushing and face washing subsided, footsteps shuffled down the hall to Erin's bedroom and the door shut. I settled into my pillow, listening to our quiet house make its small night-time noises. Erin had made it through her first night out with the car without incident. She was really growing up. It wouldn't be long until she headed off to college. Though that night was seventeen years ago, I remember it as if it were yesterday and can still conjure up the feelings of relief, pride, and a touch of melancholy.

On Saturday morning I went to run some errands with the car. As I was unlocking my door, I noticed a scattering of empty juice cans and food wrappers on the backseat—a mess. I'm not a neat freak by any stretch of the imagination, but I don't like driving a car that emits a rattling or crumpling noise every time I take a corner. Besides, implied by the term "borrowing the car" is the sense that it be returned in the same—or better—condition as when it was borrowed. I was annoyed but not really angry. It was, after all, a minor issue.

After completing my trip to the dry cleaner and post office, I returned home. As I walked in the back door, Erin was scrambling some eggs for breakfast. I'd pretty much forgotten all about the mess in the car as soon as I'd deposited it in the trash and recycling bins out back, but seeing Erin reminded me I wanted to ask her to clean out the car when she used it. Since she was a new driver, I wanted to make expectations clear.

"Erin, I want to talk to you about something."

"What did I do wrong?" was her instant retort.

"It's not a big deal, but I would appreciate it if you would clean out the cans and wrappers you and your friends . . ."

"Why are you so upset about such a little thing?" Erin asked, her voice rising.

"Erin, I'm a bit irritated, but not really upset. It's just . . ."

"What do you mean? You're all furious about nothing."

"I'm not furious. I have to be able to talk to you about these things."

"Then why are you yelling at me?"

I tried to maintain a calm, even voice. "I'm not yelling. I'm just trying to have a conversation."

"You *are* yelling. You're always yelling at me. I can't believe you people," she shouted. Then she whirled around and stomped upstairs to her bedroom. A second later the door slammed shut.

I looked at Monica. She had been an eyewitness to the entire scene. "Was I yelling?" I asked. Maybe I hadn't noticed that I'd gotten worked up.

"Nope," was her one-word reply. She got up to turn off the heat under the eggs. I sat down on a kitchen chair to get my bearings.

"Did I even raise my voice?"

"You were as cool as a cucumber."

"Did I *look* angry?"

"No, I actually thought you were in a pretty good mood."

———

Scenes like these are common in many households. The incidents seem to come out of nowhere. Somehow the smallest incident gets misinterpreted and rapidly escalates into a big deal. Any trivial matter can be kindling for the sudden inferno of adolescent emotion, just because of a simple misunderstanding. And although an incident like this can begin in any number of ways, it often ends the same way, with stomping feet and slamming doors. The most frustrating part for adults is that it can feel as if two completely different conversations just took place.

Parent-adolescent miscommunications are legendary. For years parents and psychologists alike chalked them up to hormones or "attitude." If parents were in a particularly suspicious mood, we blamed a communication breakdown on a "guilty conscience." These explanations weren't always on target or fair to teens. Miscommunication is actually another mystery that can be explained, at least in part, by what's going on in the adolescent brain. Once again the prefrontal cortex is involved. Before turning to the science behind miscommunication, let's assess the condition of the communication skills compartment of the survival kit.

The Parent Survival Kit: Communication Skills

Good communication is a critical item in the survival kit. Assess your status by answering *yes* or *no* to the following statements.

PARENT SURVIVAL KIT

Communication Skills

Yes No

☐ ☐ 1. I am a good listener.

☐ ☐ 2. I can tolerate some adolescent "mouthiness."

☐ ☐ 3. I am able to avoid power struggles with my teenager.

☐ ☐ 4. I am able to remain calm even when my teen son or daughter isn't.

☐ ☐ 5. I understand the brain's role in teen miscommunication.

☐ ☐   6. I can avoid generalizations when talking with my
            adolescent.

☐ ☐   7. When communication becomes tense I can stay
            focused on one issue at a time.

☐ ☐   8. I never engage in name-calling or put-downs when
            talking with my teenager.

☐ ☐   9. I never swear or use foul language toward my
            adolescent or other people.

☐ ☐   10. I do not accept foul or abusive language from my teen.

Yes answers mean the communication door with your teen is wide open. *No* answers will shut that door and prevent open and productive conversations with your teen.

Miscommunication and the Brain

Deborah Yurgelun-Todd, a researcher at the McLean Hospital outside Boston, and other brain scientists have discovered that the adolescent brain interprets emotional expressions differently than an adult's brain. The most important of their experiments involved test subjects looking at a series of photographs of other individuals. Each person in the pictures had been photographed in the midst of a particular emotional state, including anger, sadness, surprise, and fear, which the test subject was asked to identify. "Was that fear or surprise?" Brain scans from these experiments show that when adults are asked to interpret facial expressions they use their prefrontal cortex to read emotions and distinguish subtle differences. Adults could correctly identify different emotional states in the pictures, but adolescents often mistook fear or surprise for anger. As scientists studied the data more closely they found that adolescents frequently misread emotional signals.

Then came the big surprise. As they tried to read emotions, adults and adolescents used different parts of their brains. While adults relied on their prefrontal cortex, the most active part of the adolescent brain was the amygdala, the seat of fear and anger. Adults use the rational part of the brain to read emotions, but adolescents basically do it with a gut reaction. And they are frequently wrong. Unfortunately their mistakes are not random; they often misinterpret the cues as anger or aggression.

As adolescents get older, the amygdala response gives way to the prefrontal cortex. In adult brains, the amygdala continues to be on the alert to others' emotions, particularly fear and anger, but the PFC's more reasoned—and, as scientists have shown, more correct—interpretation overrides the amygdala's. But in the midst of adolescence, while the PFC is still developing, the amygdala may have free reign to interpret others' emotions.

This new discovery means Erin did misinterpret my expression of irritation as one of fury. Most likely, she did hear my talking as yelling, even though no other adult in the room would have interpreted my words that way. Like any typical adolescent, Erin felt that her reaction, based on the information she was getting from her amygdala, was completely justified.

Misreading emotional cues can lead to some real problems.

When I was a high school teacher, I walked out of my classroom one day and heard two of my students shouting at each other, on the verge of blows. I rushed over and got between them just in time to head off a brawl.

"Calm down. What's going on here, fellas?" I said.

"He's looking for a fight! He just shoved me," said one.

"What are you talking about? I didn't shove you!" said the other.

"Yes, you did, you liar!"

"I am not lying! You can ask anybody here. I barely brushed up against your arm." It went back and forth like this for a while before I separated them and gave them time to cool down.

Scenes like this happen all the time with adolescents. An accidental bump in the crowded hallway is interpreted as a challenge. An offhand comment is taken as a grave insult. An innocent joke by one person is thought to be a dig at someone else's expense. Students are often upset about getting "dissed" by others, and are often on the watch for it. The amygdala—also called the brain's watchdog—functions to protect us, keep us alert to danger, and help define what is safe and what is not. But its misinterpretations can lead to real violence with tragic outcomes.

Communicating emotions is always tricky, but it is especially challenging for adolescents, who are faced with a triple whammy. First, the adolescent brain is likely to misread an emotion. Even though an adolescent feels she knows exactly what just happened, she doesn't have reliable analytical equipment in her brain. Secondly, her response from the amygdala is going to be emotional, not evenhanded or well thought out; the amygdala reacts first and asks questions later. Third, the brakes are on back order. The prefrontal cortex isn't really open for business, so the work it would normally do, modulating the emotional impulse, is not getting done. To put it into something like a mathematical equation: misinterpretation + gut response + lousy brakes = poor communication.

When a seemingly normal conversation with an adolescent suddenly spins out of control, it's not just because a kid is being difficult or having a bad attitude. He may really be interpreting the outside world, especially emotional messages, differently. He's not exactly the one we should blame; it's his brain's fault.

When people who live and work with adolescents don't know that kids are subject to interpreting emotions incorrectly, things can escalate. Here's how it happens: The teen overreacts because his brain misinterprets a comment as a threat or insult. His emotion pushes the button of the parent or teacher, who also becomes upset. The adult's expression of emotion, in turn, prompts the teen to misinterpret the situation still further. This back-and-forth can lead to serious escalation of a trivial matter resulting in some regrettable consequences.

So what should you do? Teaching your teen how to communicate in a respectful, productive manner is the most effective way to prevent miscommunication from leading to unfortunate words and hurt feelings. But teaching effective communication skills can seem impossible when adolescents feel justified in exploding like fireworks factories every time something doesn't go their way. Miscommunication, a serious matter, becomes a secondary problem when kids haven't learned to control their anger.

Take this example. Judy, a single parent with three children, came to my office for counseling with her oldest daughter, sixteen-year-old Laura. Our goal was to improve communication, because almost every conversation between the two of them turned into a fight.

"I am so upset about the way Laura treated me on Saturday night, I can hardly look at her," said Judy, as she sat down at one session.

Laura sank into her chair and pulled her jacket up around her neck. She cast an icy glance at her mother and then stared at the floor.

"Laura was headed out the door to hang out with her friends at ten o'clock. I asked her where she was going. She said that she was going to Tania's house and then to a movie. I told her it was too late for a movie because she needed to be home by her curfew at eleven. She tried to sweet-talk me into extending the curfew till midnight. I said no, because if they had really wanted to see that movie, they could have gone to the earlier show. That's when she blew up."

"What do you mean 'blew up'?" I asked.

"She told me I was ruining her life and that she was the only one with such a ridiculous curfew. I remembered what you had said last week about not losing my temper, so I tried hard to stay calm. I started to remind her that we had already talked about the curfew, when she screamed at me and ran out the door."

I turned to Laura, who was still glaring at the floor. "Is that what happened?"

"No one else in my class has to be home at eleven," Laura answered.

"Let's stick to one thing at a time. I asked if your mom's description of what happened Saturday night was accurate."

"Yeah, probably," Laura mumbled. "But I came home at eleven. If I didn't, she'd ground me."

I asked Laura what she had said to her mother, but she just shrugged.

"She swore and screamed that she hated me," Judy said softly. "Then she ran out of the house. She was gone before I knew what happened."

"Was she home by eleven, Judy?" I asked.

"Yes, she was."

"Okay," I said. "Then let's get to work. The issue we're going to work on today is not curfew and it's not breaking rules. The only issue we are going to deal with today is how to handle angry outbursts."

Laura started to protest. "But eleven o'clock is ridiculous."

I had to keep everyone on task. "We'll discuss *reasonable* and *unreasonable* some other time. Today we're going to stay focused on how to handle anger, okay?"

For the rest of that session the three of us did just that. Laura admitted that even she was surprised at how angry she got and how quickly it happened. "I was furious as soon as she started to ask where I was going."

"Is that happening more frequently these days?" I asked.

She thought before she answered. "I guess so. I get really mad at my family a lot. I don't yell at my friends, but I get pretty angry with them sometimes, too."

"You don't yell at your friends, but you do yell at your mom, brother, and sister. Why?"

"I guess because I'm afraid my friends wouldn't like me."

"And you don't have to worry about that at home, do you? You think that no matter how you treat your family, they'll still be there for you." Laura didn't say a word, but I knew that she was getting the message. I spent a lot of time in that session explaining to both Judy and Laura that one of the challenges of adolescence is managing the anger that seems to run quicker and hotter than ever before. I gave them a minilesson in adolescent brain development so they could understand why Laura felt the way she did. Laura seemed to brighten as I concluded my explanation.

"See, Mom, I'm just being normal," Laura said with the first half smile of the session.

I gave Laura some tips on managing anger. "As soon as you feel yourself getting angry, picture a big stop sign. Then take a deep breath. Then say to yourself, 'Self, just chill.' Repeat the sequence until you feel like you're in control. Stop, breathe, chill."

Laura asked, "So am I never supposed to get angry?"

"I didn't say, 'Don't get angry.' Anger is not the problem. How you're expressing it is what we're trying to change. There's nothing wrong with your feelings. You just have to learn how to express them without swearing, screaming, and acting like a maniac."

Laura was not going to give up too easily. "When do we get to talk about how unreasonable my mother is?"

I explained to her that we could only work on communication and negotiation skills after she made a commitment to work on the way she expressed anger. I asked her what she thought would happen to our communication if there was a possibility that I might burst into a swearing fit at any moment during our counseling sessions. She said she wouldn't come back if I ever started to scream and swear at her.

"Right, and I wouldn't blame you," I responded. "So how do you think your mother feels when you unload on her?" The room was silent.

Judy hadn't said anything while I was talking with Laura. When I turned to her she looked relieved. She could see I was getting through to Laura. "Have you been walking on eggshells lately, Judy?" I asked.

"All the time."

We finished up the session when Laura agreed to work on her anger. I gave her paper and a felt-tipped pen and she wrote out in big letters "Stop. Breathe. Chill." I reminded her and Judy not to expect perfection. They both agreed that progress would be the goal. With Laura listening to every word, I suggested to Judy that she not let Laura get away with out-of-control tirades. "The next time something like Saturday night happens, tell Laura she can't go anywhere until the two of you can have a discussion and even a disagreement without her swearing and screaming." I looked at Laura and smiled. "Okay?"

"Okay" was her barely audible reply.

Laura wasn't perfect after that session. She and Judy had more episodes, but little by little things improved. One of the early changes was Laura's ability to take responsibility. During a counseling session not long afterward, Laura started off by saying that she had blown it earlier in the week. "I started swearing and yelling at my mom again the other night when she made me get off the phone."

"Laura, I'm proud of you," I responded. She looked confused, so I added, "Because you took responsibility. You said, 'I blew it.' You didn't come in here blaming your mother for your bad behavior. That is the first step to turning things around."

Once Laura started to get her angry outbursts under control, we were able to start working on improving communication. During a private session I had with Judy I explained that establishing good patterns of communication with adolescents is not something that can be done in a day. It takes time and effort, a lot of each, to help them get into the habit of giving those around them the benefit of the doubt.

The most important thing is to remember that adolescents aren't great at interpreting other people's emotions. This awareness can help you avoid escalation. It's the parent's job to keep cool. Because it's a lot harder for an adolescent brain to "be reasonable" in these situations, you have to provide a fully functioning pre-frontal cortex, to remain calm and rational. Spell out your feelings to help your adolescent understand the correct interpretation of what you're saying. For example, when I was talking to Erin about the trash in the car, I probably should have said right away, "I want to let you know that I'm not mad, but I am irritated you left the car a mess last night." This could have helped her make the correct interpretation. If you're surprised or worried, say so. Keeping that to yourself is usually not worth the risk that you will be seen as angry.

Educating your teen, as I did with Laura, about what is going on in his or her brain, can mitigate miscommunication. Teaching adolescents about their brain development will help them keep in mind that they can tend to misinterpret others and overreact. When they know that they may not always be reading your or other people's emotions correctly, they can learn to check things out before they go with their guts. You can help them with this by practicing and modeling good communication yourself. For instance, in the middle of a conversation in which your child says nothing happened all day, you can check things out by asking, "When you say nothing happened today, do you mean that the whole day was boring or that you'd just rather not talk about it right now?"

If you're in a potentially difficult exchange, you should show them exactly how you hope they would talk to you. After all, we are all capable of misreading emotions, so before you proceed as if your interpretation is correct, it is a good idea to check it out. You could say, for instance, "It seems to me that you're getting angry. Is that right?" Such a question gives the other person the opportunity to correct any misreading. By modeling reasonable dialogue with our kids, we give them a script for doing this in their relationships with us and with others. The teenage years are a window of opportunity to learn communication skills that will serve your children well for the rest of their lives. It's the best time to teach them how to handle conflict and help them learn how to relate to others. Talk with adolescents and listen as much as possible. The more you keep in touch with them, the easier it is to help them through difficult times.

Whenever you yourself misinterpret or get carried away, make an effort to apologize. Adolescents aren't the only ones who can misread a situation and get all worked up. Sometimes it seems like an adolescent prefrontal cortex with its incomplete wiring can cause all the other PFCs in the room to go haywire, just by proximity. Apologizing and admitting when you've spoken in haste or anger is a good way to defuse a tense situation and a good model of behavior for adolescents to follow. Because they are prone to stubbornness and independence, adolescents need to learn to acknowledge when they falter. This sort of realistic perspective will help them become happy, healthy adults.

Communication Tips

Here's a summary of tips to improve communication with your adolescent.

1. Begin statements with "I" rather than "You." Starting with "You" triggers defensiveness. Instead of saying, "You're really rude," say, "I'm angry that you walked out of the room while I was talking with you."

2. Avoid generalizations. As soon as an adolescent hears one, her mind starts to search for the exception to refute you. Instead of saying, "You never clear the table," say, "You forgot to clear the table this evening."

3. To eliminate confusion, be as specific as possible when asking for something. Instead of saying, "Don't forget to take out the garbage," say, "Please take out the garbage before you go to school."

4. Ask a question that requires more than one word to answer. That will increase the chances of a longer conversation. Say, "Tell me about your day at school" instead of "Did you have a good day at school?"

5. Stick to one topic at a time. Avoid this kind of sentence: "I want to talk to you about your report card, and by the way, I don't like the way you treated your brother last night." Instead say, "I would like to talk to you about your report card. When would be a good time to do that?"

6. When there is tension between you and your teenager, avoid attacking. Remember these three steps:
   • Name your feeling.
   • State the reason for your feeling.
   • State what you would like. Here's an example. Don't say, "You're so inconsiderate. You knew I'd be worried when you weren't on time for dinner." Instead say, "I'm angry because you were late for dinner. I'd like you to call to let me know you're going to be late so I don't worry."

7. Listening is more important than talking. Research shows that listening attentively communicates respect. That automatically sets a more positive tone and lowers the defenses. When your teenager is talking with you,
   • establish eye contact but don't stare,
   • don't interrupt,
   • use short phrases like "Uh-huh" or "I see" (they encourage your teen to keep talking),
   • keep an open posture; don't cross your arms,
   • ask clarifying questions like "I don't quite understand what you mean. Could you explain that again?"

- check to make sure you're understanding correctly. For example, you might say, "If I'm hearing you correctly, you're angry with me because you feel like I put you down last night."

Of course, even if you religiously follow all of the advice I've just given you—a feat I've never been able to fully accomplish myself—you'll still run into the problems of misinterpretation, escalation, and stomping feet. While the prefrontal cortex and amygdala in the adolescent brain are often the culprits behind an emotional explosion, sometimes these outbursts occur for other reasons. Adolescents are a potentially volatile bunch, and some of their instability isn't just due to misfiring neurons and half-constructed brain centers. Sometimes exploring their own explosiveness is the way adolescents figure out who they want to be.

I was chatting recently with Jordan, a man I work with, about adolescents and their tendency to misinterpret emotions. Jordan was particularly curious about how scientists themselves had interpreted their findings and how they had conducted the experiments. Did they only use photographs, he wondered, or did they try real-life situations, too? I told him that this was done with photographs because it's easier to make sure the emotional expressions are the same for everyone in the study. Then he asked me, "Did they try to account for adolescents who might be misunderstanding the emotion on purpose?"

"What do you mean 'on purpose'?" I asked.

"Well, when I think back to those sorts of arguments with my parents, I can remember willfully misinterpreting what they were getting at just to have an excuse to fly off the handle. It almost felt like another part of me was controlling my actions, while I sat back and watched it all happen. My stepfather would remind me to empty the dishwasher, say, and I'd flip out on him, claiming he was giving me a hard time and always finding fault. At least part of me knew he was being completely reasonable, but I acted like he'd just spit on my shoes or something. It's possible part of my brain really was misinterpreting his comment, but even in the heat of the moment, I understood that my reaction was totally out of proportion."

"Do you think there was anything else going on?" I asked.

"Maybe," said Jordan. "I suppose I could have been expressing anger over something else in my life, or even tapping into some other issue I was having with my stepdad. But I don't think that was it. I think there was something about expressing anger like that to him that made me really want to do it . . . that made me really like doing it. It was a completely new thing, I guess, and getting into a real shouting match where I felt like I held my own made me feel more grown up somehow."

Jordan stared off into space. After a moment he looked at me and continued.

"It sounds silly, I know, but purposefully misinterpreting my parents made me their equal. It was a way I could practice being an adult."

Challenging figures of authority, even on the flimsiest of pretenses, is one of the quintessential activities of adolescence. Whether its root causes are found in the human brain or in human culture is not clear. As with the nature-versus-nurture argument, the explanation probably lies in both. Most likely Jordan's notion that his brain was both misinterpreting and correctly identifying the emotion behind his stepfather's comment is right on the money. His trigger-happy amygdala probably prompted his zero-to-sixty, angry response. Then, a moment later, when his weak prefrontal cortex took stock of what was really going on, he made a conscious decision to run with the situation. It really was part of the way he helped himself grow up. Learning how to express anger, as well as the rest of the emotional palette, is essential to functioning in the adult world. Of course, learning to keep emotions to ourselves is important, too, but adolescence lasts awhile, and there's time to get good at both.

Jordan's stepfather may have actually done his son a favor in letting the kid blow off some steam over dishwashing, yet Judy was also right to confront her daughter over curfews. Communicating with adolescents requires a judicious balance. If you jump down your teen's throat every time she raises her voice, you'll have a constant battle on your hands or, worse yet, you'll effectively cut off communication altogether. As parents, we need to let our kids have an outlet for their anger, up to a point. When you feel anger and miscommunication beginning to derail a conversation with your adolescent you can say, "I want to talk about this, but I'm not going to get into a yelling match with you. We'll talk when you're ready to talk without yelling." It is tempting as a parent to think, "If I only say it louder or emphasize it loudly again, the kid will hear me and do what's right." But all that will get you is a shouting match. Once the screaming starts, nobody is going to listen to the other person. And if no one is listening, then no one is communicating. To get you and your kid into an emotional state where your rational minds, your prefrontal cortices, can engage, you need to tell yourself, "I am going to try to understand what we are really talking about here."

We also need to let our adolescents know that they step over an important line when they swear or throw and break things. We have to make it clear that we will not accept those behaviors. The first step in preventing out-of-control behavior in our teens is modeling. We'll be less able to confront our teen's bad behavior if we end up swearing or throwing things ourselves. Secondly, we should never let our kids get what they want if they can't act in a civil way. Conversations should end, for example, if swearing starts. An adolescent who throws or breaks things should be held accountable by your enforcing the loss of privileges and restitution for any damage.

We parents put a lot of our effort into making ourselves clear, but we also need to remember that it is just as important to listen. If we've taken the time to listen—and haven't judged or offered advice at every exchange—to our teen, we might be able to hold a real conversation when it comes time to talk. When we can really talk and listen to one another, everything else gets easier.

For teens to establish a new, adult relationship with their parents, they do require some freedom to explore new boundaries and approaches. I implied earlier that my altercation with Erin might have gone better if I'd been clearer about my emotions. That might have defused the situation, but as it turned out, no real harm was done. A little while later Erin came downstairs and we talked about what had happened. She was calm enough to hear me when I reasserted that I had not been angry. Eventually, she apologized and we went back to a fairly peaceful morning. It wasn't the first such incident of mistaken emotion and escalation, and it wasn't the last. But in letting it play out as it did, with as much effort to stay calm as I could manage, I think I helped Erin learn about how to be angry with someone while still loving them, and in the end, figure out a way to get along again.

DO

✓ Listen, listen, listen.
✓ Say clearly what you are feeling to reduce misinterpretations.
✓ Model good, clear communication skills.
✓ Expect and tolerate a little adolescent "mouthiness."
✓ Apologize to your adolescent if you need to.
✓ Call a time-out if communication is badly off track.

DON'T

✗ Don't swear or use abusive language toward your adolescent son or daughter.
✗ Don't accept swearing and other abusive language.
✗ Don't engage in name-calling or put-downs.
✗ Don't get caught up in a yelling match.
✗ Don't leave conflict unresolved.

What do I want to continue?

_____
_____
_____

What do I want to change?

_____
_____
_____

SIX

Stress and the Teen Brain

"I don't feel like going to soccer practice today," Maria told her grandfather over breakfast. "I'm just not up for it."

"But you worked all summer to make the team! Now you are on it and you don't want to go?" he replied.

"Listen, Grandpa," Maria said, "I don't know why; I just don't feel like it!" Then she stormed off.

Baffled, Maria's grandfather walked into the next room to talk to his wife. "I don't understand it—" he began.

"I think I do," she gently interrupted, having overheard the entire conversation. "She's been more and more anxious all weekend. She spent most of the day in her room yesterday and was more irritable than normal when I asked her even simple questions. Making the junior varsity team was probably exciting at first, but she has to be nervous to play with a whole new group of girls. She's been all mixed up since she made the team—both nervous and excited at the same time."

"That's ridiculous. She has to go to practice! She made a commitment to that team. I didn't raise a quitter and she can't be that nervous after counting down the days to soccer season all summer long," Maria's grandfather retorted. "I'll talk to her."

"She certainly does need to go to practice. But I'd be careful not to come down too hard on her. Like you've never been scared to do something? We have to find a way to help her cope with her anxiety. These transitions aren't always easy."

By the time Maria's grandfather was driving her to school he had had time to calm down and think about what his wife had said. He ended up sharing a story about the time that he had faked being sick before his band's first big performance in front of a crowd. It wasn't the end of his musical career, but it was something he regretted for some time. "Maybe you aren't feeling nervous like I was, but if you are, you should know that sometimes the things that we grow from the most scare us the most, too. That's why we need to do them."

Maria didn't say much in the car but she did end up lacing up her cleats for soccer practice that afternoon. It wasn't long before she was chattering on the phone with her teammates at night and helping organize team fundraisers, her initial anxiety a thing of the past.

Stress is a part of life. New experiences, transitions, real and perceived dangers, deadlines, unknowns, and pressure can all evoke feelings of anxiety. Stress regulation is one of the brain's primary "executive functions," centered in the prefrontal cortex. Given that a teenager's prefrontal cortex is under construction, teens often have extra difficulty gaining perspective on their emotions and coping with anxiety, which also means that this time is a "window of opportunity" for teens to get extra practice in calming themselves, considering alternative actions, and adapting to new and sometimes overwhelming situations.

Helping youth cope with stress is a balancing act because stress is tricky. Too much stress shuts down the executive center and disrupts the brain's developing architecture. Too little stress robs the brain of practice in handling life's challenges. As Dr. Bruce Perry shares in his book *Born for Love,* "Just as you wouldn't build muscle by resting all week and then trying to lift a hundred pounds just one time every Friday morning, you can't build a healthy stress response system by complete protection from stress or occasional exposure to an overwhelming dose." Understanding how the brain is built and how it responds to stress can help inform how we strike that balance.

The Parent Survival Kit: Stress and the Teenage Brain

The items in this kit will help you learn about the effects of stress—too much or too little—on adolescent brains and how you can help teenagers cope.

PARENT SURVIVAL KIT

Stress and the Teenage Brain

Yes No

☐ ☐ 1. I understand that some stress is unavoidable and my job is to teach my teen coping skills so he or she can handle it.

☐ ☐ 2. I know stress affects how the brain functions.

☐ ☐ 3. I realize intense stress can affect memory, learning, and emotional regulation.

☐ ☐ 4. I understand that extreme or long-term stress can be toxic to the brain.

☐ ☐ 5. I do not rush in to rescue my teen from unhappiness or disappointment.

☐ ☐ 6. I realize that real self-esteem comes from achievement and competence.

☐ ☐ 7. I praise my teen's efforts as opposed to his or her natural talent.

☐ ☐ 8. I understand that resilience helps my teen handle stress and bounce back from setbacks.

☐ ☐ 9. I know how important caring relationships are to my teen's ability to handle stress.

The more positive answers to the items in this tool kit, the better equipped you are to raise resilient teenagers.

Too Much Stress

While the brain allows us to do all sorts of amazing things, its primary job is to keep us alive. That's why it comes equipped with early warning detection systems that scan the environment for potential danger and threat. This has served us well for thousands of years. Imagine that I'm hiking on a beautiful day enjoying the sights, sounds, and smells of the forest when I hear a loud *crack* of a stick snapping behind me. As we learned in chapter 4 my stress response immediately hijacks my thinking brain. Three hormones rush into my bloodstream. First, the hypothalamus releases the hormone CRF, corticotropin factor, which in turn stimulates the release of the hormone adrenaline. Adrenaline prepares the body for energized action by speeding up the heart. The third hormone, cortisol, alters the blood sugar level providing a quick burst of energy and lowers pain sensitivity. These hormones coordinate the well-known fight-or-flight response. Once my brain registers that a friendly hiker snapped the branch instead of an angry bear, my stress response system calms down and my cortex reengages. Within minutes I am once again enjoying my hike.

We may not be confronting large carnivorous animals on a regular basis anymore, but there are plenty of threats and stressors in our modern environment that our brain responds to in the same way as it did to predators. How these hormones affect the brain depends upon how long the stress lasts. In his book *Why Zebras Don't Get Ulcers,* Stanford neuroendocrinologist Robert Sapolsky argues that our stress response system evolved to handle the kind of stress a zebra experiences when chased by a lion. If the zebra is lucky enough to get out of the chase alive, his fight-or-flight response would fade as soon as he was out of harm's way. In other words, the time between activation and calming of the stress response could be measured in minutes or hours. We were not designed to endure the kind of stress that some children experience today, which can go on for weeks, months, or even years.

Not all stress is bad. Consider, for example, the stress that a teenager might experience on the first day of school. Learning how to handle positive stress is a healthy and normal part of development. There are, of course, events that activate the body's stress response system to a greater degree. Losing a loved one, surviving a natural disaster, or witnessing a frightening incident are all examples. Even these stress experiences, however, can be tolerable for adolescents if they are time limited and buffered by caring adults who can help young people cope and adapt. Toxic stress results from prolonged, frequent, and intense experiences of adversity without any adult support. Examples might include child abuse, living with a family member with mental illness, exposure to violence, ongoing bullying, or the burdens associated with poverty.

Toxic stress wreaks havoc on both the body and the brain, especially the executive function. While cortisol initially boosts immunity, prolonged cortisol elevation weakens it and increases fat storage, leading to weight gain. In the brain, cortisol lingers much longer than adrenaline and can eventually damage the hippocampus, the brain's memory registration center. In addition, the brain produces less "brain-derived neurotrophic factor," or BDNF, when stressed. As we'll see in chapter 11 BDNF is considered "Miracle Gro" for the brain. The combination of brain cell damage and BDNF deficiency reduces the brain's ability to produce enough dopamine, serotonin, and other chemicals to maintain cognitive efficiency and emotional stability. Attention and memory suffer. Depression and anxiety follow. Sleep difficulties, behavioral challenges, concentration problems, social isolation, headaches, stomachaches, and other physical ailments are all symptoms of chronic and severe stress.

In addition to increased risk of long-term health problems, young people who are in a constant state of fight or flight have difficulty accessing their cortex and the executive functions that go with it. When we respond to threat in our environments, activity shifts to other parts of the brain more central for survival. It makes sense then that if a student is harassed, bullied, and made fun of in the hallways every day, he is hard pressed to concentrate during even the most engaging math lesson. Likewise, it isn't surprising that a student who listens to her parents have another screaming match over breakfast has difficulty regulating her own behavior on the school field trip later that afternoon.

Protecting teens from toxic stress is important for their health, development, and academic achievement. This is why you should act right away if you find out that your child is being bullied or is bullying another child. From the brain's perspective, improving school climate and making sure that all students feel safe and supported is not an extracurricular afterthought; it is central to academic performance. Basic feelings of safety and security enable young people to harness the power of their cortex for new learning and emotional regulation. This is why efforts to ensure that youth have adequate food, housing, and safety from violence are also so critical. Brain science begs us to ask big and pressing questions about how we care for and protect young people in this country.

We can buffer young people's experience of stress by surrounding them with strong, caring relationships. In chapter 14 we will explore further the protective power of connection, but it is clear that caring relationships with adults shield teens from the most noxious effects of toxic stress, enable them to cope with tolerable stress, and help them thrive under positive stress. In fact, the brain regions involved in relationships are the same ones that regulate our stress response. From the start of life, we rely on others to help us manage stress.

This is most obvious in little babies. While it may not always be comfortable for Mom, a baby enjoys a safe, secure, and tranquil environment in the womb. Then comes a rude awakening called her birthday. The journey from womb to world is challenging in and of itself, but life on the outside doesn't get any easier. There are bright lights, harsh noises, fluctuating temperatures, and feelings of intense hunger. Needless to say, these experiences trigger the baby's stress response system. So what does she do? Her capacity to handle this kind of stress is underdeveloped, so she protests in the way human infants have been doing for millennia—by crying. Infants cannot calm themselves, so they outsource this to caregivers. The baby relies on a parent or other caregiver to pick her up, hold her close to his chest, rock her back and forth, and whisper, "Shhh, shhhh." When sensitive and caring parents do this, they are instinctively trying to re-create the environment that the baby associates with safety and security. Thousands of interactions like these, where babies experience appropriate doses of stress and then are calmed down by caregivers, eventually help the baby internalize the ability to calm herself on her own. But this is a long, multiyear process.

As a child's cortex matures, she gets better at regulating stress and managing her emotions. A tired and hungry three-year-old may have a total meltdown at the grocery store but we expect better stress regulation from our fifteen-year-olds. Teenagers' maturing cortexes help them gain perspective. In addition, they can adopt all kinds of different coping skills, including getting enough sleep, exercising, eating healthfully, or practicing mindfulness to manage stress. That said, in the absence of close, caring relationships, these stress-relief strategies are rarely very effective. This is why the strategies we will discuss in chapter 14 for staying connected to your teen are so important. Teens continue to rely on caring relationships as their primary shield from toxic stress and as their grounding for learning to handle positive stress. We couldn't concoct a more powerful antidote to stress if we tried.

Too Little Stress

"I grew up in a really stressful home and I was determined to do something different for my kids, but I think I took my role as protector a little too far," a parent told me a few years back.

"What do you mean?" I responded.

"I worked so hard to shield my daughter from stress that I did everything for her. It almost became an obsession. The worst part is that the more I protected her, the more anxious she seemed about even the smallest things. By the time she got to middle school, we were both a wreck."

The parental urge to protect children from harm is strong. Protection, however, can be overdone, too. Remember our mantra: *Whatever the brain does a lot of is what the brain gets good at.* Adolescents who haven't had practice handling stress or taking responsibility for their actions, even when it is difficult, can become more anxious and risk averse. As my school superintendent friend Phil Ledermann liked to tell parents, "Your job is not to smooth out all the bumps in the road for your kids. It's your responsibility to equip your children with good shock absorbers so they learn to handle the bumps themselves."

Stress has a bad reputation in our culture. Everywhere we look we see products designed to "eliminate stress" and "get rid of stress once and for all." Clearly toxic stress is harmful but good stress can be energizing and motivating. Young people need some stress to exercise their psychological muscles for resilience, stamina, perseverance, confidence, self-reliance, and diligence. It's okay for kids to feel bad sometimes. Each time they recover from appropriate levels of stress, they get stronger and more responsive.

Myths of the Self-Esteem Movement

The modern self-esteem movement has made it difficult for many parents to let their children experience feelings of sadness, disappointment, and challenge. Unfortunately, in the quest to save our children from these feelings we have inadvertently made them more vulnerable to them. Self-esteem is an important but often misunderstood concept. The movement launched by Nathaniel Brandon's book *The Psychology of Self-Esteem* equated self-esteem with feeling good. As it spread, millions of parents and teachers were told that the key to success and happiness was "feeling good about yourself." This led to a couple of enduring and damaging myths.

One myth is that self-esteem comes before success. This sounds good but it isn't borne out by the research. It turns out that the opposite is true. For example, studies involving thousands of children demonstrate that self-esteem does not boost academic achievement. Real self-esteem is born from feelings of achievement and competence. When a teenager is successful, he feels good about himself. Not the other way around. Competence doesn't mean getting things right all the time. Mistakes can be great teachers as long as young people keep trying. Achievements don't need to be big but they do need to be real. It may mean meeting a personal goal, completing a difficult school project, or following through on a hard conversation with a friend. The same skills that enable a teenager to do these things also help him get along better with others. Accomplishments and strong friendships will do more for self-esteem than a year's worth of self-esteem-building exercises.

Once self-esteem became equated with feeling good, then another myth emerged: challenge and disappointment damage self-esteem because they don't feel good. As a result, many parents developed an allergic reaction to their kids' unhappiness. There is nothing wrong with being happy, but learning how to meet life's challenges and disappointments is part of the important work of growing up.

This lesson doesn't always come easily to us parents. I remember clearly the first day my daughter, Erin, set foot in a geometry class. She had always loved math and it came easily to her—until geometry. For the first time, she had to struggle through problems and had difficulty tracking concepts in class. Erin's anxiety about math class was palpable around the house. She cried, picked fights with her brothers, and tried to find excuses to miss school. She was miserable. It took nearly all my strength not to do her homework for her. I had all kinds of worries. I was worried that she would start to hate school, start believing that she was stupid, and that the class would destroy her self-esteem. Luckily Monica expertly handled the situation. She acknowledged Erin's stress and reassured Erin that as long as she worked hard in the class that we would be proud of her. Then she encouraged Erin to come up with some solutions including meeting with the teacher and using lunch hour to get a little extra help. It was painful at the time, but Erin eventually did just fine in the class and gradually learned to even enjoy it.

This challenging class didn't destroy her self-esteem, and it was probably one of the best things to influence her confidence as a student. Because she had always excelled in math and received a lot of praise for her high grades, Erin had started to avoid challenging herself. "It was easier to be a 'math whiz' if I kept to the easier stuff. I was good at math and I didn't want anything to damage that reputation," Erin recalls now. "Geometry changed all that. There was no avoiding the hard stuff because it was all hard stuff." She went on, "Looking back, it was during that class that I started realizing that mistakes and challenge were part of learning. I got a little better at handling the tough stuff because it didn't throw me into a total meltdown and identity crisis. I even began seeking out more difficult classes. I guess I'm glad now you didn't do my homework though I would have given anything for you to do it for me at the time!"

If I had swooped in and tried to save Erin from the stress of difficult assignments, she would have missed out on a lot more than geometry. She would have missed out on the opportunity to build real self-esteem. The ingredients that compose real self-esteem, things like persistence, resilience, resourcefulness, and self-reliance, serve teens far beyond any single math assignment. They lead to success in both school and life.

Praise and Mindset

Erin's experience in math class taught me about more than just the importance of not rescuing her from difficulty. It was also a good lesson in the power of praise. Praise comes easily to us parents. It is a nearly effortless way to remind our kids that we support them and love them. This is, of course, not a bad thing! But it turns out that all this verbal encouragement can backfire on us if we aren't careful. The kind of praise that Erin received regularly growing up about her natural gifts as a mathematician may have actually undermined her confidence.

Psychologist Carol Dweck and her team at Stanford University have been studying the impact of praise on children and youth for well over a decade. Her initial experiments illustrate the striking difference between helpful and unhelpful praise. The researchers gave a group of students a set of puzzles that they all successfully completed. At this point their experiences diverged. Randomly splitting the group in half, they told one half that they were really smart for having solved the puzzles. They told the other students that they must have done so well because they worked so hard. Both groups were then told that for the next round they could choose between two more sets of puzzles. They described one set as very challenging and the other as fairly easy. While the only difference between the two groups was a single line of praise, the effects were powerful. Most of those praised for their intelligence chose the easy task. However, the majority of those praised for their effort chose the more challenging task.

At first the results seem counterintuitive. Why would the "smart" kids take the easy way out? Much like Erin's experience when it came to math, the kids who were deemed smart didn't want to risk that identity by tackling a more difficult problem. Students praised for their work ethic were given license to take this risk. As long as they tried hard, their identity was secure.

Dweck's experiments did not stop there. In the third round of puzzles, none of the students was given a choice. They all were instructed to do very difficult tasks and, not surprisingly, all of them failed. In response, the "hard workers" assumed that they needed to just work a bit harder. They became very engaged in testing out different solutions and seemed to take pride in troubleshooting what went wrong. The "smart kids," on the other hand, appeared stressed, anxious, and downright despondent. From their perspective, they had just received confirmation that they weren't smart after all. But Dweck's battery of tests was not over yet. In the final round all of the students completed another round of easy puzzles, similar to the first round. Here again, we see the legacy of a single line of praise. The "hard workers" improved on their initial scores while the "smart kids" did worse. My guess is that in addition to the blow to their confidence their stress response systems were interfering with their thinking.

This initial experiment launched an entire field of research on praise and what Dweck calls a student's mindset. She has shown that young people with a *fixed mindset* believe that their intelligence and abilities are fixed traits and that talent is what leads to success, not effort. In contrast, a growth mindset celebrates struggle. Teens with a *growth mindset* believe that abilities can be developed through persistence and hard work. They understand that their brain is like a muscle and that exercise and practice strengthen it. They see that falling down and getting back up again are part of living and learning. Consequently, Dweck has begun teaching young people about their brains. She has found that when kids learn that their brains are a work-in-progress, as opposed to a finished product, they tend to adopt a growth mindset. We can nurture a growth mindset through praising effort and allowing our kids to struggle, thereby building resilience. This teaches them that being their best selves can be found through practice, effort, and often in mistakes.

Here are some tips for helpful praise:

1. *Praise the effort.* Rather than saying "I saw your grade in physics, you are so smart!" it is helpful to say "You must have worked really hard to get this grade. I am proud of

you!" There are lots of other ways to encourage effort,
including "Nice job hanging in there," "I love that you
stuck with it," and "You did a great job figuring that out."

2. *Make praise specific.* Praise is one of the ways that we hold
up a mirror to our teens. Instead of saying "You are really
good at soccer," it is more helpful to say "Your practice is
paying off! Nice passes out there today! Great job."

3. *Praise should be sincere.* Young people can sniff out insincere
praise from one hundred yards away. I overheard a student
once say, "Oh, she always says that. I don't even think she
would notice if I wasn't on the stage! Everyone knows I
totally messed up my lines today," in response to what felt
like insincere praise. It might have been more helpful to
hear, "I know you are probably disappointed that you forgot your lines. That's tough. You've got tomorrow evening's
performance to try again."

4. *Encourage teens to self-assess.* Sometimes we jump in with
praise before teens have time to reflect themselves on their
performance and how they feel about it. Asking questions
like "How did you feel about your exam today? What was
hard? What went well?" can be more helpful than saying
"Oh, don't worry. I am sure that it went well. You are so
smart."

5. *Don't overdo the praise.* We shouldn't use praise like a fire
hose. There is nothing wrong with kind and encouraging
words, but they mean more when we use them carefully.

Raising Resilient Teens

The road from childhood to adulthood is full of joy, fun, challenge,
stress, disappointment, elation, and struggle. It is absolutely our job
as parents and as a society to do everything in our power to protect
youth from toxic stress. It is also our job to make sure that our teenagers learn how to handle positive stress. When they learn to deal
with small setbacks, they are better prepared to deal with bigger
ones later on in life. On the other hand, if they're never disappointed, they never learn how to deal with setbacks. If they never

lose, they don't learn how to handle defeat. If they are never frustrated, they never learn persistence. By handling life's ups and downs, teens build the psychological muscles they need for life.

The ability to overcome adversity and to bounce back from challenge is called resilience. Resilience is not hardwired. It is highly impacted by young people's circumstances and supports. Resilience can be nurtured and learned. There's been a growing interest in resiliency, protective factors, and positive youth development. While the latest research on the teenage brain helps us better understand why young people engage in risky behavior, focusing on reducing risks alone doesn't get us very far. Karen Pittman, one of the most influential leaders in the field of youth development, reminds us that "Problem free is not fully prepared. And fully prepared is not fully engaged." Our goal as parents isn't solely to prevent our teens from taking risks but to prepare them for life. This means that we need to recognize their strengths, capacities, and possibilities. This begs that we ask, What is it that enables some teens to successfully navigate the challenges and stressors of adolescence? Why is it that some teens not only survive this journey, but seem to thrive?

The late Peter Benson of Search Institute reviewed the research and came up with a list of forty Developmental Assets, the external supports and internal strengths that young people need to live productive, meaningful, and successful lives. The assets are in many ways intuitive; they fall under categories like support, empowerment, social competencies, and constructive use of time. Search Institute's team has spent more than fifty years helping parents and other caring adults understand how to nurture these assets, both in their own children and others, sometimes through simple, everyday actions. As Dr. Benson liked to remind adults, "If you breathe, you are on the team."

Bonnie Bernard, one of America's leading researchers on resilience, has also synthesized decades of research and provides a useful road map for parents who want to help their teens cope with stress, step up to challenges, and recover from mistakes or setbacks.

SUPPORT AND CONNECTION

Resilient teens have relationships with caring adults who believe in their ability to succeed, listen to them, and ask about and support their interests. I will talk more about the importance of support and connection in chapter 14.

HIGH EXPECTATIONS

Elijah, a high school sophomore, was trying to convince his friend to skip class with him one afternoon. "No way, my parents would kill me if they found out," Zach responded.

"Really? My parents don't mind. As long as I don't get into too much trouble, they don't care what I do. Your parents are so uptight," said Elijah.

"Maybe," Zach responded. "But it isn't so bad. Going to class is better than having to catch up later anyway."

Resilient teens have parents, teachers, mentors, and other adults who believe in their ability to succeed and have reasonable but high expectations for their behavior. Making it clear that you expect your child to attend class every day communicates that you believe in his capacity to succeed academically. When Maria's grandfather encouraged her to attend soccer practice, he not only reinforced the message that he expected her to follow through on her commitments but also that he believed she could do it. On the other hand, unrelenting pressure can backfire and make kids stressed out, not stress resistant. The popular documentary *Race to Nowhere* chronicles the price of being obsessed with straight A's, being the best in the class, hanging out with the "right" group of friends, and getting into the "best" college. Like many things, it is a balancing act. Setting unachievable or unrealistic expectations sets our kids up for failure and shame but we don't do our kids any favors by lowering the bar so much that they could trip over it.

COMPASSION

A certain amount of self-centeredness comes with the territory of adolescence, but resilient teens also take interest in others, reach out, and get involved in their communities. If we send the message that the entire world should revolve around them, we give them a false sense of importance. Resilient teens are compassionate, willing to help out, and take other people's feelings into account.

Amina overheard some girls near her locker making fun of Sasha, a girl Amina shared two classes with. Noticing that Amina looked uncomfortable, one of the girls shifted the conversation to her and said, "Why are you staring at us? You aren't friends with her, are you?"

For a split second, Amina considered coming to the girl's defense. Sasha was shy and a bit awkward but there wasn't a mean bone in her body. Amina actually enjoyed the times they did group projects together. Realizing the girls were waiting for a response, Amina laughed and said, "No way! How could anyone be friends with her?" The group of girls was already moving down the hallway laughing together. For them, Sasha had been just one target in a long line of gossip that morning.

The school social worker overheard the entire interaction. She gently asked Amina if she could talk to her for a bit in her office.

"I'll follow up with the other girls later, but do you want to talk about what just happened?" the social worker prompted.

"I didn't have anything to do with it!" Amina replied. The social worker waited. Amina went on, "I mean, those girls don't like Sasha but I don't have a problem with her. It is no big deal. We were just joking around anyway. Sasha didn't hear any of it."

"It may not feel like a big deal to you right now, but how do you think Sasha would feel?" the social worker responded. She succeeded in helping Amina imagine how painful this experience must be for Sasha. Before long, Amina's cheeks burned with embarrassment.

"I knew it wasn't right; I was just thinking about myself, I guess. I knew that if I didn't join in, I'd be next." They went on to talk through other ways that she might have responded. It became a lesson in both compassion and courage.

The next time that Amina heard the girls making fun of another kid at school she made sure not to join in. She also made sure to reach out to the targets of their ridicule and by the end of the year she even had the courage to intervene. "Don't you have something better to do than make fun of other people? It is really mean and no one deserves that."

AUTONOMY AND RESOURCEFULNESS

"I hate Mr. Harrison and he hates me!" seventeen-year-old Henry exclaimed. "He is always picking on me and I can't do anything right in his class. It's stupid."

Henry's mom, Julia, took a deep breath. Her first instinct was to march into the school and give Mr. Harrison a piece of her mind. None of Henry's other teachers gave him a hard time. It did seem like this teacher had a chip on his shoulder. She took another deep breath and squelched her impulses. She decided to let Henry work on it a bit before she intervened. "That sounds really hard. What are you planning on doing about it?"

"I have no idea! What can I do? I'm not going to talk to him," Henry retorted. "He probably wouldn't listen to me anyway."

"Talking to him actually sounds like a great idea. It may just be a miscommunication," Julia prodded. "You have no idea why he is so tough on you?"

"No! I mean, all my friends are in that class so we talk a lot. But that's no excuse for always picking on me," he replied.

Julia took another deep breath. "Well? What are your options?"

"I could drop the class!" Henry said eagerly. Seeing that that wasn't an option, Henry reluctantly conceded, "Or I could talk to him. I don't know about that, though. We'll see."

A week went by and there was no mention of history class at home. Julia didn't press it. Finally, the following Tuesday, Henry casually mentioned that he had talked to his teacher after class the day before. "Turns out Mr. Harrison isn't so bad. He is actually pretty nice. I realized I've been a pain in the neck and he admitted to coming down a bit hard on me. He said it is because he knows I could really succeed if I just stopped messing around with my friends. We've got a new plan. I'm going to tone it down and he's going to give me the benefit of the doubt more often." Before Julia could respond Henry was on his way out. "I've got history home-work to do with my friends!" he yelled back just before the door closed.

Resilient teens are given the chance to take initiative and figure things out for themselves. Parents support their efforts and encourage them to come up with ideas and solutions to their challenges but avoid taking over. Setting goals, working toward them, and learning from mistakes build confidence and competence.

OPTIMISM

Resilient kids focus on strengths rather than weaknesses. They find value even in difficult situations and search for the silver lining when things go wrong. Psychologist Martin Seligman spent his career studying optimism. He found that optimistic young people experience less stress because they believe that things will eventually turn out okay. We can help nurture optimism by encouraging our teens to focus on strengths. This doesn't mean that we ignore feelings of sadness, anger, or frustration, but we don't reinforce them. Pessimistic teens lose perspective very quickly. For example, a disagreement with a friend can quickly turn into "I don't have *any* good friends" or "I am so stupid my friends always end up hating me." The strong emotional responses that we discussed in chapter 3 only amplify these pessimistic feelings. We might respond by saying, "It sounds like your conversation today with Sheila was really hard. What can you do today to repair your friendship?" Acknowledging your teens' negative feelings but working to prevent them from going into a downward spiral goes a long way toward nurturing optimism.

DO

✓ Protect your teen from toxic stress. Address bullying, violence, poor caregiving, and other threats immediately.

✓ Acknowledge feelings of sadness, grief, anger, and stress.

✓ Model and teach your teen coping skills including
  • exercise
  • sleep
  • nutrition
  • balanced media diet
  • self-talk
  • mindfulness.

✓ Support but don't rescue your teen.

✓ Celebrate mistakes and encourage a growth mindset.

✓ Make sure that your teen is connected with caring adults.
✓ Set reasonable but high expectations for your teen's behavior.
✓ Encourage your teen to find the strengths in challenging situations.
✓ Expect your teen to volunteer, get involved in school or community projects, and think about the experiences of others.

DON'T

✗ Don't ignore sources of toxic stress.
✗ Don't demand perfection or set unrealistic expectations.
✗ Don't assume that poor behavior is the result of a bad attitude. First ask if there is anything else going on.
✗ Don't ignore signs that your teen is too stressed, including sleep problems, overeating, undereating, lost interest, or increased irritability.
✗ Don't try to talk your teen out of his feelings.
✗ Don't do something for your teen that she can do for herself.
✗ Don't add to stress by overscheduling.
✗ Don't allow your teen to evade responsibility or reasonable consequences.

What do I want to continue?

_____
_____
_____

What do I want to change?

_____
_____
_____

SEVEN

Understanding Male and Female Brains

On a cold Minnesota night in the dead of winter, our kids Brian (age six) and Erin (four) were playing a game they had just invented. The family had finished dinner. Monica and I were downstairs in the kitchen, clearing the table and washing dishes. As we went about our chores, we heard much more than the pitter-patter of little feet upstairs. Brian's bedroom was in the front of the house and our bedroom was in the back. The object of the game was to be the first one to get from the front wall, through the door, down the hallway, through our bedroom's doorway, and all the way to the back wall. They had to begin with at least one hand touching the front wall. Both would count down, three, two, one, and then . . . they were off like a shot, laughing and shouting all the way to the other end of the house. We looked at each other nervously every time the dishes in the cupboard rattled in time with the pounding feet overhead, but we did nothing. Erin and Brian needed to blow off some steam because a prolonged, bitter cold spell had kept them inside for several days in a row and both had a lot of pent-up energy.

After several heats, Brian had a few wins and so did Erin. This wasn't definitive enough for either of them. A winner-take-all championship was the only way to settle the question of who was faster. One race, one winner, one champion. They counted down in unison, three, two, one, and were off. As they raced down the hall they were neck and neck, but when they took the turn into our bedroom Brian inched into the lead. In a split second, Erin decided victory would require urgent action. While Brian scrambled around the queen-size bed, she leapt across it and stretched out horizontally for the finish line.

Erin would want me to give you the most important fact before any others: she did reach the wall first. Unfortunately, she also smashed her forearm into the windowsill at an awkward angle and broke it.

Brian raced downstairs to tell us about Erin's injury. His first words were "I didn't do it."

By then we could hear Erin's wails. We were upstairs in a flash. After a quick parental medical evaluation, we bundled Erin up and headed for the urgent-care center.

Two hours later we returned home with Erin's broken arm in a cast. She was only four years old, and this was her third broken arm! Monica and I were pretty sure that social services had a thick file on us. How could a sweet little girl like our Erin have three broken arms before she even started school?

Her early familiarity with roughhousing probably came in handy when Erin got to high school and joined one of the first girls' high school hockey teams in the state. By the time she was a senior she and her best friend, Gretchen, were captains of the team.

Anyone who says that girls do not like rough-and-tumble play certainly has not met many girl athletes. Attempting to describe *absolute* differences between girls and boys is always a tricky business. Any statement about what all girls or all boys are like will be proven false by a multitude of exceptions. Few individuals fit neatly into any category, typical or not, but sexual stereotyping has often been used to denigrate girls and women. For example, scientists learned long ago that male brains are on average 10 to 15 percent larger than female brains. Some misguided people claimed that information as proof that men were more intelligent than women and therefore superior to them. Scientists now know that conclusion is preposterous: a bigger brain does not indicate more brain power.

In attempting to correct the mistakes caused by stereotypes, some people went too far in the opposite direction and suggested we erase distinctions between the sexes altogether. For a time in the 1970s and '80s, a politically charged argument held that male and female brains were exactly the same. This noble but flawed approach to thinking about sexual identity and the brain tried to correct centuries of sexism. If there were no differences between male and female brains, the thinking went, then there could be no arguments that men were superior. The problem is, there *are* significant differences, and simply ignoring them does a disservice to both sexes.

The Parent Survival Kit: Understanding Male and Female Brains

The statements in this kit are designed to help you pay attention to your teenager's gender-based needs.

PARENT SURVIVAL KIT

Understanding Male and Female Brains

Yes No

☐ ☐ 1. There are biologically based differences between girls' and boys' brains.

☐ ☐ 2. I realize it is important to keep brain-based differences in mind.

☐ ☐ 3. I encourage my teens to pursue their interests regardless of sexual stereotypes.

☐ ☐ 4. Our sons and daughters face different academic challenges.

☐ ☐ 5. I help my teenage daughter identify solutions and actions she can take when she feels down or discouraged.

☐ ☐ 6. I help my teenage son manage his aggression and anger.

☐ ☐ 7. I realize that the dramatic changes at puberty affect girls and boys differently.

As the items in this kit suggest, openness is crucial to parenting adolescents. All teens need love, acceptance, and support for who they are. If you find yourself disagreeing with the statements, you may find that you need to adopt a more open attitude in order to provide the support your teen needs in forming his or her identity.

Boy Brains and Girl Brains

In this discussion of male-female differences, please keep in mind that no two brains are alike. We are trying to identify general differences, but anytime I use words such as *boy, girl, male brain,* and *female brain*, you should mentally add the word *average* before the term. Statistically speaking, the distinctions I make about the sexes are correct, but what is true for most girls may also be true for some boys you know. The differences I will describe are only tendencies. Some distinctions are strictly physical; some, behavioral. They do not imply any system of hierarchy or morality. In other words, there is no better or worse sex—they are just different. Boy brains are larger than girl brains, but neither can be said to be better than the other.

Biology is not the same as destiny. Experience plays a big role in the shaping of the brain—the neurons that fire together wire together—and can even change hormone levels and brain structure. Girls' brains seem to be equipped to acquire language skills faster than boys' brains, but that doesn't mean that an individual boy will be unable to learn languages quickly if his experiences support such learning. With some exceptions, many of the differences between girls and boys can be eliminated or changed through individual experience.

Finally, I want to stress that all implications drawn from differences between the sexes are tentative and open to further research. For example, thirty years ago many scientists believed that boys as a group were better at math than girls as a group, even though there were obvious exceptions. They had research to back up this theory. Objective test scores and grades showed that indeed boys did better than girls on math tests. Since then teaching approaches have changed, and we have seen the supposed male math superiority melt away. It turns out that the discrepancy between boys and girls in mathematics was more sociological than biological. That may be true of some other traits as well.

With so much focus on differences, it is easy to lose sight of the many ways girls and boys are alike. For instance, boys and girls are equally intelligent. Various brain-based differences have been used throughout history to make the claim that either boys or girls are smarter. Boys have slightly bigger brains, but there is no evidence that that makes them smarter. Girls' brains develop faster than boys' brains, but there is no evidence that that makes them smarter, either.

With all these caveats it may sound like I'm suggesting that a child's sex doesn't matter. On the contrary, every year we have more and more evidence that it does matter. It's just that we need to be careful how we use that evidence, because we're only beginning to understand *how* sex-based brain differences matter. As long as we don't use this new knowledge to limit our sons or daughters or to place them in a box, exploring some of their differences can help us better understand the adolescents in our lives.

The simple explanation for the jump that girls' brains get developmentally on boys' is that they reach puberty earlier. The gradual shift of emotional processing from the amygdala to the prefrontal cortex happens earlier for girls than it does for boys. So while a fifteen-year-old boy is prone to an angry, quick-judgment outburst when you ask him to clean his room, a girl of the same age, with her more fully wired PFC, is more likely to comply with the request (or weasel out of it more subtly). Part of this story is the fact that the myelination—the insulating of the neuron cables—proceeds faster for girls than it does for boys. So the short-circuiting in the brain typical of adolescence is more likely to afflict a teenage boy than it is his twin sister. At the end of adolescence, most boys' brains have caught up to girls'.

During infancy, when the brain is undergoing its first major period of development, the left hemisphere develops before the right hemisphere in baby girls. For boys just the reverse is true. In them the right hemisphere develops before the left. Among many other things, language is centered in the left hemisphere. Development of a girl's language center so early in the growth process seems to bring a long-term tendency to verbal fluency that carries into adolescence. Because boys' right hemispheres mature quickly, they usually have an early capacity for spatial thinking. One of the right hemisphere's tasks is determining spatial relationships like navigation and mental rotation of objects. Boys in general tend to do better at these tasks through adolescence into adulthood. There are obvious exceptions to these rules, of course—there are great male poets and astounding female engineers—but in general girls have a knack for language while boys have talent for manipulating objects in three dimensions.

The corpus callosum, the bridge of nerve fibers between the right and left hemispheres of the brain, tends to be thicker in the female brain than in its male equivalent. Research suggests that the thicker the corpus callosum, the more it facilitates communication between the two hemispheres. Women therefore seem to have an advantage in linking both the analytical and verbal left brain with the intuitive right brain. Not surprisingly, brain scans of men and women performing identical mental tasks show women's brains using both hemispheres simultaneously while men tend to focus their brain activity in one hemisphere or the other for a given task. For the most part this difference merely points to the fact that there are different ways to do the same thing.

A part of the hypothalamus with the unglamorous name of third interstitial nucleus of the anterior hypothalamus (the INAH-3) is pretty much the same size in boys and girls—until they approach puberty. Then the INAH-3 becomes larger in boys' brains. The brain scans of the last few years have revealed that the INAH-3 is involved in sexual interest, desire, and sex drive. So boys' preoccupation with sexual thoughts and fantasies as they enter adolescence is more than just hormones. It is due to a structural difference in the brain.

Hormones play a big part in the differences between male and female brains because of the different levels of testosterone, estrogen, and progesterone that both sexes have. The concentrations of each hormone increase at puberty and throughout adolescence.

For boys, testosterone levels are much higher than levels of estrogen and progesterone. Known as the male hormone, testosterone seems to be related to a number of male traits—for example, the competitiveness and rough play typical of many boys. The combination of the tendency toward aggression brought on by testosterone and the poorer verbal skills caused by slower development of the left brain leads many boys to have difficulty in school and to act out when they are frustrated. The net result of this is that today boys are struggling to keep up with girls academically. This may come as a surprise, since in many cultures men are supported in striving for academic achievement while girls and women are not. In twentieth-century America girls and women won equal access to education, but for a while they still did not perform as well as boys in most subjects. Today that has changed, however, and boys are falling behind girls in many areas. For example, reading and language arts classes have become problem subjects for many boys. Test scores are down and so are grades. For every 100 boys earning their bachelor's degrees, 132 girls are getting theirs. Seven out of ten kids in special education classes are male. Anecdotal reports from teachers show that boy pupils are much less likely to be engaged and participatory in class than their fellow female students. By any measure, this new educational gap is a growing problem.

One theory for the falling achievement rates is that, ever since the '70s, educators have made an effort to use teaching methods that encourage girls—a necessary antidote to years of teaching girls in ways that made it hard for them to learn. Unfortunately, a similar effort to tailor teaching styles for adolescent boys has not been made. Another possible explanation is that the differences in male and female brain development make English class easier for the average girl than for the average boy.

Whatever the causes for boys' faltering academic performance, you can take steps to help the adolescent boys you know. Stay in touch with their teachers, and attend teacher conferences and school events. Encourage boys to read by providing books and magazines about their interests, such as nonfiction books or articles about sports, cars, or hobbies. When boys do read fiction, think the Harry Potter series; they tend to prefer stories with a lot of action and adventure. Point out and discuss articles in the news that you think might interest them. Reading sports articles will build their reading skills. Be willing to help them when they run into trouble with writing assignments. You can help boys wire in the capacity for language through such experiences.

Physical activity is another key to helping boys learn. Recess, maybe a couple of recesses a day, could end up being one of the most important methods of helping boys become literate. Boys need the large motor exercise their brains are dying to practice: exercise can actually wire their brains to do better in school. Some experts think that making students sit still in a desk all day isn't good for either sex, but girls are better able to tolerate it. Boys are more likely to get frustrated by school and lose interest.

As research on the academic gap between the sexes continues, educational leaders will continue to push for changes in the way our kids are taught. The Common Core State Standards, adopted by almost all states, put more emphasis on problem solving—something boys and girls seem equally good at. But the full impact of these standards may not come for years. Parents, teachers, and others who care for adolescents need to help boys stay engaged in school. As important as it is for us to liberate our daughters from the stereotypical limits that have historically existed, it is as important to help our sons. Many parents encourage their sons to get involved in athletics, but we need to do a better job supporting their interests in other after-school activities such as drama, art, music, the school newspaper, community service volunteering, and student government. A well-rounded education will help them become men who are more likely to have stable families, earn good salaries, and be happier than less fortunate, undereducated men.

Testosterone and Boys

As boys' testosterone levels ramp up at adolescence, their tendency toward anger and aggression increases. The amygdala—the anger and fear center of the brain—is rich in testosterone receptors. For some teen boys, the tendency toward aggression can lead to violence. That was the case with Allen, a fourteen-year-old I counseled. Big and strong for his age, Allen had developed a reputation as a bully in junior high school. He had been suspended on several occasions for fighting, but the really serious incident happened a few months after he entered high school. Allen thought that another boy at a party had insulted him so he challenged him to a fight. The other boy foolishly agreed. As they went outside, someone called the police, but before they arrived Allen had seriously injured the other boy. Within minutes Allen was in handcuffs and his victim was being taken to the hospital. Assault charges were filed and Allen was assigned to a juvenile probation officer. His mother brought him to see me.

I quickly discovered that Allen was usually very angry, and before long I had a good idea why. He had spent his entire childhood caught between two battling parents. Many nights, while trying to fall asleep, he had listened to his parents' loud arguments. He also recounted the times he had gotten between his parents to plead with them to stop arguing. He had hoped things would improve when his mother filed for divorce, but that did little to end the turmoil. A long custody battle ended with Allen dividing his time equally between two warring adults. He listened for hours each week as his father complained bitterly about his mother and vice versa. Neither parent was aware of how angry and bitter Allen was about being put in the middle. His seething anger boiled over into violence when testosterone lit up his amygdala at adolescence.

Fortunately, Allen and I hit it off well and quickly came to trust each other. Within a couple of sessions I was ready to confront him. "Allen, I don't blame you for being angry. It's not fair for your parents to put you in the middle of their problems. I'm willing to see if we can fix that, but first we have to do something about your fighting."

"I don't go around starting fights. I can just take care of myself, that's all."

"That's not the way I see it, Allen. From what your teachers tell me you've been threatening kids and picking fights since junior high."

Allen looked at the floor and said nothing. I let the seconds tick by silently. Then I asked, "Do you want to stop it?" Allen remained silent so I tried another approach. "Allen, you've listened to your parents calling each other names, threatening each other, and arguing since you were little. I know you're too young to think about marriage, but can you imagine having kids and putting them in the same spot you've been in?"

Allen finally broke his silence. "I would never treat kids like they did,"

"I hope not. But don't you think that what you've been doing is the high school version of the same thing?" I explained to Allen that fighting was a way to let out some of the anger inside and to be in control. "I'll bet you know when other kids are afraid of you, don't you?" I asked.

"Yeah," said Allen.

"Doesn't that feel kind of powerful?"

"Yeah," Allen admitted.

"Well, maybe that's your way of having control since things have always been out of control with your parents."

Allen made good progress. First of all, he agreed to let me talk with his parents privately. I have seen divorced parents battle through their kids so many times that I have lost a lot of patience for it. So when I met with Allen's father and mother I read them a version of the riot act. I told them how destructive their behavior was and I pleaded with them to take Allen out of the middle. "I'll do my best to help Allen deal with his anger better, but the two of you have to stop undermining him. Keep him out of your fights. He was lucky that the boy he beat up this time will recover. Unless Allen turns this around, he is going to get in a lot more serious trouble." The message got through.

Then Allen and I began to get down to work on stopping his fighting. I explained that learning to manage anger is a skill that needs practice. "The first thing you have to do is know when you're getting angry before it gets out of control. Anger always gives physical signs like a racing heart, a tight stomach, and shallow breathing. As soon as you notice any of these, take a deep breath to slow your body down. Counting to ten really helps because it not only calms you down, but the extra oxygen helps your brain think better. And better thinking is key because the next step when you're angry is to ask yourself, 'Why am I angry and how can I handle it without violence?'" I also had three school strategies to support Allen. His teachers and the school counselor all agreed that Allen could come to any of them at any time to get help calming down if he felt like he was going to blow up at school. Second, Allen joined a group that worked on conflict resolution skills. Third, Allen joined the wrestling team so he could let out some of his aggression in an appropriate way.

Staying physically active can help all boys deal with aggression. My theory is if boys exert enough energy out on the field or track, in the gym or on a bike or hockey skates, they may be less likely to release it in an inappropriate moment. If nothing else, the exercise can tire them out to the point that throwing a punch just seems like too much work.

Aggression isn't the only danger associated with testosterone surges. Another is risk taking. Enrique was thirteen when he and his friends decided to skateboard in and out of moving cars down a steep hill. Apparently they gave a few of the drivers quite a scare, because someone called the police. A squad car was waiting for the boys when they hiked back up to the top of the hill. The officer was friendly enough, but she made it clear that skateboarding on the hill was reckless and dangerous, and if they didn't stop, she'd be back to lay down some serious consequences. Enrique and his friends told her they understood and would find something else to do.

As soon as the police car was out of sight they recommenced bombing the hill on their boards. Ten minutes later Enrique zigged when he should have zagged. In an instant he bounced off the hood of a car and was thrown ten feet in the air. Fortunately, he escaped permanent injury, but he did spend the rest of the summer with an itchy cast around his badly broken leg. Enrique got off easy, but if his adolescent brain hadn't served up a big testosterone cocktail, he might have never taken such a foolish chance. He was lucky to avoid death and brain damage after a spill like that, but he could have averted injury altogether.

Estrogen, Progesterone, and Girls

Estrogen and progesterone spikes in the female brain during puberty can have a powerful effect on girls' brains and behavior, too. These hormones affect the group of neurotransmitters that influence mood; consequently, the risk for depression rises for girls during adolescence. Teen girls are more likely to feel depressed than boys.

When Marta was little, she was one of the happiest kids you could ever meet. Her mile-wide smile dominates every picture of her as a child. When Marta hit adolescence, however, she stopped smiling. Depressed, she began to have trouble making friends at school. When she had her period—that's when estrogen and progesterone levels are the most in flux—she would sometimes spend days in bed, doubled over with cramps, sobbing into a pillow. Her parents were at a loss. They found her after-school activities and helped her devise strategies to make new friends. They encouraged her to go out for sports teams to keep herself fit and be a part of a group. She went into therapy and changed schools. Some of these things seemed to improve her mood for a while, but then, out of nowhere, she'd sink back into depression. The world's happiest kid had become one of the saddest.

Marta had a particularly extreme case of adolescent hormone fluctuation. Her neurotransmitters were bombarded with confusing messages. Now a young adult, she is doing much better. She still has bouts of unexplained sadness, but they are fewer and farther between. Fortunately, when she does hit a rough patch it doesn't seem to get as bad as it did when she was a teenager. For the most part, she is happy and successful, known for her charismatic smile and contagious laughter. Now that her brain is done with its adolescent development, she is no longer a victim of the chemicals at work in her head. We will discuss adolescent depression more in chapter 12.

The differences between boy brains and girl brains present some real challenges that can be met with the support and guidance of parents and other adults. Even though every adolescent is different, sex-based brain characteristics will surface at some point during adolescence.

Girls need help through adolescence to overcome the cultural barriers to their sex that still exist. For all the work that Title IX has done to encourage equal participation in sports, for instance, girls are still underrepresented in athletic activities in our society. That's too bad, because getting girls into sports isn't just a matter of justice and equality. Physical activity is the key to physical and mental health. Exercise is good for more than the lungs and muscles—it's good for the brain. Rigorous exercise increases the neurotransmitters linked to happiness, elevated mood, and energy—which may partly explain why girls who play sports tend to feel better than their nonathletic counterparts. Sports also give girls a chance to be part of a social group. One of the important tasks of adolescence is socialization, and firing those social neurons will help wire in the ability to have healthy adult relationships.

Our culture and most others place enormous value on the physical appearance of girls, which can lead to problems such as eating disorders and pressure to dress and act glamorous well beyond their years. Poor nutrition, premature sexual activity, and a flawed sense of self-esteem often exacerbate these issues. We all need to encourage girls to develop their entire personalities, not just look good for the boys. What they learn to do as teenagers will help them as young women.

Here's how a friend of mine, Bonnie, handled the situation with her fifteen-year-old daughter, Melanie, when they went dress shopping before a school dance. Before they entered the store, Bonnie made it clear that she was not going to argue about dresses that were too revealing. "I want you to find something pretty that you really like. There are dresses that are plain and there are dresses that are way too skimpy for someone your age. We need to find something in the middle. I won't push for plain if you won't push for skimpy. I reserve veto power, okay? If we can't come to an agreement, the shopping trip is over, and we'll have to try another time."

Even in our highly technological culture, girls tend to avoid science and technology and thus may need help to become more comfortable in those areas. Boys are encouraged more than girls to dive deeply into computers and to explore science and math and the way mechanical objects work. For example, when a boy asks for help on a science experiment, teachers will more often give him suggestions for how to proceed. When a girl asks, teachers are more likely to complete the experiment for her, leaving her to watch. As a result, adult men are usually more comfortable than adult women with technology. Technoliteracy is becoming more and more important to leading a successful, productive life and adolescence is an important time for picking up skills and trying new things.

Because teen girls tend to verbalize their moods, they are also in danger of talking themselves into a depression. When they have something on their minds, some teen girls begin to talk about it, then talk about it, and talk about it, and before long, all this verbal attention to the problem blows it out of proportion. As a result, their perspective becomes so altered that everything looks grim and the condition appears permanent. Girls have enough of a challenge overcoming hormones and neurotransmitters to stay in a good mood, so they need all the help they can get when they start to sink into a verbal mood whirlpool. While we need to listen to our daughters when they are emotionally hurting, we also need to encourage them to work toward solutions to lift themselves out of a downward spiral. A conversation with a girl about something that is bothering her should include talk about how to feel better, not just be a list of all the things that are wrong.

Here's a sample dialogue of how a parent can help a daughter put the brakes on negative feelings: "I can understand how disappointed you are that you didn't make the basketball team. I'd be sad, too. With the new girls coming from the other junior high school this year it was very competitive. It's too bad that the high school doesn't offer more opportunities to play. But you know, some of your good friends didn't get on the team either. Maybe you could get a group together to enter a team in the park board league. Or perhaps you could look into the cross-country ski team. I hear that the kids on that team really have a good time."

"Dad, you don't understand. I really wanted to play basketball. I don't even know how to ski."

"Yeah, I know. I'm sorry it didn't work out. Please understand that I'm not trying to push you into skiing. I just think that it's helpful to start to think of some other things you can do this winter. The disappointment will hurt for a while, but whenever that happens to me I find it helpful to start to think about some other possibilities. Of course, you don't need to decide anything tonight. For tonight suppose we just find something fun to do. I was going to try to bake an apple pie tonight. How about helping me?"

"Aw, Dad, I don't think so."

"I'll tell you what; if you help me a little with cutting up the apples, you can play whatever music you want while we do it."

"But you hate my music."

"What are you talking about? I just say that to give you a hard time. When you're not home I play your music all the time. I just don't want you to know it."

"Yeah, sure you do."

"Listen, here's the deal. If you help me, I promise I won't say one word about your music and you can play it as loud as you want. Come on, we usually have fun doing some baking together."

"Can I invite Lisa to help? She's bummed out, too."

"Sure. Call her now and see if she can come over."

For years we've heard about the battle between the sexes, and this martial language is supported by our sense that boys and girls think differently, act differently, and care about different things. As recent research has shown, these differences do exist, but that doesn't mean that boys and girls should be seen as at odds with one another. The differences that divide us into sexes should be seen as an opportunity to help each other with what we do best rather than a reason to pit ourselves against each other. Because of their brain development differences, boys and girls need specific care from adults. But that shouldn't distract us from doling out the guidance and love that all of them need.

DO

✓ Encourage your daughters to get involved in sports.

✓ Encourage your sons and daughters to be involved in a wide range of activities.

✓ If your sons or daughters are reluctant readers, make an effort to find books and magazines about topics they are interested in. For example, if your son likes music, buy music magazines for him.

✓ Pay attention to your son's and daughter's school performance and intervene early if you see him or her starting to turn off.

✓ Encourage daughters to find solutions when they are feeling down or discouraged. Ask them what they can do about a situation that is bothering them.

✓ Encourage your sons to name and talk about feelings. Model emotional literacy for them with phrases like "I'm feeling frustrated that I can't figure out these directions" or "I'm excited to be going to the play tonight." Ask them questions to encourage talking about feelings, such as "Tell me how you feel about getting a low grade on the math test."

DON'T

✗ Don't limit your adolescent by only encouraging traditional gender interests and goals.

✗ Don't tolerate your son's aggressive behavior if it turns destructive to either property or people. Intervene early and tell him exactly what behavior is out of bounds. You might say, for example, "I understand that you're angry, but you may not hit your brother." Instead of issuing an ultimatum, tell your teen what the consequence will be. "If you hit your brother again, you will not be able to go out with your friends this weekend."

What do I want to continue?

_____

_____

_____

What do I want to change?

_____

_____

_____

EIGHT

Love, Sex, and the Adolescent Brain

In November during my first year as a high school counselor, I began working with a student named Mark, who came to see me because he was feeling "down" and didn't seem to be able to shake it. I had taught Mark the previous year and in my class he'd usually been good-natured, if a little quiet—a fairly happy kid. After talking with him for a few minutes, it was clear that the old Mark was gone and the one in my office was really suffering. We talked a couple of times over a period of weeks, but nothing in particular seemed to explain his depression. When our meetings were interrupted by a two-week winter break, we still hadn't made any real progress.

In our first meeting after the holidays Mark seemed to be a different person, just like his old self—but better. Upbeat, energetic, and happy, he told me he didn't think we needed to meet anymore because he was feeling just fine.

"Well, if you really are feeling okay, we probably don't need to get together anymore," I said. "But tell me one thing, Mark. What's her name?" I had seen him the previous day talking animatedly with a girl in the hallway, and I had a hunch about what was going on.

"Whose name?" Mark said, an embarrassed blush blooming on his cheeks.

"The girl who brought so much excitement into your life."

He blushed even more and then proceeded to tell me about Stephanie. She had transferred to our school in late October. Mark had noticed her the first day she walked into history class. Every day he thought more and more about her, but he did not have the nerve to strike up a conversation. He had said hello a couple of times but decided that she was more interested in the other guys in the class, who were more outgoing and cool.

That's when Mark had come to see me. He knew he was having a tough time, but he wasn't sure if it was due to a girl he didn't even know. Consequently, he had never hinted at the fact that he was lovesick. He had only been able to talk in a general sense about feeling down. No wonder we never got anywhere with our meetings.

Then over the holidays he had run into Stephanie at a party. The most amazing thing was, he told me, *she* came over to *him* and started a conversation. They spent the rest of the party together talking, laughing, and getting to know each other. When Mark left the party that night, it was as if he had never been down at all. Everything else in his life seemed inconsequential compared to Stephanie's interest in him. Over the next two weeks things with Stephanie just kept getting better and better. They talked on the phone. They worked on homework together. They laughed together. Mark was happier and more excited than he'd ever been in his life.

As I listened to Mark, I began to smile. After he finished I asked him a couple of questions.

"Do you think about her all the time?"

"All the time."

"Is she the neatest girl you have ever met?"

"Neatest?" He smiled. "I don't think I'd put it that way, but, yeah, she is. She's the nicest girl anyone has ever met."

"Mark, that's great. I'm really happy for you. Bring her by sometime and introduce me. I've seen her around school, but I haven't met her yet."

He promised he would and we finished our conversation. As Mark walked down the hall I shook my head. Why hadn't I thought of it earlier? Mark was in love and that had made all the difference.

The Parent Survival Kit: Sex, Sexuality, and Values

Sex is one of the trickiest and most difficult issues that parents have to deal with, but making sure your adolescent has good information and healthy attitudes means the topic must be broached. Use this kit to see if you are helping your teen in this important area.

Sex, Sexuality, and Values

Yes No

☐ ☐ 1. I have talked with my teens about sex and sexuality.

☐ ☐ 2. I've told my teens about the dangers of sexually transmitted diseases.

☐ ☐ 3. I am aware of the statistics about teen sexual behavior and know that teens tend to be sexually active.

☐ ☐ 4. My spouse and I are consistent in communicating the values our family has about sex and sexuality.

☐ ☐ 5. I am willing to deal with my own discomfort talking about sex, because I know how important it is for my children to get information from me and not just from peers, media, or the Internet.

☐ ☐ 6. I can talk with my adolescent about sexual identity questions.

☐ ☐ 7. I talk about gays, lesbians, and transgender people with respect.

☐ ☐ 8. I will love and accept my adolescent regardless of sexual identity.

Answering yes to the statements in this kit means that you are helping your teen figure out important sexual issues. If you have to answer no to several items, you are in danger of abdicating your position of influence over your child and allowing the media, the Internet, and peers to provide your teen with his or her sexual values and information.

Romance and the Brain

All parents who want the best for their children want them to be happy and fall in love . . . someday. We tend to be ambivalent, however, when it happens to our own teenagers. On the one hand, we are happy for our child's excitement in discovering one of life's greatest gifts and most exciting adventures. On the other hand, adolescent love gives us a laundry list of new worries. Will my son or daughter get hurt? Just who is this person he or she is falling in love with? How serious should she or he be at this age? The potential for sexual contact, teen pregnancy, and sexually transmitted diseases is troublesome and real.

When it comes to adolescent romance, all adults feel that they're experts. Most people, however, don't know the brain science behind the phenomenon. Brain structures and brain chemicals both affect the way an adolescent first dives into romance.

The awakening of romantic infatuation actually begins even before puberty. Around the age of ten, the body increases production of a group of hormones in the brain collectively known as androgens. As these androgens increase, especially DHEA (dehydroepiandrosterone), boys and girls experience their first crush. The first crush has some of the same ingredients as the full-scale romance to come, but it is just a preview of coming attractions. The main act, romantically speaking, comes with puberty and the beginning of adolescence. This is when the real awakenings of sexual interest and sex drive occur. It is also when that first intoxicating experience of "falling in love" usually kicks in.

For boys, the rapid development of the hypothalamus's INAH-3 (third interstitial nucleus of the anterior hypothalamus) prompts sexual thoughts to begin crowding out thoughts of studies, chores, and many other things in a boy's brain. The combination of the maturing INAH-3 module in the hypothalamus and the surges in testosterone—a real double whammy—results in a great interest in sex, which takes the form of sexual fantasies, thoughts, and curiosity. At this stage an adolescent boy will usually start to have erotic dreams, culminating in orgasms, "wet" dreams, which can be confusing and embarrassing for a boy unused to this new hormonally propelled sexual development. Masturbation often becomes common for adolescent boys. At times they are obsessed with sexual thoughts and fantasies. Dopamine, the hormone related to good feelings, also spikes. The sex drive in boys and girls is linked to dopamine. Since sex is very pleasurable (and necessary for the human race to continue), it makes sense that the reward, or feel-good hormone, dopamine, is involved.

The hypothalamus also drives changes in hormone levels that are responsible for the sexual awakening in adolescent girls. Present in boys and girls, men and women, testosterone provides the sex drive, although the concentration of the hormone is much higher in boys. Thus, interest in the physical aspects of sex is stronger in boys, who are more likely than girls to sit in class fantasizing about their classmates. Of course, girls also have erotic fantasies, but they don't seem to be as all-consuming as boys'.

Because of their developmental differences, boys and girls have a different attitude toward sex and romance. Because of their testosterone surges, adolescent boys tend to view girls as sexual objects. Adolescent girls are more prone to focus on the relational aspects of sexual attraction, such as spending time together and talking.

The nascent sex drive is only part of the romantic awakening for every adolescent. Although sexual interest is always part of falling in love, falling in love is not always part of the sex drive. An adolescent boy can, and often will, have erotic fantasies about girls or women who are total strangers. The erotic interest may be purely physical with no romantic overtones. Falling in love, however, involves more than a sexual interest. Falling in love is more powerful, more consuming, and involves more of the adolescent brain. As Mark found out, it is truly a mood-altering experience and for adolescents the experience is brand-new.

Andreas Bartels and Semir Zeki, brain scientists at University College, London, have conducted the first brain-based studies on what's happening inside the brains of young people who are madly in love. The scientists scanned the brains of young men and women while they looked at pictures of their girlfriends and boyfriends. To make sure they were seeing the brain pattern associated with romantic love they also scanned the kids' brains while they looked at photos of close friends to whom they had no romantic attraction. The results of this experiment showed a very distinct pattern of brain activity. When the young lovers thought of their boyfriends and girlfriends, four separate areas of their brains became very active. Two were in the cortex and two others, deeper within the brain. The study found that the prefrontal cortex—the seat of reason—was inactive. When we fall in love, we aren't using our rational brain, and our impulse control—the job of the prefrontal cortex—is not very high. Falling in love is more emotion than thought. Its active neural circuits are not the same that fire during sexual arousal. Falling in love is not all about sex. Although the pattern of brain activation associated with falling in love is unique, it was not completely unfamiliar to the scientists. The brain activity in someone in love is very similar to the neural firing pattern of someone under the influence of cocaine, and some researchers believe that the hormonal interplay can be somewhat addictive, as Dr. Stanton Peele wrote in his book *Love and Addiction*. From the brain's point of view, at least, falling in love is as powerful as a cocaine high: dopamine (feeling good), norepinephrine (reacting quickly), and serotonin (mood) are all in play while falling in love.

Dr. Helen Fisher, an anthropologist at Rutgers University who specializes in the brain chemistry of love, confirms that falling in love elevates dopamine, which explains the euphoria; elevates norepinephrine—commonly known as adrenaline—accounting for the racing heart and sweaty palms; and decreases the levels of serotonin. Serotonin is the mood stabilizer hormone. Decreasing the level of serotonin results in some of the sadness and obsessive behavior typical of falling in love, as well as the roller coaster of emotions we experience.

As exhilarating as it is, the brain can't sustain this level of hormonal fireworks forever, so the experience of falling in love is short. The duration of the intense feelings associated with falling in love is even shorter for the adolescent brain than it is for the adult brain. The average length of infatuation for an adolescent is three to four months.

That sounds about right, when you think about it. Most intense adolescent romances don't last much longer than a few months. When I was a high school teacher, I had a student who seemed to follow the three-to-four-month rule exactly. Sara had been going from one intense relationship to another since I first met her as a ninth-grader in my homeroom. By the time she was a senior, I realized that she had averaged a couple of boyfriends per school year during the four years I had known her. During a class discussion in her senior year, we were talking about dating and marriage issues. Sara commented that she didn't think she would ever get married. Some classmates asked her why. She said she realized that she always eventually became bored with her boyfriends. As one relationship cooled, someone else always came along. Since she always felt bad about breaking up with guys, she couldn't imagine how hard it would be to go through a divorce.

"I think the best thing for me to do is to never get in such a serious relationship as marriage," she said. "The problem is that I love kids. I really want to have kids of my own. So I don't know what I'm going to do about that."

When falling in love is a brand-new feeling, a person can be extremely disappointed when it passes. He or she is tempted to look for it somewhere else. But even adolescents who tend to skip from one relationship to the next usually figure out how to get past the need to fall in love constantly when they grow up.

Back in the classroom that day with Sara, I used her comments to initiate a discussion with the class about the difference between falling in love and what I call standing in love. Some adolescents like Sara move quickly from one romantic relationship to another. Others transition smoothly from the tumultuous and exciting experience of falling in love to the calmer and more comfortable standing in love.

Falling in Love and Standing in Love

Compared to falling in love, standing in love is less euphoric but happier, less intense but more solid, less breathtaking but more satisfying—more warm than hot. Standing in love is the basis of long-term commitments and lifelong romantic relationships. No one (and no one brain) can sustain the intensity of falling in love. Some people, however, keep searching for that high, seeking out intense relationships that they abandon when they eventually and inevitably cool. It is only after the cooldown begins that the brain can fully engage the prefrontal cortex and make judgments about the viability of a long-term relationship. Of course, not every love relationship should become a standing relationship. Once the prefrontal cortex becomes active, the adolescent may begin to think, "What did I ever see in that person?" I've talked to many parents who are more worried about their adolescents standing in love than falling in love.

"I don't want her to get too serious too early," they say. "She's got her whole future to think of." This is a well-founded concern. Plenty of teens become consumed by serious romantic relationships when they would be better off trying out different kinds of relationships. Sometimes hopping from one intense experience to the next helps an adolescent decide what he or she is looking for in adult life. Others, like my friends Eileen and Michael, move from falling in love to a standing in love that lasts for a lifetime together.

Eileen and Michael met in high school. They knew each other from hanging out with a larger group of friends. In their senior year they started to date. Going to different colleges was difficult for them, but they kept in touch and got together during breaks and over summer vacations. They each agreed to date others during college and in the years immediately following graduation. But inevitably they would end up back together again. Michael and Eileen decided to get married when they were twenty-four. Now they've celebrated their fifteenth wedding anniversary and have two sons and a daughter.

Not surprisingly, standing in love involves a different set of brain chemicals than does falling in love. For girls the hormone associated with a warm (standing) love relationship, forming close intimate bonds, is oxytocin, which is also involved in childbirth and in nursing. Susan Barker of the University of Maryland refers to oxytocin as the "cuddle hormone." Naturally increasing in the female brain as adolescence progresses, it is responsible for the fondness many adolescent girls have for cute, cuddly animals and little babies. Meanwhile it is preparing them for long-term, committed love relationships.

For boys, the attachment hormone is vasopressin, which also regulates the proper concentration of water in the human body. As levels of vasopressin rise in boys and men, they are more apt to be protective and attentive to their partners' needs. In addition, animal studies reveal a connection between elevated vasopressin and faithfulness to one partner.

Romantic Pitfalls

How do you keep your adolescent out of all the trouble that can come from romance and love? One of the most common worries can be summed up by this question: What if my son or daughter falls in love with someone who is not a good match?

I once counseled a sixteen-year-old girl named Elizabeth who had been arrested for serious vandalism at her high school. She and her boyfriend had broken into the school late at night and done several thousand dollars' worth of damage with spray paint and a baseball bat. Her parents and teachers were shocked. It was the first time Elizabeth had ever gotten into any trouble. The courts made her pay restitution and referred her to a youth diversion program. Her parents also insisted that she see a psychologist, which is how I met her.

Elizabeth explained to me that her boyfriend, Brad, had talked her into it. She had resisted, but he pressed and assured her that he had done the same sort of thing before, no one would get hurt, and they would never get caught. She asked him why he wanted to do it.

"If you come with me, you'll find out what a rush it is," was his response.

Elizabeth was really in love with Brad, so she reluctantly agreed to go along. Elizabeth explained to me with tears streaming down her face how much she regretted it. She had lost the trust of her parents, and everyone at school thought she was a loser. She told me that although she had broken up with Brad and was determined to repair her reputation, she secretly worried that this episode would haunt her for the rest of her life.

It was a bad decision on her part, yes, and if she hadn't been in love, she probably wouldn't have gone through with it. Her prefrontal cortex would have kicked in and said, "You know what, Brad? I'm going to take a pass." Elizabeth admitted that her parents had expressed concerns about Brad, but she hadn't listened.

Falling in love can blind teens to another serious problem: physical or sexual abuse. One of the darker sides of romantic love is jealousy and possessiveness. A girl I counseled, Jane, found herself enmeshed in a smothering and controlling relationship with a boy during her junior year in high school. Raymond was polite, funny, and very attentive to her. She looked forward to the time they spent together. Little by little, however, Jane started to withdraw from her other friends. She felt guilty because Raymond became sad when she did things without him. It was easier to reserve all her time for him than it was to bring him out of his funk. His phone calls became more frequent, and he wanted to know whom she was talking with when her line was busy. On one occasion he wouldn't talk to her for two days after seeing her laughing and talking with another boy at school. He eventually convinced her that she was at fault because she was such a flirt. Jane grew nervous that Raymond would see her talking with other guys, so she started to avoid all of her male friends.

In her ninth- and tenth-grade years Jane had enjoyed playing minor roles in the school plays. She was excited when the drama teacher encouraged her to try out for a major role in the spring musical. When she shared her good news with Raymond, he became furious. "What am I supposed to do for the next two months?" he screamed as they sat in his car. "We'll have time together," Jane insisted. Raymond got out of the car and stormed off. Jane chased him, but he wouldn't stop. "Raymond, can't we talk about this," she pleaded. She caught up with him and put her hand on his shoulder. He wheeled around and in one motion punched her hard in her stomach. With the wind knocked from her lungs Jane dropped to the ground. "Look what you made me do," Raymond shouted.

Jane did not try out for the play. Raymond had convinced her that she was being selfish.

A year later, after she was finally able to extricate herself from Raymond's emotional clutches, Jane described this scene and many others like it. I asked her if Raymond had ever sexually abused her. "No," she answered. I pushed a little further. "Did he ever persuade you to do sexual things that you didn't want to do?" Jane was quiet. After a few moments she admitted he had. "He complained a lot that

I was uptight and a prude. A lot of times he would get me to do sexual things by nagging, but that's not sexual abuse, is it?" I asked her if it felt like abuse. She thought for a long time. She started to cry and finally managed to say, "I hated it" between sobs.

No one is sure how many teen victims of emotional, physical, or sexual abuse there are, but we do know that every day there are more. It is safe to say that many kids like Jane suffer in silence. What should parents look for to prevent their daughters or sons from getting caught in such a trap? Unexplained cuts or bruises raise obvious red flags, but those marks are not nearly as common as the more subtle signs of being under the influence of someone else's controlling behavior. Parents should pay attention when teens start to cut themselves off from other friends and activities in order to please a boyfriend or girlfriend. Abuse victims often become moody or depressed; you may overhear them accounting for their whereabouts or justifying their actions.

It is very difficult for teens to extricate themselves from abusive relationships. Enlisting friends and encouraging your teen to talk will help her or him begin to see the reality of the relationship. In serious cases parents need to directly intervene by seeking professional help.

Worries about a boyfriend or girlfriend can bring about some of the most difficult, potentially explosive situations in parenting adolescents. Encourage your son or daughter to bring boyfriends or girlfriends over to your house as much as possible. Establish a relationship with the person in your adolescent's life. Opening up that line of communication can help when dealing with difficult issues later on. Don't put down your adolescent's boyfriend or girlfriend. Attacks will almost guarantee resistance, because a teenager in love will defend his or her romantic partner to the end. Instead of saying, "I can't stand your boyfriend and I forbid you to see him again," say "I know you really care about him and I can tell you see a lot of his good qualities. Tell me some of the things that you really like about him." Make sure you listen without getting angry or judging. Acknowledge his good points and then share some of your concerns calmly. For example, you might say, "You don't spend any time with your other friends since you started this relationship. Do you ever feel pressured to avoid your friends or to do something you know isn't right?" If she answers yes, then you have the opportunity to talk about it. If she says no, then make sure you let her know that you're ready and willing to talk about it if the situation arises.

As always, be clear about your expectations, rules, limits, and the consequences of breaking them. For instance, you can say, "I know you don't want me to hassle you about your boyfriend. I'll be a lot easier to get along with if the two of you comply with the curfew and other rules that we have. I've shared my concerns with you, but you can prove me wrong by keeping up your responsibilities at home and school." Opening up this kind of respectful dialogue can help your adolescent feel okay about raising concerns about a relationship later on down the line.

Another worry that parents have is "What if my son or daughter gets hurt?" The best thing to do for an adolescent who gets hurt in love is to listen, empathize, and support. Try to help the hurting adolescent regain perspective, but also realize that Cupid's wounds take time to heal. If months pass and the sadness of a breakup is intensifying rather than abating, it might be wise to schedule an appointment with a counselor to help get past the hurt or to make sure the disappointment has not triggered some depression. We'll discuss depression further in chapter 12.

Teens and Sexual Behavior

Probably the biggest set of your worries concerns your child's sex life. All of the volatile emotions of romance can seem multiplied in intensity and duration when teens get sexually involved. Most parents think that sex should be left for adulthood or marriage, but whether we like it or not, many adolescents have sex and get into trouble because of it. It may sound strange, but we parents need to come to terms with the fact that we are part of the problem. A growing body of evidence shows that American parents stop short in providing complete guidance about sexual behavior for our adolescent sons and daughters. Fortunately, teen pregnancy rates in the United States have started to decline, by 29 percent between 2007 and 2012. Nevertheless they are by far the highest of all Western industrialized countries. In addition, the United States has the highest rates of sexually transmitted diseases, such as syphilis, gonorrhea, and chlamydia, in the Western industrialized world. Every year, four million U.S. teens contract an STD.

Adolescents in the United States engage in sexual intercourse at about the same rates as adolescents in other Western industrialized countries. The average age for the first experience of sexual intercourse in the United States is fifteen for males and sixteen for females, about the same ages as their counterparts in other countries. Almost two out of three American teens have had sex by the time they graduate from high school, again, about the same as other Western industrialized countries.

So if teens in the United States have sexual activity at rates similar to those of other industrialized nations, why are pregnancy and STD rates so much higher here? For starters, our teens have more sexual partners and are less likely to use condoms than teens in other countries. In addition, American teens are less well educated about birth control and STDs than their foreign counterparts. It's not just that teens here don't know about STDs; they have a lot of incorrect information. In the United States misconceptions about STDs abound among teens. Let's consider some examples.

Chlamydia, known as the silent STD, is the most frequently reported bacterial sexually transmitted infection in the United States and is most common among young people. An estimated three million Americans are infected each year. Teenage girls have the highest rates of infection. The Centers for Disease Control (CDC) reports that as many as one in fifteen sexually active adolescent girls is infected and that 50 percent of sexually active women under thirty have had chlamydia at some time in their lives.

Most adolescents do not realize that chlamydia can be transmitted during oral sex. Many adolescent boys and girls are unaware that they have the disease and are transmitting it to others. Teenagers are particularly susceptible because they are unaware of the risks and because the cells in a young girl's cervix are especially vulnerable to the bacteria. Left untreated, chlamydia can cause a number of serious health problems later in life. For men the long-term risks include urethral infections and potentially infertility.

Untreated chlamydia in women can cause a painful, chronic infection called pelvic inflammatory disease and can permanently damage the reproductive organs, leading to infertility.

Genital herpes is also widespread among adolescents. And again, many adolescents are unaware that genital herpes can be spread through oral sex.

Another disease that is extremely easy to spread is genital HPV infection, a disease caused by human papillomavirus (HPV). One of the ways it manifests itself is best known as genital warts. They are so common that the Centers for Disease Control reports almost eighty million American females carry some form of this virus, most in their late teens and early twenties. There is growing concern about the escalation of the rates among both adolescent boys and girls. Although genital warts can be removed by a specialist, they can develop into precancerous or cancerous cells if untreated and are frequently associated with cervical cancer, which is deadly if untreated. In 2006 an effective vaccine was introduced to reduce the incidence of contracting HPV by 56 percent among the girls who were vaccinated. In spite of the demonstrated effectiveness, however, only 30 percent of American girls have taken advantage of this breakthrough.

Many teens are unaware of the dangers of contracting HIV/AIDS because they think only adults, gay people, and drug addicts are at risk. This complacency is dangerous because, according to the latest data from the CDC, the rates of HIV/AIDs among teens are increasing while rates for other age groups are dropping. There were 2,200 new cases of teen HIV/AIDS in 2009. Teens need to know that this deadly disease can be transmitted through intercourse, oral sex, and shared needle use.

We parents need to do a better job educating our adolescents about sex. The countries with low rates of teen pregnancy and low rates of STDs deal with sex more openly. It is not uncommon for adolescents to talk frankly and frequently about sex with their families and in schools. It may be counterintuitive that these more open societies have fewer problems associated with adolescent sexual activity. This is because in the U.S. many fear that if we talk to teens about sex, sexuality, and birth control, the information will somehow trigger their interest in it—as if teens have not heard about sex before taking a health class on it. Having bought into this misguided notion that information would promote sexual promiscuity, political leaders in this country have spoken and voted against funding for sex education.

Here's a news flash for policy makers and many parents alike: teens already have sex on the mind. It doesn't matter where they come from, what their beliefs are, or how they were raised: adolescents have natural processes at work in their brains and bodies that prompt an interest in sex. Talking about it will not *make* them interested. They are *already* interested.

Research shows that if trusted adults don't talk to adolescents about sex, then the adolescents will get their information from peers, the media, and the Internet. More than half of teens report looking up information on the Internet for themselves or a friend. Unfortunately, the sites they view often give inaccurate sexual health information. And other studies confirm that the information adolescents get from peers—such as their understanding of how diseases are spread—isn't the real deal. Any adult who remembers the kind of information available in the schoolyard knows that it is largely based on hearsay, ignorance, and bragging. Unfortunately, only 19 percent of teens get accurate information on sex from their families. With restrictions on sex education in schools, many of the other 81 percent rely on often flawed information. Keeping kids in the dark in an attempt to guide them to a healthy lifestyle without sex is obviously backfiring.

According to the Centers for Disease Control and Prevention, 47 percent of American teenage boys and 41 percent of teen girls have received oral sex. Teens know they can't get pregnant from oral sex and mutual masturbation. Many also believe incorrectly that they can't get an STD from either oral sex or mutual masturbation. To repeat, they can; chlamydia, human papillomavirus, herpes, and gonorrhea are all on the rise among teens. Many teens also do not consider oral sex and mutual masturbation to be "real" sex, which they define as only sexual intercourse.

The debate between comprehensive sex education and abstinence-only advocates has raged for more than thirty years. The abstinence school teaches children and teens the importance of not engaging in sex until marriage. The comprehensive camp includes information about birth control and contraception in its lessons. A large national study showed that teaching about contraception did not increase adolescent sexual activity or STDs. The teens that received comprehensive sex education also had a lower risk of pregnancy than their peers who received abstinence-only teaching. Although this has resulted in fewer federal and state dollars for the abstinence-only approach, no one expects the debate to end.

Talking with Teens About Sex

All responsible adults, teachers, and parents, regardless of their position on the sex education debate, need to have open and honest conversations with our adolescent sons and daughters about sex and about sexuality. Sex is about biology. Sexuality is about biology, psychology, values, and spirituality. When adults ignore the reality of our children's awakening sexuality, we are ignoring what is going on in their brains. Even if we adults do not explain what sex is and how we want our children to behave, teenagers will think about sex, they will talk about sex, and they will probably engage in some sort of sexual activity—just as most of their friends do. If we don't want them to have oral sex or mutual masturbation, we have to discuss that with them and explain why it is not good for them. If we want the sex our children ultimately do have to be physically, psychologically, and morally healthy, then we'd better start talking with them.

Here are some tips for talking with teens about sex.

1. *Get motivated.* Some parents don't talk with their teens about sex because they are afraid that it will spark their kids' curiosity or give them ideas, thereby causing their kids to engage in early sex. The reality is just the opposite. Kids who have good communication with their parents delay sexual activity and are more responsible and safe. Remember, if you don't talk to your teens about sex, someone else will and they probably won't have your values.

2. *Get educated.* There are good books and Web sites that provide solid information as well as tips for talking with teens about sex. Being well informed builds confidence and helps to overcome the nervousness that many parents feel.

3. *Get comfortable.* Most parents feel uncomfortable discussing sex with their kids. Even if you can't overcome your discomfort, don't hesitate to share that with your kids. It might help to say something like "You know, it's hard for me to talk with you about sex because we never discussed it when I was growing up. But it's a really important topic so I'm going to do the best I can." Your kids will appreciate your candor and your interest.

4. *Make it an ongoing conversation.* Don't approach discussions about sex as the "big talk." Look for opportunities to have many shorter conversations that begin in preteen years and continue throughout adolescence. Sexual topics come up regularly in the media. Use these to start short discussions. For example, "Did you see that item in the news today about how many teens are engaging in oral sex? What did you think of that? Do you think it was realistic based on what's going on in your peer group?"

5. *Don't try to cover too much in any one discussion.* For example, you might have a discussion like this with your son about sexual fantasies: "One of the things that happens at your age is that the part of your brain that triggers sexual interest kicks into overdrive. So don't be surprised if you seem obsessed with sexual thoughts and images. That's normal for someone your age."

6. *Choose appropriate times when you and your teen have some privacy and are not rushed.* You'll both be more comfortable.

7. *Discuss sexuality, not just sex.* While it is important for kids to have accurate biological information, they also need to know that a healthy sexual relationship entails respect, caring, and responsibility. You might say something like "One of the things I try to remember is that sex is just one part of a good relationship. If I'm just out for my own pleasure, then I'm using the other person."

8. *Discuss dating.* For example, you might say something like "It really bothers me the way the media portray dating. On TV, couples who go out usually end up in bed together. Dating should be a time to get to know someone else and have fun together."

9. *Don't preach.* Teens hate long-drawn-out lectures. Say what you want to say and then let it go. The odds are a lot better that your kids will listen.

10. *Make it a dialogue.* Ask questions and then listen. You will know if your teen really heard what you were saying. Try to understand your teen's concerns, questions, and opinions. Don't cut off your adolescent with a statement like "I don't care what you think, I'm your parent and I know a lot more about this than you do." Teens who hear such comments learn to keep their thoughts to themselves.

11. *Multiple messages are okay.* We can tell our kids why we think it is important to delay sexual relations until they are adults or married while also making sure they have accurate information about safe sex, birth control, HIV/AIDS, and other STDs.

12. *Share your values.* We need to teach our kids that healthy, satisfying relationships include respect and responsibility. We need to teach our sons and daughters that while the changes in their brains increase their interest in sex, we don't want them to rush into sexual behavior. If they work on developing communication and relationship skills, they will be better prepared for the adventure that love brings and the joys that healthy relationships bring.

Recently, I ran into Mark. He was decades older, as was I, and I'm not even sure how I recognized my former student. We chatted a bit, catching up on each other's lives. He had become a doctor and had his own practice. As we were about to go our separate ways, I told him he looked like he'd come a long way indeed from those days when he'd moped in my office and wouldn't tell me what was really wrong.

"Must have been Stephanie's influence," I said. "You know? You never did bring her to my office like you said you would. Did you two stay together for long?"

Mark smiled. "No, we broke up a couple of months after I last saw you. It was pretty hard. But since I had already had you along for the ride on my first emotional roller coaster, I was too embarrassed to come to you for help again."

"You should have. I wouldn't have given you a hard time."

"Yeah, I know that now, but at the time . . . The funny thing is, though, in retrospect, I'm glad I went through all of it, even if I was alone at the end. After I got over Stephanie, I realized I had had a girlfriend. I turned a real corner then. I was more willing to take chances to get what I wanted, and I became a lot happier. That first love gave me a big push."

Mark's story, like others, shows how we begin to understand the power of love for our teens.

Sexual Identity

Deciding how to guide teens is especially important as they begin to explore issues of sexual identity. One of the important tasks of adolescence is what the developmental psychologist Erik Erikson calls "identity formation." Teens try on different roles at different times to see what fits and what feels comfortable. They're trying to figure out "What role makes me feel the most relaxed or at home?" Is it leader, rebel, intellectual, geek, athlete, party animal, or one of hundreds of others?

One day I overheard one of my ninth-grade students regaling his peers with a tale about how he had been drinking over the weekend in the local park with a group of older students when a police car pulled into the parking lot. He went on to recount in great detail how they had fled and eluded capture by outsmarting and outrunning the police. The other students were mesmerized with his adventure. As I learned later, the entire episode was fabricated in order to impress his peers. This boy was trying on the role of party animal with his new classmates to see how it fit. Fortunately for him it wasn't comfortable. He gradually developed another role, as leader. He was student council president as a senior, graduated with honors from college and law school, and today is a well-regarded patent attorney. The reasons that some roles feel more comfortable than others include temperament, upbringing, social expectations, peer approval, and, of course, brain wiring.

Since adolescence is a time of sexual awakening, questions about sexual identity take center stage in the adolescent mind as well. For most adolescents these questions involve figuring out how to relate to the opposite sex. But sexual-identity questions don't just concern how to relate to others sexually; they focus on whom to relate to. Everyone has a sexual orientation. The majority of girls are sexually attracted to boys and vice versa. But some adolescents find that their feelings of sexual attraction run toward members of their own sex or toward both boys and girls. Still others feel that their gender identity doesn't fit neatly into the binary categories of boy and girl. Because of cultural issues these realizations can be very scary and painful for adolescents.

Homosexuality, bisexuality, and transgender issues are emotionally and politically charged topics. Some people have a deep-seated, even violent prejudice against gay, lesbian, bisexual, and transgendered people. Even in today's changing social climate many adolescents grow up hearing jokes, derogatory comments, or hate-filled speech about homosexuality. So the adolescent who discovers that he or she is attracted to someone of the same gender can be terrified. It can be difficult for an adolescent to deal with his or her sexual orientation at the very time of life when it is so important to fit in and be accepted. The emotional and psychological torture that many gay and lesbian adolescents experience can be overwhelming. Studies suggest that one third of all teens who commit suicide are gay or lesbian. For them death can seem preferable to the pain of accepting a sexual identity that some of their friends or family or culture find perverted, sinful, or shameful.

Brain science can help adolescents and parents sort through the confusion around sexual orientation, help eliminate any shame, and confront discrimination. Same-sex orientation is not new. Anthropologists have shown that homosexuality has been part of human cultures throughout recorded history. In fact, same-sex attraction is not even unique to humans. Scientists have observed same-sex attraction in as many as sixty different animal species. Sexual orientation, heterosexual or homosexual, has its origins in the brain, and is very complex. Twin studies and other genetic research point in the direction of a genetic component to sexual orientation. Most geneticists now think that a combination of genes triggers different concentrations of sex hormones in the brain during a series of critical periods when the brain is being wired. Some have identified critical periods during pregnancy, while others think the critical periods occur during the first years of life. Both groups may be correct, because sexual orientation is the product of an unfolding series of three or four brain events.

A combination of the genetic, hormonal, and brain anatomy discoveries together lead most scientists to conclude that sexual orientation is rooted in the brain: it is not a matter of choice or the result of sexual abuse or parent-child interactions early in life. None of the major scientific societies, including the American Medical Association, the American Psychiatric Association, the American Psychological Association, and the American Academy of Pediatrics, considers same-sex attraction a disorder. Like heterosexual youth, gay, lesbian, and bisexual young people discover how their brain is wired for sexual attraction as they mature. They are not recruited, seduced, or taught to be homosexual.

So how can adults help and guide adolescents as they sort out their feelings of sexual attraction? First and foremost, parents and teachers should sort out their own attitudes toward gays, lesbians, and bisexuals. Adolescents will find it very intimidating to bring up questions or concerns if they aren't sure where their parents stand. It will be even more difficult if they have heard negative comments about gays and lesbians at home. Second, it is important to let adolescents know that it is common to have questions about their sexual orientation. It is also common for adolescents to have feelings of attraction toward members of their own sex, which older generations called schoolgirl crushes. Wonders and worries are normal and may continue into young adulthood. Most importantly, let adolescents know that they are accepted, loved, and cherished for who they are, no matter what the outcome of their sexual or gender identity search is.

At seventeen, Linda was worried that she was a lesbian. She only felt romantic attraction and sexual desire for girls, something she had noticed for several years but worked hard to ignore. Very popular with boys and girls, she was a leader in her class. She had an active social life with many friends, staying busy enough to reserve thoughts about sex and her attraction to girls for late at night when she was alone with her thoughts and feelings. She frequently cried herself to sleep with the secret she could not bear to share with anyone, not even her best friends.

Toward the end of her junior year in high school, Linda realized that she was falling in love with Karen. She thought about Karen all the time and felt her heart skip a beat whenever Karen so much as looked in her direction. It was very exciting and very frightening. Eventually she decided to go see her parish priest. She knew him from the church youth group, and all the kids said that he was very easy to talk to. She thought maybe he could help her sort things out. It took her three tries before she summoned up the courage to show up to an appointment with him. When they finally met, Linda was extremely nervous and jumped from topic to topic before the priest finally interrupted her.

"Linda, you look scared to death. What's the matter?"

She panicked. She wanted to bolt for the door, but the expression on his face somehow encouraged her to take a chance. Within seconds she was in tears, pouring out her story and her fears. After a minute she stopped to gauge his reaction. She expected him to look away, to yell at her, to tell her that she was a sinner, to do anything but what came next. He calmly looked at her, smiled, and said, "You know, Linda, you're a wonderful young woman. You will sort this out in time, and no matter what the outcome, God loves you." When Linda recounted this story to me years later, she said she didn't know how long she had cried when she heard those words.

After a month of weekly meetings with the priest, he persuaded her that it was time to talk with her parents. "You need to let them in on what you are going through." She reluctantly agreed and several days later asked her parents if she could talk with them after dinner. The three of them sat down in the living room. Linda couldn't even breathe she was so scared. She started to sob uncontrollably. Her mother hugged her and kept asking, "Linda, what is it?"

Linda finally blurted out, "I'm a lesbian."

The look on her parents' faces immediately told Linda that she had made a big mistake. They both looked stricken. The questions and comments tumbled out. "What do you mean? You can't be. How do you know? You're just confused. Oh, my God, no!"

The hours-long conversation did nothing to improve the situation. Linda's parents refused to even consider that she might indeed be lesbian. They told her that they would find a counselor and she should not talk about this with anyone else.

Linda recounted this story to me when she was twenty-one, four years after the night she came out to her parents. I asked her how her relationship with her parents was now.

"You know, they haven't really changed that much. They refuse to talk about it and completely ignore any references I make to the women I'm dating. They made me see a counselor that first year until I refused to keep going. The arguments have stopped, so that's good. But both my father and mother still pray that I'll wake up 'straightened out.'"

"So how do you feel?" I asked.

"About what? About being lesbian? About them?"

"All of it, I guess."

"I'm comfortable being a lesbian. My brother, sister, and friends have been fabulous. I'm happy with my life except for my parents. I feel so distant from them that I can hardly believe it. We used to be really close before I came out. I'm still really sad that they won't accept me."

As I listened to Linda's story I felt sad for her parents, who were robbing themselves of the joys of a relationship with an adult daughter who clearly wanted to be close to them but who was forced to keep part of her life separate from them to avoid the conflict that she knew it would cause. Linda had sorted out her sexual orientation and sexual identity during adolescence and blossomed into a mature, loving adult. But her parents had built up barriers that prevented them from sharing in her life.

Science will continue to shed light on the complexity of human sexuality. For some parents, this provides much-needed under-standing. For others, it doesn't matter. The most important question for all is not whether our children are gay, lesbian, bisexual, or straight but rather whether they will live out their sexual identity in an honest, respectful, and loving way. They all need parents and adults who will help them do that. Whether our children are girls, boys, gay, straight, or something else, they need our support.

DO

- ✓ Emphasize the importance of respect and honesty in all relationships.
- ✓ Have regular conversations with your sons and daughters about sex and sexuality.
- ✓ Communicate about the values you consider important in romantic relationships.
- ✓ Provide your teen with accurate information about birth control.
- ✓ Make sure your teens have accurate, complete information about sexually transmitted diseases.
- ✓ Get to know your adolescent's friends, especially when there is a romantic interest.
- ✓ Listen, listen, listen.

DON'T

- ✗ Don't get angry and use put-downs about a boyfriend or girlfriend you have concerns about.
- ✗ Don't ridicule or make fun of crushes or romantic attachments.
- ✗ Don't assume that your son or daughter won't engage in sexual behavior.
- ✗ Don't keep quiet and let TV and movies become the only teachers your kids have about sex and sexuality.
- ✗ Don't use disparaging remarks about gays, lesbians, or transgender people.

What do I want to continue?

_____

_____

_____

What do I want to change?

_____

_____

_____

NINE

Monkey Wrenches in the Brain: Alcohol, Tobacco, and Other Drugs

I met hundreds of adolescents in the early '90s during my tenure as the executive director of the largest (and one of the best) chemical dependency treatment programs for adolescents in the country. Our program at Fairview University Medical Center in Minneapolis took the best of the adult recovery centers and tailored it to the unique problems of young addicts.

One of the patients, Lisa, seemed to have everything going for her. She was seventeen, smart, popular, pretty, but she was an alcoholic. Sad to say, Lisa's story—par for the course at Fairview—is widespread among teenagers today. In a recent study, 24 percent of high school seniors qualified as heavy drinkers. Even more alarming, many of these underage drinkers did not perceive their binge-drinking habits as unsafe. Unlike Lisa, many kids who get in over their heads with alcohol and drugs don't get the help they need. As alarming as her story may be, Lisa is one of the lucky ones.

When I met Lisa, she was a senior at an exclusive private high school in the Twin Cities. Her father was a prominent physician and her mother, an active volunteer at the school Lisa and her sisters attended. Lisa told me she had her first "real drink" when she was twelve and spending the night with a group of classmates at her friend Kathryn's house. Kathryn's parents had gone out for the evening "to give the girls some privacy." Before leaving they told the girls the ground rules for their home. They also said they would be back by eleven o'clock. Within fifteen minutes of their departure Kathryn was opening a bottle of wine. She had taken it out of one of the boxes that her father had recently purchased at a big wine sale. "They bought cases of the stuff. They'll never miss it," she assured her wary friends. Kathryn's parents didn't miss it. They never knew. And so Lisa found something she liked a lot. Drinking on the sly was a bit of naughty mischief that made her feel grown up. The adrenaline rush of the forbidden adventure and the good feeling she got from the wine made for a great combination. Best of all, getting away with it was so easy.

For the next five years Lisa's drinking continued—and increased. By the time she was fifteen, the weekend parties she attended routinely involved alcohol, pot, and occasionally some other drugs. Lisa tried everything that came her way, but her favorite was alcohol. She prided herself on the fact that she could hold her liquor as well as the guys. Sometimes she'd get into contests with the boys to see who could drink whom "under the table." Before long, on nearly every Saturday morning she felt sick and had only a foggy memory of what had happened the night before.

In addition to her drinking, Lisa made a habit of other risky activities including unprotected oral sex. Like the alcohol use, her sexual activity became more and more frequent. Her boyfriend, Toby, talked her into sexual intercourse while she was drunk shortly before her sixteenth birthday. After crossing that bridge she often combined drinking with sex with Toby. Eventually, having sex while drunk was something she did with other boys, too.

After more than four years of alcohol use, Lisa's relationship with her parents began to deteriorate. The heated fights about curfews, declining grades, and blowing off chores escalated. If Lisa's parents suspected alcohol abuse, they never said anything about it to her, until the night came when Lisa's problem with alcohol was impossible to ignore. Luckily, her parents were home when the call came from the hospital emergency room. Lisa's friends had taken her to the ER after she passed out from heavy drinking. When her friends realized they couldn't wake her up, they hauled her unconscious body into a car and rushed her to the hospital. She was admitted with alcohol poisoning. Neither Lisa nor her friends could remember exactly how much she had to drink that night, but the doctor said it had to be a lot to get her blood alcohol level up to .40, five times the legal limit for intoxication in most states. When she did regain consciousness and was lucid enough to understand what he was saying, the ER doctor told Lisa how much danger she had been in. To put it simply, she was lucky to be alive.

Lisa's parents were shocked but relieved that she had escaped her brush with death. Lisa promised them that she had learned her lesson. She also told them this had been her first experience with drinking and she would never do it again. Three months later the police caught Lisa and a group of her friends with an open liquor bottle in their car. Released without charges, she once again escaped relatively unscathed. And once again she promised her parents that she would steer clear of alcohol and any situations where it was present.

Early in Lisa's senior year, the assistant principal of her high school called her parents in for a conference. Lisa had been caught drinking on school grounds. The principal told Lisa's parents that teachers were hearing rumors that Lisa was drinking every day. He also told them that Lisa was suspended from school. He would not allow her to return until she had a complete chemical-dependency evaluation.

Lisa was referred to Fairview. The first several sessions of the evaluation didn't get very far. Lisa racked up hours of denial, inconsistent stories, and pleas to get off her back, directed at her parents as well as the staff. But when Lisa walked into her last session with the evaluation team, she saw one of her best friends sitting in the room. The girl had tears streaming down her face. Lisa, taken aback by the presence of her friend, almost didn't notice that sitting beside her were her parents and two sisters.

"What are you all doing here?" Lisa demanded.

"Lisa, I'm sorry. But I've agreed to tell your parents and the counselors everything," her friend said in a shaky voice.

"Why don't you mind your own business?" Lisa said.

"Because I'm afraid you're going to end up pregnant, hurt, or dead!"

During the next hour the real story of Lisa's drinking finally started to come out.

The staff at Fairview Health Services comprises doctors, nurses, and counselors who try to repair the damage done by the ravages of alcoholism and other drug addictions. By the time young people get into treatment, they've usually left a long trail of damage—their family relationships, schoolwork, legal status, and health are parts of one big mess. The big hope, on the part of both the program staff and the parents, is that they have intervened early enough to prevent the damage from being permanent. In my experience, there is nearly always hope that recovery can repair the damage done to relationships and can get school performance back on track. When it comes to their brains, however, adolescents aren't always so lucky. Recent research suggests that drugs and alcohol can cause permanent damage to the adolescent brain.

The Parent Survival Kit: Alcohol, Tobacco, and Drugs

No family is immune to the dangers of alcohol, tobacco, and other drugs. Use the statements in this kit to determine how much you are doing to minimize the risk associated with the teen use of these substances.

PARENT SURVIVAL KIT

Alcohol, Tobacco, and Drugs

Yes No

☐ ☐ 1. Adults in our home model responsible use of alcohol.

☐ ☐ 2. Adults in our home do not use illicit drugs.

☐ ☐ 3. I have frequent discussions with my teenager about the dangers of tobacco, alcohol, and drugs.

☐ ☐ 4. I am clear with my adolescent about my expectations for substance abuse.

☐ ☐ 5. There are consequences in our family if a teen uses alcohol or drugs.

☐ ☐   6. I know the signs of teen alcohol and drug abuse.

☐ ☐   7. I have curfews that I enforce with my teenager.

☐ ☐   8. Adults in our home are careful about keeping
         prescription medicines safe.

If you can't agree with every statement, there is increased risk for problems with alcohol, tobacco, or drugs. This is an important area of parenting teens because the stakes can be so high.

The Vulnerable Teen Brain

For years one argument against doing alcohol or drugs was based on a belief that everyone has a finite number of brain cells. No new brain cells would ever grow, no matter what. For the rest of your life, you could only maintain the number you had or lose them. Once they were gone, you weren't getting them back. Therefore, scientists recommended that any activity that caused brain cell loss should be avoided. Drinking and doing drugs, which kill large numbers of brain cells, are dangerous partly because, it was thought, they quickly deplete our finite supply. Doctors and counselors would typically say, "You shouldn't get drunk: It's just like hitting your head against the wall. You're killing parts of your brain that you'll never get back. Basically, you're just giving yourself brain damage."

From research conducted by a team of neuroscientists in Sweden and the United States, it turns out that our brains can regenerate cells throughout the course of our lives. And as we've seen in the previous chapters, the number of brain cells you have isn't as important as how you fire and wire the ones you have. Even so, alcohol and drugs are probably even worse than we thought. Drugs and alcohol do more in the brain than simply kill brain cells.

By now practically everyone knows that a pregnant woman should not drink, smoke, or take any drugs not prescribed by her doctor. These prohibitions are not for the sake of the expectant mother; they're for the fetus inside her, which is particularly vulnerable to any foreign chemicals floating among the cells as they divide, multiply, and form organs and tissues. Alcohol and drugs can have a dramatically negative effect on fetal development. Fetal alcohol syndrome and "crack babies" provide tragic evidence that the brain and central nervous system are among the most vulnerable parts of the growing organism. There is no greater period of sensitivity than when the brain is growing during gestation. Foreign chemicals that work their way into the environment in which the brain is growing act like poison.

Prenatal and childhood development aren't the only important periods of blossoming and pruning of neurons and their structures in the brain. The adolescent brain also has one of those intense developmental periods and is also very sensitive to foreign substances. In the following pages we shall see how recent research confirms that ingesting powerful chemicals such as alcohol, tobacco, and other drugs during the "window of sensitivity" in adolescence has very harmful effects.

Alcohol and the Adolescent Brain

Alcohol is the drug that is most likely to hurt an adolescent you know. Talk of cocaine, heroin, methamphetamine, and ecstasy strikes fear into the hearts of most parents, but the facts are clear that alcohol has been, and continues to be, the substance that does the most damage to the most kids.

When I was a high school basketball coach, I had to suspend one of my star players, Kyle. Even though his absence on the court was going to hurt our chances for victory, I knew he needed consequences. He had been caught drinking beer at a party after I had laid down very specific rules at the beginning of the season: "If you want to play, don't drink. If you get caught drinking, you will not play."

When I called Kyle's parents in for a meeting to discuss both the penalty and my concerns for their son, I wasn't encouraged by their reaction. After I told them the whole story, Kyle's father said, "Thank God it's only beer. I was afraid it was going to be drugs." I didn't know then what I do now about the detrimental effects of alcohol on an adolescent brain, but I did know drinking could lead to serious problems. The conference with Kyle's parents lasted longer than I'd planned, but by the end I knew they at least understood that I thought Kyle's drinking should be taken seriously.

Adolescent drinking should be taken seriously because it is so prevalent. The "heavy drinkers" I mentioned at the beginning of this chapter were no slouches with the bottle. The study in question defined heavy drinking as five or more drinks in a row within the past two weeks. With this sort of habit and culture, when kids get to college, no wonder so many of them have problems with alcohol. Recent studies show that half of U.S. college students binge drink, with almost 20 percent meeting the criteria for abuse. Tragically, alcohol-related causes claim the lives of 1,825 college students every year. If alcohol were the relatively harmless substance so many people assume it to be, it wouldn't have such a potentially tremendous negative impact on the adolescent brain. Chronic use is particularly dangerous.

Most of the damage done by alcohol, tobacco, and other drugs during adolescence is due to their interference with neurotransmitters, the chemicals that transmit important messages across the synapses from neuron to neuron. Alcohol, nicotine, and other drugs inject chemicals into the brain, and these chemicals mix with the brain's chemical neurotransmitters, wreaking havoc on some important developmental processes.

For example, alcohol stimulates the release of dopamine, the feel-good neurotransmitter. That good feeling Lisa got when she drank was caused by alcohol-fueled surges of dopamine. Whenever you constantly use a foreign substance like alcohol to trigger dopamine surges, the body stops producing the levels of dopamine that it normally needs. As a result, you will feel worse and worse when you don't have alcohol in your system. Just at the time when your brain is trying to figure out how much of each chemical is needed— a crucial task of adolescence—alcohol gums up the works. Chronic drinkers like Lisa may feel great when they drink, but when they are sober and there's no alcohol-triggered dopamine, they feel awful.

Heavy alcohol use also interferes with the encoding of new memories. That's why it's hard to remember what happened after a night of heavy drinking. Alcohol's effect on short-term memory comes from its interference with a neurotransmitter called glutamate, which aids the neurons in storing new memories and in learning. When neurons fire together, glutamate helps them wire together, and thus makes them more likely to fire together in the future. Without glutamate the neurons that fire together would not wire together. Alcohol makes it harder to learn and store new memories for anyone with a brain, young or old, but its effect on glutamate is *most* pronounced in the adolescent brain. Because adolescent brains are furiously blossoming, pruning, firing, and wiring, glutamate is even more crucial to adolescents than it is to people in other age groups. If glutamate effectiveness drops even a little bit, it can have a very negative effect on the sensitive adolescent brain. This teenage susceptibility to the negative effects of alcohol on glutamate functioning, and therefore on learning and memory, persists into the early twenties.

The results of alcohol use begin to add up. Research shows that heavy alcohol use can impair adolescent memory function by as much as 10 percent. Additional evidence shows that adolescents who are heavy drinkers have a smaller hippocampus, the brain structure key to the process of recording new memories, than nondrinkers. Thus, *adolescents who drink a lot of alcohol end up having more memory and learning impairment than adults who drink the same amount,* because their brains are more susceptible to damage.

Alcohol's negative effect on learning and memory is bad news, but that's not the only problem. Adolescents are *over*sensitive to damage and *under*sensitive to the warning signs. For reasons that we do not yet understand, the sedation effects of alcohol are not as pronounced in the adolescent brain. The impairment of motor coordination is also delayed. That means that adolescents don't experience the two major warning signals that go off in the adult brain—sedation, or tiredness, and motor problems, like slurring words or stumbling—which indicate "I've had enough." It takes an adolescent drinker a lot more alcohol before sedation and motor coordination problems take effect. By then, they can be dangerously drunk. In the absence of warning signals that tell them to stop, adolescent drinkers tend to drink more and do more damage to themselves. Adolescents like

Lisa brag that they can "hold their liquor," but the fact that they're not showing outward signs of alcohol impairment doesn't mean they're *not* doing themselves serious damage. By the time the warning signals telling them to slow down show up, the physical harm of impaired reactions and memory damage has already occurred.

There's one more piece of bad news for adolescent drinkers. The earlier a youngster starts to drink, the higher the probability that he or she will have alcohol problems or alcoholism as an adult. This correlation probably occurs because drinking while the brain is developing encourages the brain to decide, through the firing and wiring process, that it needs alcohol. Adults would have to drink more heavily to be as likely to wire a tendency for alcohol use into their mature brains.

Teenage Driving and Alcohol: A Fatal Combination

Late one night Stanley and his wife, Colleen, got the type of call that all parents dread. "This is Sergeant Chalmers," the voice at the other end of the phone began. "I hate to bring you this news but your son Tyrone has been involved in a serious auto accident. He's been taken to Ramsey Hospital."

"How seriously is he hurt?" Stan practically yelled into the phone.

"He was alive and able to talk when the ambulance pulled away," the officer responded. "His injuries, however, looked pretty serious."

By the time Stan and Colleen arrived at the hospital their son was already in surgery. It was more than three agonizing hours later before the surgeon emerged to meet with them. "Your son is very fortunate given the extent of his injuries," he began. "He will survive and I think he will eventually, over time, make a full recovery." He went on to explain Tyrone's injuries to two frightened but relieved parents.

"How did this happen?" Stan eventually asked.

"The police can give you a lot more information than I can, but from what I've been told it was a single-car accident. He lost control as he came around a bend on County Road 19." He hesitated before adding, "Your son had been drinking."

In the days following Tyrone's near-death accident the details began to emerge. Tyrone had just dropped off the last of his friends and was heading home in the family car when he went off the road into a stand of trees. He admitted to his parents that he had had "a couple of beers" at the party. The blood alcohol level, as measured by the hospital lab, was .07, below the legal limit.

Tyrone's story is similar to that of many teenage drivers who end up seriously or fatally injured in traffic accidents. In 2010 22 percent of teen drivers in fatal crashes had alcohol in their systems, the highest of any age group. Even though Tyrone was not legally drunk, the "couple of beers" impaired his concentration and reaction time. In addition, like other teens he was most likely less sensitive to the brain's warning signs. Research shows that teenage drivers are at much greater risk for accidents at lower levels of alcohol than older drivers. Their passengers are also at more risk because adolescents are much more likely to get into a car with an impaired driver. In a 2011 study 24 percent of teenagers reported that they had ridden with a driver who had been drinking within the previous hour. The vulnerability of young drivers and their passengers is the reason that the National Transportation Safety Board is urging all states to lower the legal limit from .08 to .05, the limit in most other industrialized nations.

Tobacco

Tobacco contains chemicals that damage the adolescent brain. During the tobacco lawsuits in the mid-1990s tobacco companies were forced to turn over internal documents that revealed that they had deliberately targeted children and adolescents in their marketing and promotion efforts. They targeted the young because, although they may not have known brain science, they did know statistics. Research showed that if a young person got to the age of eighteen without lighting up, the odds were five to one that he or she would never use tobacco. Most habitual smokers began to use tobacco when they were adolescents. Big Tobacco targeted kids because they had to get them hooked by the time they graduated from high school or risk losing a lifelong customer.

A recent spate of adolescent tobacco use studies has shown that nicotine, like alcohol, affects the adolescent brain differently than it affects an adult's. Adolescents are much more likely than adults to get addicted to nicotine, the most prominent and powerful chemical in tobacco, and they get addicted much more quickly.

Nicotine's potent effect on the brain is due to its effect on almost two dozen neurotransmitters. Nicotine quickly increases the number of receptors (docking stations) for itself in some key brain areas so that the brain quickly adapts to the presence of nicotine and reacts negatively when it is absent. Each time a person smokes, in other words, his brain will extend its desire for more nicotine. And when he is not smoking, he will crave the drug and have physical symptoms of withdrawal that make quitting cold turkey so difficult.

At the same time that nicotine makes a home for itself in the brain, it also behaves like alcohol and increases the production of dopamine. Smokers really do feel good when they have a cigarette because their dopamine levels rise. And because their bodies depend on nicotine for that dopamine surge, they begin to feel lousy if they go a long time without a cigarette.

Nicotine has a triple whammy effect on adolescents, making it extremely addictive: it increases dopamine; it increases the number of nicotine receptors in the neurons; and it affects the mix of neurotransmitters. This triumvirate of trouble makes it especially hard for adolescents to quit.

Making matters worse, adolescents are more likely than adults to use tobacco as a springboard to using other, more powerful drugs. Tobacco is truly a gateway drug: smoking makes it easier for adolescents to try other drugs. Research shows that kids who smoke are at higher risk for using alcohol and other drugs.

Of course, there are many health reasons to be concerned about tobacco, too. The link between nicotine and a host of diseases, including some types of cancer, heart disease, lung disease, and overall susceptibility to disease, is undeniable. More than 400,000 people die of tobacco-related illnesses every year in the United States. It's a shame, then, that 4,000 kids start on this deadly addiction every day.

Yet there is some good news about adolescents and cigarettes.

Tobacco is the only drug for which usage by adolescents actually decreased dramatically. The percentage of high school students who smoke dropped from 27.9 percent in 2000 to 15.8 percent in 2011 before plateauing in 2012. That's an amazing and inspiring initial improvement. Reasons for the drop include the advertising campaigns against smoking, many of which are funded by the tobacco lawsuit settlements. It is discouraging, however, that many state legislatures cut these programs in order to solve their budget problems. In doing so, they—and the citizens who elected them—are dismantling one of the most successful public health initiatives of the past twenty years.

Unfortunately a threat to this downward trend in smoking is seen in the increasing popularity and sales of electronic cigarettes. E-cigarettes are battery-operated, barrel-shaped devices that contain a nicotine-filled cartridge along with other chemicals and flavors that are turned into vapors and inhaled by the user. Unless regulated by the Federal Drug Administration, e-cigarettes will continue to be marketed in the media and online and readily available to children and teens. There is a legitimate fear that e-cigarette use will lead to more teenagers getting hooked on nicotine. In 2012, 1.8 million middle and high school students said that they had tried e-cigarettes.

Drugs

Alcohol and nicotine are two big, real problems for teens, but most parents are more concerned about their kids getting into other, "harder" drugs. Even though we shouldn't forget how serious alcohol and nicotine are, we have reason to be concerned about other drugs as well. The common thread among all these drugs is their effect on neurotransmitters, especially increasing the levels of dopamine. Each drug has its own unique chemical interaction, but dopamine figures into every picture.

Kids get very mixed messages about marijuana. Many parents have used marijuana themselves when they were younger. It didn't seem to hurt them much, if at all, at the time they used it, and adults who used the drug back then, for the most part, do not notice any lingering effects. But what adults and parents need to remember is that marijuana today has 500 percent more THC, the active ingredient in marijuana, than the pot they smoked in decades past.

The liberalization of marijuana laws and the increase in medical marijuana have also convinced many teenagers that there is no risk in smoking pot. As one teenager told me recently, "If doctors recommend it, it's got to be safe." So after years of decline, the rates of teens smoking marijuana have increased dramatically. In 2012, 28 percent of tenth-graders and 36 percent of high school seniors reported using marijuana.

The problem is that as THC increases levels of dopamine, it can adversely affect how the brain makes its own dopamine. This means that today's teens who smoke pot are more likely to become addicted to it. In addition, the evidence is growing that marijuana use impairs working memory, which is where we hold and process information for understanding and learning. In other words, working memory is the brain's "think pad." This explains why pot smokers often come across as spacey. Problems with concentration and coordination have long been associated with marijuana, and neuroscientists have discovered why. The brain networks affected by marijuana bear a resemblance to those associated with schizophrenia.

One of the biggest worries about marijuana use is its effect on motivation. That was certainly the case with Rashon, a high school student I counseled some years ago. His parents couldn't figure out why their son gradually lost interest in his schoolwork, sports, scouts, and other activities he had previously enjoyed. Rashon slouched in his chair staring at the carpet during our first session as his father complained about his son's lack of motivation. "He doesn't seem to care about anything anymore, Dr. Walsh. His grades are slipping, he's dropped out of soccer, and he just seems so lethargic."

"Is your dad exaggerating, Rashon," I asked, "or is he painting a pretty accurate picture?" Rashon's response to my question was to shrug his shoulders. I asked his parents to give us some time alone, but my attempts to find out what was going on with Rashon went nowhere. "My parents just need to get off my back" was about all I got.

The next day I touched base with a couple of Rashon's teachers to see if they could provide any insight. His math teacher seemed as bewildered as his parents. "He's going to fail this term because he's stopped turning in assignments. I've talked with him, but nothing's changed. He doesn't seem to care."

What his chemistry teacher told me, however, turned out later to hit the nail on the head. "He's a stoner," Mr. Conroy said bluntly.

"What do you mean?" I asked. "How do you know that?"

"Dave," he began, "do you know whom Rashon has started hanging out with?" Mr. Conroy then ticked off the names of a half dozen other students. "They're all into pot. I saw the whole group heading for the woods the other day as soon as classes got out. You and I both know what they were doing there." I did indeed have a good idea since neighbors had recently complained to the principal about students smoking pot in the small strip of woods separating the campus from their homes. When I confronted Rashon with this circumstantial evidence, he completely denied using marijuana. Two weeks later, however, the police rounded up Rashon and his friends as they were lighting up in the woods once again.

Fortunately this story has a happy ending. Rashon eventually admitted to me and his parents that, despite his earlier denials, he was smoking pot regularly. Although he insisted he could stop on his own, his parents followed my recommendation for treatment. He successfully completed an outpatient program and got things back on track. Although I've since lost track of him, I remember how proud his parents were when he graduated with honors and won a scholarship to the University of Minnesota.

New research explains why regular marijuana users like Rashon are prone to "amotivational syndrome," as it is sometimes called. Neuroscientists have discovered that dopamine levels are lower in younger marijuana users, especially in a part of the brain called the ventral striatum. The circuits there are directly involved with enjoyment and motivation, explaining why teens like Rashon lose interest in activities that they used to find pleasurable.

Cocaine is physically and psychologically dangerous because it affects three neurotransmitters. It interferes with the reabsorption of dopamine, causing the levels of the neurotransmitter to keep increasing, which leads to a state of euphoria. Cocaine also increases serotonin, which can lead to an inflated sense of confidence and to higher levels of another neurotransmitter, norepinephrine, resulting in greater energy. Together, these three neurotransmitters contribute to the infamous cocaine high.

Ecstasy, often referred to as Molly, is especially dangerous because brain studies have shown that it interferes with the normal transport of serotonin, an effect that can permanently damage learning and memory. There has been mention in the popular press that ecstasy causes "holes in the brain." While not true in a literal sense, this metaphor refers to evidence of long-term damage to the cells that release serotonin. In addition, reports have shown that some people who use ecstasy heavily as adolescents go on to have chronic, severe problems with depression in their adult lives.

Prescription and Over-the-Counter Drugs

A recent trend in drug abuse among adolescents is the use of prescription and nonprescription medications. Between 2008 and 2013 there was a 33 percent increase in prescription drug abuse. At the top of the list is the growing popularity of ADD and ADHD medications like Ritalin and Adderall. One out of eight adolescents has admitted to misusing them. Young people who have legitimate prescriptions either give or sell them to classmates and friends. Sadly, many of these teens are abetted by their parents, a third of whom believe that the ADD and ADHD stimulants will enhance their sons' or daughters' academic performance by improving their concentration and focus. These and other medicines can only be legitimately obtained by prescription for good reasons since scientists have a growing concern about the long-term effects. In addition, there are worrisome side effects, including appetite and growth suppression as well as sleep disturbances. Even cases of psychosis have been traced back to overuse of ADD and ADHD stimulants.

Cough and cold medicines easily available in supermarkets and drugstores everywhere pose a threat as well. Most of these remedies contain dextromethorphan, or DXM, a cough suppressant that can produce hallucinations in high doses. Web sites tell kids how much medicine they need to get high depending on their weight. "Robo-tripping," or "dexing," requires less than a bottle and costs only a few dollars. Overdosing is on the rise, with some emergency rooms reporting as many as four cases a week among adolescents as young as twelve. Symptoms of abuse include sweating, fever, dry skin, blurred vision, hallucinations, nausea, irregular heartbeat, and loss of consciousness.

The Partnership at Drugfree.org has launched the Medicine Abuse Project and offers parents three suggestions. First, monitor the supply of all the family's prescription drugs. Second, put medicines that could be misused in a secure location. Third, safely dispose of all expired or unused medications.

Because of the adolescent brain's sensitivity while important neural circuits are being formed, the negative effects of alcohol, nicotine, and other drugs—legal or not—on the adolescent's brain are faster and more severe than on the adult brain, and they occur with less warning. The negative effects of these chemicals aren't just temporarily altered states of mind or behavior problems; they can damage a developing brain permanently. Drugs and alcohol can be a serious problem for anyone, but for adolescents, they can become a serious problem forever.

Parents, the Antidrug

How is it that parents don't read the behavior signs that their kids are drinking or using drugs? Why did Lisa's parents not catch on sooner?

During Lisa's outpatient treatment for alcoholism, her father, Mark, came to see me. Racked with guilt, he told me that on some level he had known all along that Lisa was probably in trouble with alcohol or drugs, he didn't know which.

"As the missed curfews and arguments got worse I began to worry more and more about Lisa," he said. "When she was out with her friends on weekends I was so worried that I couldn't fall sleep until she got home. I would lie awake, blinking at the ceiling, waiting for her to get home. Sometimes I'd go downstairs and sit in the dark looking out the front window. Then, when Lisa got home, I would quick run up to my bedroom. I'd get into bed, so she wouldn't know I'd been waiting up for her, and I'd just lie there.

"I was too worried to sleep, but too afraid to confront her. I didn't want to know if she was drunk or high because then I would have had to do something about it. I was so scared of the conflict, it was easier for me not to know."

Many parents can fall into this paralyzed trap of willful denial. It's very difficult and painful to confront adolescents on these tough issues, so many parents find it easier to stay in the dark. Like Mark, parents in willful denial usually suspect or even know that their kids are up to something dangerous, but they're scared of conflict or just unwilling to admit that their children can have a serious problem and so they act as if nothing is wrong. Denial is just about the worst reaction a parent can have to a kid who is mixed up in drugs or alcohol.

The research is very clear about what parents should do to protect kids from the dangers that chemicals pose. We *have* to stay connected to our kids. Whether or not they ever get involved with alcohol or drugs, adolescents need to know that their parents know about and care about what goes on in their lives.

This advice is confirmed by the results of a study from the National Center of Addiction and Substance Abuse at Columbia University. The study found that a teenager with "hands-on" parents is four times less likely to become involved in smoking, drinking, and drug use than kids who don't have hands-on parents. The scary part is that only 27 percent of American adolescents described their parents as "hands-on."

What does being "hands-on" really mean? For starters, it means knowing where your kids are. In addition to carrying their own cell phone, if they have one, have them leave a phone number of where they will be. Before giving permission for them to attend a party or an overnight, call the parents and ask if the parents will be there and what the house rules are on drinking and drug use.

Being connected means asking your kids about their day, knowing who your kids' friends are. What do they like to do? Where do they like to go together? Why are they friends? These are the kinds of questions to which you should know the answers. When your kids' friends come to your home, try to engage them in conversation. You don't need to grill them to get a good sense of what makes them tick. If your teenager doesn't bring friends by the house, find out why and try to make it clear that you want to know who his or her friends are. Make sure your home is a friendly place for your kids' friends. Stock up some extra snacks so they will be comfortable coming around. Our kids' friends nearly ate us out of house and home, but we got to know them all. And in luring them to our house with food, we were glad to know they were in a safe place instead of out on the street somewhere.

Having curfews and enforcing them sometimes feels like it puts barriers between you and your teenager, but curfews are very important. Teens with curfews have a greater sense of accountability. They know that parents who wait up will be much more likely to figure out what condition they are in when they come home. In addition, if an adolescent knows that curfews are serious business, he will be more likely to tell you where he is going if he is lobbying for an extension. Most important, he won't be out doing who knows what all night. Kids without curfews are less accountable and less connected to their parents.

Parents often ask me about setting curfews. There are no hard-and-fast rules, but here are some suggestions: Find out what other parents are doing with curfews and decide if you think their approach is reasonable. Don't base your decision on what your teen says "all the other kids are doing." Get some feedback from teachers. Once you decide on a curfew time, make it clear to your son or daughter. A phone call thirty minutes before curfew asking for a sleepover can be a signal that something else is going on. Let them know in advance what the consequences will be if the curfew is broken. Be willing to negotiate only around special events or circumstances. One suggestion is to multiply the amount of time they are late by four and subtract that from their curfew for the next night. The loss of privileges, such as use of the car or permission to attend an upcoming event, is another remedy for repeated violations.

Having a network of other adults who are connected to your kids is important, too. Ask teachers and administrators about the school's policies on supervision at school dances and other functions. Join the school's parent organization. Get to know the parents of your kids' friends. Find out what kind of rules they have. That makes conversations about drinking and supervision much easier to have.

Talk to your kids about smoking, drinking, and drugs and make sure your kids are clear about rules and consequences. This doesn't mean that you just bring up the subject once. It means maintaining an open dialogue. If you see an article on drugs or alcohol, encourage your adolescent to read it, and then talk with him or her about it. Ask questions about the school and what goes on there and what goes on when kids from other schools get together. Some schools are notorious for their drug scene.

In a large national survey of kids who had successfully steered clear of trouble, the teens were asked what was the most important thing in keeping them on the straight and narrow. The most important protective factor that emerged was connected parents with clear rules and guidelines. The kids usually put it more like this: "No, if I ever got caught drinking or smoking dope, my parents would kill me." That's kid talk for connected parents with clear rules and consequences.

If you follow this advice, you'll go a long way to staying aware and avoiding slipping into willful denial. But you have to stay actively on the watch for what is really going on in an adolescent's life. There's a middle ground between being too nosy and intentionally turning off the lights to stay in the dark. Knowing where your kids are, who they are with, and what they are doing is key. You do need to respect an adolescent's privacy—because establishing independence is one of the key psychological processes of adolescence—but that doesn't mean you can allow him to get away with drinking and doing drugs.

Will your kids experiment with smoking, drinking, and other drugs? Kids have been doing it for generations, and they will continue for generations to come. But there is a big difference between knowing they will probably experiment at some point and sanctioning it through willful denial or a wink. Kids need clear messages. Allowing some substance use or looking the other way mixes up

your messages and messes up your kid. Give your teen clear boundaries. If you don't, then they will push out further and further on
their own until they do real damage to their brains.

For some, like Lisa, experimentation can lead to problem drinking or using drugs. A savvy parent should know some of the signs
that indicate a problem. These include drops in grades and school
performance, unusual secretiveness, a habit of borrowing money or
being broke in spite of having a reasonable allowance or income
from a part-time job, changes in friends, a loss of interest in previously enjoyed activities, resistance to any conversation about alcohol or drugs, mysterious phone calls, and some telltale physical
signs. Tobacco carries an unmistakable odor, as does most, but not
all, alcohol. Drug use often causes the pupils of the eye to become
small and unresponsive to changes in light. Parents should make it
a point to talk to adolescents when they get home at night, even if
they have to get out of bed to do so. Besides being a chance to talk
about the evening, this will give parents a chance to check for
bloodshot eyes, slurred speech, or odd behavior.

What do you do if you suspect a problem? Later in the session
when Mark told me about his willful denial I suggested that we do
a role-play to learn what he could have done when he first suspected
Lisa had a drinking problem. "I'll play you, Mark. And you take the
role of Lisa." Mark agreed, so I started. "Lisa, I'm very concerned
because when you came home after your curfew last night, your
eyes were bloodshot and your breath smelled of alcohol."

Mark knew exactly how Lisa would respond. "What are you
talking about? I was a little late, but I wasn't drinking. You were
imagining things if you thought I had bloodshot eyes and alcohol on
my breath."

"Lisa, we both know that you drank last night. I am not going
to debate that. Our discussion has to focus on what we do now."

"Dad, you're wrong. I wasn't drinking. You can call my friends
and ask them. Here, I'll give you their phone numbers."

"No, Lisa. I'm not calling anyone. I know you were drinking.
Period."

"Okay, so I had one drink. That's all I had. I just did it to stop
the other kids from pressuring me."

"I don't care what the reason was. You made a commitment not to drink and you broke it. I've already told you before that I will not accept or discuss excuses. I want to know if you are willing to make a promise to me that you will not drink again. Yes or no?"

"I promise. No more drinking."

"I'm really glad to hear that. So here is what's going to happen. You're grounded for the next week because you drank last night. In addition you cannot use the car for two weeks. If you drink again, you and I will immediately make an appointment with a counselor for an evaluation. Is that clear?"

"Dad, why are you being so unreasonable?"

"Lisa, do you understand what will happen if you drink again?"

"Yes, I understand. But you haven't told me why you are being so unreasonable?"

"Lisa, I love you too much to let you hurt yourself with booze. I don't expect you to agree with me. I just want you to know that I love you and that I will follow through on exactly what we are agreeing to."

That was the end of the role-playing. I asked Mark if he thought I was being unreasonable. "No, I just wish I had done that with Lisa two years ago."

It's never too late to get serious about drugs and alcohol with your kids. Even if damage is done, it's possible to recover. Mark had made a big mistake in looking the other way, but now he is both equipped and motivated to help Lisa lead a healthy life. Lisa will be an alcoholic for the rest of her life, and she has to be on the watch for addictive tendencies until the day she dies. However, thanks to a good treatment program and a father who finally saw the light, she had the resources and support to get better. She is now a healthy adult who leads a happier life.

DO

✓ Model responsible use, the most important thing for a parent to do. Our actions related to alcohol, tobacco, or any drugs speak much louder than our words.

✓ Set clear expectations with your sons and daughters about drinking, smoking, and using other drugs. Describe the damage that chemical use does to their developing brains and explain that because of the potential harm, you do not want them to drink until they are adults and that you hope that they never smoke or use drugs.

✓ Since the adolescent brain is more susceptible to impairment caused by alcohol, even at low levels, be crystal clear about the rule to "never drink and drive."

✓ Set and enforce curfews.

✓ Get to know your adolescent's friends.

✓ Get to know your adolescent's friends' parents.

✓ Have regular conversations about alcohol, tobacco, and drugs. Take advantage of opportunities that arise from news reports or media portrayals to talk about alcohol and drug effects. Ask your kids what they know and think. Listen to their answers carefully so you understand their attitudes and the peer pressure they might be under. Make sure you let them know that you welcome their questions or concerns.

✓ Monitor, secure, and dispose of prescription and over-the-counter medicines.

✓ Seek professional guidance if you are worried about your teen's chemical use.

DON'T

✗ Don't send mixed messages about adolescent drinking, smoking, or drug use. Tolerating some use, making jokes, or bragging about your own use confuses kids and erodes your credibility.

✗ Don't ignore signs that your son or daughter is drinking, smoking, or using drugs.

✗ Don't accept excuses for repeated drinking, smoking, or drug use.

✗ Don't leave psychoactive, expired, and unused medicines where they could tempt experimenting teens.

What do I want to continue?

_____

_____

_____

What do I want to change?

_____

_____

_____

iTeens: Media and Technology

Roger laughed as he described a scene with his two teenage kids. "I thought my daughter, Emma, was doing homework. When I knocked on her door she gave a cheery 'Come on in,' so I entered. I have to admit I was surprised by what I saw. Emma held her phone in one hand, was tapping out a response to a friend online with the other, while watching a music video. The only thing in the room resembling homework was an open math book on the table next to the keyboard."

"'I thought you were doing homework,' I said. She gave me a puzzled look and responded, 'I am.'

"I left the room shaking my head. My son, Henry, was supposed to be doing his homework, too, and I wondered if his version was any more believable. I found him in the family room with legs crossed, a notebook in his lap, a pencil in his mouth, and his eyes locked on the TV. When I reminded him he was supposed to be doing homework I got the same response: 'I am.'

"Before we all headed out the door the next morning, I asked the kids if they'd had a chance to finish their homework.

"'Of course, Dad,' said Emma. 'Yeah, that's all I did last night.' 'You saw me,' said Henry."

"Do you think they really did do their homework?" I asked.

"Yes," said Roger. "They did. They both get good grades, so I've got nothing to complain about. The thing is it seems like every time they do their homework, they're plugged into five different digital tools at once. I don't think I could pay attention to music, TV, laptop, and text messages all at the same time. The idea that they can manage all that and do math problems simultaneously baffles me. Can they really do it?"

We are hurtling through the Information Age, the Age of the Internet, or the Digital Revolution at lightning speed. By any name, it has changed the way we live and communicate, and as its dazzling array of digital tools gets seamlessly integrated into our kids' daily lives they can't imagine life without them. Adolescents today spend more time with these media than they do engaging in any other activity in their waking hours, including school.

Because this incredible revolution surrounds us, we do not always appreciate just how life-changing it is. You don't have to look far for evidence, though. Just three decades ago the only people who knew what the Internet was were the scientists and academics who had been using it to communicate with one another for years. Now the Internet is accessible to all of us through devices small enough to fit in our pockets. Stories break on Twitter before the traditional news organizations can get the word out. Books are considered boring if they don't contain hyperlinks. Babies eagerly swipe their fingers at screens squealing at the results while teens make up and break up via text.

Youth take to digital media like fish to water. Indeed, it's hard to imagine some of them surviving without their digital lifelines to family, friends, and cultural heroes. Because today's teens grew up in a connected world, they are very comfortable with it; it's part of every facet of their lives. And as a result, they use it—more than anyone else on the planet.

Media in Teens' Lives

Teens in this country have more than a full-time job consuming technology. Young people ages eight to eighteen spend an average of fifty-three hours a week with entertainment media. Teens have also gone mobile. Seventy-eight percent of twelve- to seventeen-year-olds now own their own cell phone and exchange an average of 167 texts per day. Ninety-five percent of teens are online and three out of four access the Web using cell phones, tablets, and other mobile devices. Far from being passive consumers, almost a third of young people record and upload video to the Internet and 40 percent use video chat to connect with their friends. No matter which way you slice the data it is clear: young people spend an extraordinary amount of time with technology, transforming the way they learn, share, connect, and grow.

Good? Bad? That's Not the Point

Parents today are inundated with conflicting messages about the impact of technology on young people's health and development. On one hand, we are promised that access to these tools will solve the achievement gap and fuel our children's economic competitiveness in a future economy. On the other hand, we are told that technologies are catalyzing a generational "dumbing down" and that other nations are jumping ahead while our kids waste away on the couch.

In between these sensational headlines is authentic ambivalence about the role of media and digital technologies in our family lives. We reap the benefits of connectivity. Our teens text when they arrive at their destination and chat online with their grandparents. We marvel at the academic gains born from digital learning. Our kids access remote libraries with a click of a button and interview national experts for their science class podcasts. We enjoy our kids in new ways as we watch their expertly produced videos and marvel at their online competence.

We also worry. We worry about our kids losing the social-emotional skills that come with working things out face-to-face. We worry about the seemingly addictive lure of technology and lament the constant power struggles that come with trying to pry the cell phones and video game controllers out of their hands. We worry about cyberbullying, violent video games, privacy, and the toll of multitasking. We worry about our own unsettling attachment to technology and its cost to family time.

This ambivalence makes a lot of sense. If you synthesize the mountain of research on technology's impact on teens, it boils down to this: there is a lot of incredible opportunity and a lot of stuff we could all do without. In other words, media and technology aren't inherently good or bad; they are powerful. The good or bad depends on how we use them.

The "Lockdown" vs. "Hands-Off" Approach

With this ambivalence, it's tempting to adopt one of equally polarized parenting strategies that can be described as "lockdown" or "hands-off." Neither is ideal for helping teens develop healthy technology habits.

Parents who fear technology and its impact on their kids are tempted to adopt a lockdown approach. They tend to assume that all online and media-related activities are a waste of time and enforce strict rules on all technology use. On the other hand, those who adopt the hands-off approach assume parents don't have much control or influence over their children's digital lives (good or bad) and do very little to try to influence their kids' online behavior and media habits.

The good news is you don't have to choose between being a digital downer or a tech champion. Neither the lockdown nor the hands-off approach strikes the balance needed to help kids reap the benefits of the incredible power of technology. Young people rely on parents to both nurture their digital skills and set boundaries for appropriate behavior. A balanced approach where parents encourage digital skill building, take interest in their teens' digital lives, and set firm limits and consequences around both time and content sets teens up for success.

The Parent Survival Kit: Media and Technology Use

Because our kids are always two steps ahead of us, digitally speaking, it is easy to be caught off guard by technology's influence or to throw up our hands in overwhelmed defeat. It is important for parents to pay attention to the role of media in their kids' lives. Use this kit to make sure you are doing everything you can to raise a responsible, caring, and competent young person in the digital age.

Media and Technology Use

Yes No

☐ ☐ 1. I understand that media is a big part of our teens' lives and ask them questions about where they go, who they hang out with, and what they are interested in online.

☐ ☐ 2. I encourage digital literacy by guiding our kids toward appropriate digital resources and talking about the Internet as a tool for learning, creativity, and participation.

☐ ☐ 3. We enjoy media together as a family.

☐ ☐ 4. I set expectations and consequences before I introduce new technologies into our family life.

☐ ☐ 5. I understand and pay attention to media ratings.

☐ ☐ 6. I set a digital curfew at night.

☐ ☐ 7. We unplug during meals in order to connect with each other.

☐ ☐ 8. My kids understand the importance of Internet safety and know not to give out personal information online.

☐ ☐ 9. I talk to our teens about expectations for online behavior including cyberbullying, sexting, and online cruelty.

☐ ☐ 10. I limit multitasking when deep focus is required.

☐ ☐ 11. I support our children's school cell phone policy.

Answering yes to everything in this kit means that you've successfully avoided the lockdown and the hands-off camps. Instead, you understand that digital technologies are a powerful force that can bring great benefits or harm and that it's up to us to decide what the effect will be. If you find yourself saying no to many of the items on the checklist, you're probably underestimating how powerful the impact of media can be.

Digital Possibilities

Clicking through online news headlines last week, I noticed a feature story about a student from my kids' high school alma mater. The headline read "15-Year-Old Astronaut Abby Fuels Her Outreach Mission with Social Media." My interest piqued, I read on. It turns out Abby has been an avid space fan since she was six years old. It's her mission to go to the planet Mars someday and she is leveraging virtual tools to get involved now. Using a personal Web site, online fundraising platforms, and social media, Abby not only connected with a real astronaut mentor but also generated the funds to travel to Russia for his launch to the International Space Station. Now acting as this astronaut's official "Earth Liaison," Abby will pass along messages from space via e-mail, blogs, Facebook updates, tweets, and the occasional Google Hangout. This is in addition to her ongoing posts on her Web site, where she shares information and links about everything from the Russian language to technology to reminders about space-related Web chats.

This is truly a young woman on a twenty-first-century mission. There is no doubt that digital technologies offer young people like Abby incredible ways to explore their interests, engage in self-directed and collaborative learning, and expand professional and personal opportunities for themselves both on- and offline. Here are just some of the benefits of growing up digital.

Connection

Adolescents have always looked for places to hang out. Just as they have done in parks and malls generations before, teens gather in online spaces to try on new identities, share ideas and opinions, flirt, joke, gossip, and support one another. Social media sites amplify the social dynamics of teen life, even in positive ways. While many parents worry that teens spend their time online with total strangers, the research doesn't bear this out. The vast majority of young people today are simply extending relationships from the "real" world into online social networks. In other words, teens seamlessly transition conversation threads from soccer practice to social media sites and back again.

Further, unknown online friends or communities are not necessarily dangerous for young people. For some teens who feel isolated or marginalized, the Internet provides a way to find important supportive connections. This is especially true for LGBT teens and other youth in nondominant groups.

Whether known or unknown, teens report other good news about their online relationships. Sixty-nine percent say that their peers are "mostly kind" to one another online, and more teens report positive personal outcomes than negative ones from interactions on social network sites. This isn't to say that we don't want to take the risks of cyberbullying and disconnection seriously, but we also need to give many of our kids credit when they do use social media in ways that strengthen their relationships.

Learning

Youth can access virtual libraries with the tap of a finger and instantly access news from around the world. They watch how-to videos on YouTube and dig into interest topics without prompting from teachers. Researchers with the University of California's Digital Youth Project coined the term "geeking out" for such self-directed learning. As teens dive deep into topics that interest them online they can gain significant expertise, form relationships with mentors, and find information that exceeds what is available to them at school or in the community. The folks at UC Berkeley argue that parents play an important role in encouraging these "interest-driven practices" by helping set learning goals and modeling ways to use the Internet not only as a portal to entertainment but also to real learning. Researchers with the Connected Learning Research Network are convinced that with support, young people can link this kind of self-directed learning to academic achievement, career success, and civic engagement. More study is needed, but you can't help but be excited about the possibilities. My guess is that a young person is going to show us the way.

Creativity and Identity

Adolescence is not only a time for neural blossoming and pruning; it is also a time to ask important questions like "Who am I?" and "Who do I want to be?" Self-expression and identity development are part of the important work of growing up. Teens may experiment with clothing, dying their hair, music, and new activities or hobbies. Young people often use online spaces to reflect and test out these new aspects of their offline selves, turning to music, video, images, writing, and animation as new tools of expression. While some of the downsides of this kind of public display are evident, many young people flourish with new avenues for creative expression.

When I first met Sandra she was slightly withdrawn and timid in her responses to my questions. Her parents informed me that she was having a hard time making friends in the transition to high school, didn't communicate with them much anymore, and her grades weren't as strong as they had been in middle school except for her freshman literature class. We worked to connect Sandra to a writing group at the school based on her interests and my knowledge that the teacher did a beautiful job noticing and encouraging students' strengths. A few months later, one of Sandra's moms came into my office with exciting news. "A poem Sandra wrote was just published on a Web site for teen writers. I didn't even know she wrote poetry, much less submitted writing for publication. It's beautiful!"

Indeed it was. Sandra's feature on the site was a multimedia exploration of her transition to high school, complete with painted illustrations, beautiful prose, and loads of comments in the thread below about how inspiring her work was to others. What an incredible space for Sandra to explore her emerging voice.

Participation

Even given the importance of social media in political campaigns and movements, researchers are hesitant to cast judgment on whether or not digital technologies are changing the quantity or quality of civic engagement for most young people. However, nearly all agree that new media are at least creating new *possibilities* for youth voices and participation in public decision making. There is emerging data to back up these hopes. Researchers with the MacArthur Research Network on Youth and Participatory Politics found that 41 percent of young people ages fifteen to twenty-five have engaged in at least one act of participatory politics in the past year including starting a political group online, circulating a blog about a political issue, or forwarding political videos to friends. Young people are also finding creative ways to harness the power of new media to spur change in their communities outside the realm of conventional politics. One of the most powerful Internet safety videos I have ever seen was filmed and produced by a group of teenagers in Ontario who organized a successful digital citizenship campaign in their community. A group of high school students in Tulsa, Oklahoma, created a campaign called "Project Unmask" to raise awareness of media's impact on teenage self-perception. Using short films, online PSAs, infographics, and live presentations these teens changed the conversation about media in their community and beyond. Examples like these abound. Getting involved in these types of projects not only gives youth a voice in issues they care about but helps them develop twenty-first-century skills including problem solving, strategizing, critical thinking, and planning.

The New Digital Divide

Unfortunately, the benefits of growing up digital are unevenly distributed among young people today. When the first edition of this book came out, there was still a lot of buzz about a digital divide based on access. Some kids were wired while too many others lacked a connection. While there is still work to be done, this gap has closed dramatically in the last decade. For the most part teens in the United States have access to high-speed Internet and computers. However, a new digital divide is replacing the old one. The University of California's Mimi Ito describes the new digital divide as an opportunity gap. Some young people have the extra support, guidance, and

resources to use technology in healthy ways that advance their academic and personal goals. Others are just hanging out online, wast-
ing time. Senior researcher at Microsoft Dana Boyd reminds us,
"Access is not a panacea. Not only does it not solve problems, it mir-
rors and magnifies existing problems we've been ignoring." In other
words, getting digital tools in our teens' hands is just the beginning
of the journey. Now our teens need support and guidance to learn
how to use them. There is no time to waste. The stakes of unsup-
ported and unmonitored access are clearer every day.

Multitasking

The scene I described at the beginning of this chapter is likely familiar to parents everywhere. Like Emma and Henry, young people
today are habitual multitaskers. Nearly a third of the time adolescents use media they are using two or more forms simultaneously.
This isn't just a trend among our kids. It's not unusual for some
adults to check their e-mail thirty to forty times an hour during the
workday! For the multitasking generation, if you have only three
balls in the air, you feel like you're slacking off.

Our kids are quick to tell us that they are excellent multitaskers.
Some go further and say they *need* to multitask. But are they really
good at it? The research so far points to an emphatic *no*. To be fair,
heavy Internet users are certainly more adept at sifting through
massive amounts of information very quickly. Young Internet users
appear to be more efficient at processing the daily bombardment of
media messages, images, and bits of information. For example, a
researcher in the United Kingdom found that frequent Web surfers
took only two seconds on any given Web site before deciding to
move on to another. Remarkably, she found the sites where surfers
stopped and focused were ones most relevant to the search terms. In
other words, our brains get better and better at synthesizing and
evaluating information at lightning speeds.

However, this speed-of-light processing has a significant cost.
When kids multitask, their brains spend so much energy making
quick decisions and responding to stimuli that they have fewer
mental resources for comprehension and retention. A couple of

researchers at Cornell proved this. They divided a class of students into two groups. One group was allowed to be online during a lecture and the other group was not. It turns out that the online group did seek out some information related to the lecture content, but they also checked e-mail, checked in on social media, and watched videos. The second group had to listen to the lecture unplugged. The unplugged students performed significantly better on measures of memory and comprehension following the lecture. Similar studies have produced the same results. Frequent interruptions scatter kids' thoughts and erode their memories.

Our brains were built for one thing at a time. It's not that we can't do some tasks simultaneously. We can all eat food while walking, and most of us can drive a car and carry on a conversation. But if we hit construction and exit in an unfamiliar neighborhood, the radio goes off and the talking stops. If two tasks are performed at once, one of the tasks has to be familiar. We perform a familiar task on "automatic pilot" while really paying attention to the other one. If they both require concentration, we're in trouble. That's why you can always tell immediately when someone is reading their e-mail while you are talking to them on the phone. They sound distracted because they are.

Many teens protest that their brains must be different from the dinosaur brains of their elders. They've told me, "You may not be able to multitask, Dr. Dave, because you're an old guy. We can do it because we're young." Again, the research doesn't back up their claims. According to Clifford Nass, one of the leading researchers on the subject from Stanford University, heavy multitaskers are actually very bad at multitasking. In every lab task, including the ability to filter out unnecessary information, the ability to store and organize information, and even to switch quickly from one task to another, heavy multitaskers performed worse than low multitaskers. As Nass puts it, heavy media multitaskers are "suckers for irrelevancy." In addition to the toll on comprehension and memory, frequent multitasking appears to give teens a lot of practice in the art of distraction. We may be living in the Information Age but our brains have not been redesigned. When a task requires deep focus, our teens suffer a cognitive cost from juggling too much at the same time. So the next time your teen tells you she can do homework while watching music videos, just say, "Sorry. One thing at a time."

Self-Regulation and Technology

Tyrus's dad knew about the research on multitasking and talked to his fourteen-year-old son about not texting while doing homework or throughout the night. Unfortunately, the frequent talks didn't seem to be getting through.

"I looked at Tyrus's call/text history after he spent two hours in his room doing 'homework' and I can't imagine how he got anything done. The crazy thing is that he knows he will lose privileges but that doesn't seem to stop him."

On one hand it could be that Tyrus is simply openly defying the house rules. On the other hand, ignoring digital distractions can be a near-Herculean task for some teenagers. Teens have to rely on their still-maturing self-regulation skills to do things like ignore a text message, continue doing homework while friends are online gaming, or resist the "ping" of an incoming chat. As I've shared in earlier chapters, parents play a powerful role in helping teens *practice* the skills of self-regulation by setting clear expectations and following through with consequences. However, as Tyrus's consistent poor choices point out, practice doesn't always make perfect.

Why is resisting digital distractions so challenging? Researchers are hard at work trying to answer that question and they've given us a couple of leads. For starters, neuroscientist Jaak Panksepp at Washington State University explains that we have a built-in reward system that encourages us to be seekers. It makes sense that we are wired to be curious about what is around the next bend. Today, this means that we get a minishot of dopamine, the "happy" neurotransmitter, as we click on hyperlinks, answer a text, or Google something. The downside of course is that our seeking brains don't differentiate between information that is crucial to our central task and information that merely presents distraction.

University of Virginia's Daniel Willingham adds that his research shows why technology is especially alluring to teenagers. He suggests that texts, tweets, and other social bits of information are "highly perishable." Checking texts even two hours after an event may reduce the social value of the information, especially when everyone else is already in the know. For young people, "always on" feels like a social imperative. That's why Willingham advises us not to expect our teens to always be able to resist digital temptations. For example, Tyrus's dad might be inadvertently setting him up for failure with statements like "You can have your phone, but don't text while finishing your homework."

Not only does Tyrus's seeking and social brain trip him up, his self-regulation is also limited on any given day. Stress and high-demand environments diminish a teenager's reserve, and they need sleep, downtime, or exercise to recharge their supply. That's why people tend to eat junk food when surrounded by it or at the end of the day, when their willpower is worn down after hours of refusing sweets. When you find that your teen responded to a string of texts while writing a paper, she may be more mentally exhausted than outright defiant.

Even if your teenager doesn't answer an incoming text while doing homework, precious resources go into this act of resistance. A recent study found that drivers were more likely to engage in risky driving if their cell phone rang, *even* if they ignored the calls. These effects were most noticed in drivers who usually answered their cell phones. This tells us that trying to inhibit a habitual response may be a distraction in and of itself.

This doesn't mean that every time your teenager cracks open a textbook he needs to enter a digital desert. Some schools have chosen to deeply integrate technology into lessons so that, far from being a distraction, tech tools are central to learning. However, if social media or cell phones aren't part of the lesson, resisting the buzz of a text message during study time might be draining mental resources away from learning. In these cases, "off and away" gives our teens' brains the space they need to think.

Social-Emotional Development

Gwen was driving her teenage daughter and two friends to a soccer game and noticed that the car was unusually quiet. "I thought that they must have been thinking about the big game," she told me. "When I glanced in the rearview mirror, however, I was able to see what was really going on. The girls were furiously texting on their smartphones in the backseat. When I asked them whom they were texting they giggled and said 'each other.'"

The idea of texting someone two feet away might seem crazy to a lot of parents. Yet teens consistently report that they are more likely to text their friends than talk on the phone or face-to-face. Is there a cost to this booming virtual social life? Does it impact our kids' person-to-person skills? Emerging research shows it does and underlines the need to balance tech enthusiasm with encouraging our kids to use age-old practices like turning toward each other, face-to-face.

This makes a lot of sense from the perspective of brain science. Our kids are born into this world hardwired for social connection, but they need a lot of practice to fully develop the skills involved. Learning to read emotions and respond to them is challenging. It is no surprise that if youth don't practice interacting with others, they won't do it as well. There is the possibility, of course, that already socially nervous or very introverted kids tend to prefer screen-based communication and that already socially confident teens prefer face-to-face interactions. Even if this is the case, technology likely amplifies these already-existing tendencies. If teens can avoid difficult social interactions by sending a text message, they never get the practice they need to build social confidence and competence. Because they don't feel confident and competent, they avoid the next opportunity by sending another text, thus creating a vicious cycle. Remember, *Whatever the brain does a lot of is what the brain gets good at.* That's why research shows that preteen girls, who are heavy technology users, report fewer feelings of social competence.

The good news is that face-to-face communication and time spent in the offline world with friends and family pays off. So let's honor the ways that our teens are using social media to strengthen their relationships. Let's also give young people the critical experiences they need to take care of their own emotions and learn about the emotions of others, even when it is difficult. Let's encourage them to face each other and connect.

Online Cruelty and Cyberbullying

"I know firsthand how mean people can be online," eighteen-year-old Manny told me.

"What do you mean?" I asked.

"When I was in tenth grade two guys from my baseball team edited a picture of a giant hog with my face on it and sent it to the rest of the team online. Within a day half the school had seen it. I felt like everyone in the school was laughing at me. The worst part was that I thought these guys were my friends. I don't think they actually meant any harm by it. They just thought they were being funny. I'm sure none of them had any idea how devastating the whole thing was for me."

Sorting out identity, friendships, and relationships during adolescence has always been a roller coaster. The difference today is that the roller-coaster ride is on display for the entire world to see. Everything young people do online leaves a permanent footprint. Many have taken charge of their digital tracks using the online world as a creative canvas and a powerful tool for learning and advocacy. Unfortunately, other young people use these tools to tease, bully, or harass their peers.

While bullying and meanness has long been an unfortunate element of adolescence, the barriers today are lower than ever and the stakes are higher. With one post a student can spread a rumor about someone to the entire school. With another, a sexually suggestive photo can be in the hands of everyone on the hockey team. Not only can this have a devastating impact on the bully's target, but the bully's digital footprint is marred as well.

There are differences between face-to-face and online bullying. The social cues that govern our interactions diminish as we use more and more digital tools. Without seeing the pain that derogatory messages or images cause on the victim's face and absent the threat of adults' overhearing, kids may not hesitate when they text, post, upload, and blog mean things. Research at the University of California helps explain why people might act differently when sending an e-mail or a text message than they do in person. In face-to-face communication a part of our brain called the orbitofrontal cortex constantly reassesses emotional signs and social cues that help us interact appropriately. The brain's social censor, however, doesn't activate in online communication. That's why people, not just teenagers, might say something online that they would never say in person.

We aren't going to eliminate all cyberbullying or cybercruelty with a single solution. We can start by making sure that kids have clear expectations and consequences around responsible online behavior. Setting parental controls can also keep you cued in to your kids' online activities. This is just the beginning, though. We need to follow up with collective conversations among teachers, social workers, law enforcement, counselors, and parents about how to best support young people and teach conflict resolution and communication both online and offline. We need to support programs that guarantee that both bullies and the bullied get the help they need and strengthen social-emotional learning within schools. Let's also not forget to include young people in the conversation about what it means to be a good friend and a good digital citizen—the quality of their footprints and their relationships depend on them figuring it out.

Sexting

Stories of inappropriate and crude texting get major news headlines as both politicians and teens alike share images and texts on their phones that come back to haunt them later. Unfortunately, the word *sexting* is fast becoming a required part of the twenty-first-century parenting lexicon. Sexting is exactly what it sounds like, sending or posting sexually explicit messages or images. But like any hot issue making a big splash in the news, is sexting really all that common among teens? Depending upon the study, anywhere from 4 to 20 percent of teenagers have sent a sexually suggestive photo or video online. The reality is probably somewhere in between. Even though most teens are not sexting, it's a serious enough issue that parents ought to be paying attention.

Our response to teenage sexting should not be driven by fears of "teens gone wild," but grounded in our understanding of the teenage brain. Young people are growing up online and smart-phones are the epicenters of their social and emotional lives. Teenagers' brains are wired to be thinking about sex and sexuality yet few teens have good conversations with parents or other caring adults about sex, sexual decision making, and health. In the absence of these important resources, too many young people turn to the Internet, movies, or their peers for guidance on sex. In addition, as you know, the "brakes" in the teen brain are under construction. Once we connect all of these dots, sexting is not necessarily a surprising phenomenon. It is the twenty-first-century digital manifestation of impulsive adolescent sexual exploration.

Just because teenage sexting is understandable doesn't make it any less concerning. A high school freshman whose parents I spoke with last year sent a topless photo of herself to her boyfriend and within a month it had made its way onto the Web for the whole world to see. Before she knew it, an image of her body was the center of a high-profile police investigation on the possession and distribution of child pornography. In some states, sexting is considered a felony while in others it is a misdemeanor. In all states, sexting can have life-altering emotional consequences.

Just hearing the word *sexting* might make you want to throw your children's cell phones out the window and send them to their room. While tempting, this strategy isn't much help. Certainly monitoring your teen's cell phone use and setting clear limits and consequences about online behavior is an important step. But as parents we need to couple that with important conversations with our kids about sex, healthy relationships, consent, and peer pressure.

Whoever Tells the Stories Defines the Culture

Old mainstays like television, movies, and advertisements continue to have a huge impact on teenagers despite the growing popularity of new media. Believe it or not, young people still spend an average of thirty hours a week watching TV content. The debate for years has been whether or not media content influences the attitudes, values, or behavior of young people. Clearly, it does. Adolescents take cues from the media, with dramatic results. For example, a RAND

Corporation study shows that teens are twice as likely to have sex or engage in sexual acts if they watch media with similar sexual content. A study I helped conduct showed that television advertising helps determine the brand of beer that underage drinkers were most likely to drink. In that study we found that Budweiser, the beer with the largest advertising budget, was the overwhelming favorite among underage drinkers. The brand with the second biggest budget was the second favorite and so it went down the list. Similarly, a number of studies have shown that movie portrayals of tobacco use lead to higher smoking rates among teens.

Perhaps the most extensively researched impact of media involves media violence. Research on the connection with screen violence and youth aggression has been going on since the 1950s. Without reviewing the hundreds of studies on the topic I will just list the organizations that have gone on record stating that the scientific evidence clearly shows a cause-and-effect relationship between virtual violence and real-life aggression: the American Psychological Association; the National Institutes of Health; the Surgeon General's Office; the American Academy of Pediatrics; and the American Medical Association. Scientifically speaking, the notion that media violence is a risk factor for kids is an open-and-shut case.

The real impact of media violence is often more subtle than many suspect. The most important effect of a diet of violent entertainment, in my opinion, isn't actually violent behavior, but the resultant culture of disrespect it creates and nourishes. I believe that whoever tells the stories defines the culture. When the stories portray aggression and antagonism again and again, young people are more apt to see the world in those terms. The storytellers have redefined how we're supposed to treat one another. We've gone from "Have a nice day" to "Make my day." Too many of our kids have learned that uncivil lesson.

The debate over violent video games and other violent media will no doubt continue. I believe that the most sensible conclusion is video games and other media are powerful teachers. Pro-social video games encourage helpful behavior in our kids. Hyperviolent games tend to do the opposite. Media violence is a risk factor. A lonely, angry teenager without any connection to caring adults who spends hours playing first-person shooter video games is at greater risk for real-world violence. A teen with good connections with his parents and positive peer relations is less likely to be affected.

A couple of key phrases will help us make good decisions as parents. "Whoever tells the stories defines the culture" and "Whatever the brain does a lot of is what the brain gets good at." When it comes to media, we should pay close attention to the storytellers in our kids' lives and make sure our teens get more practice in respect, care, and empathy than disrespect and violence.

Health and Wellness

As we talk about how media can undermine what adolescents need to thrive, it helps to divide the issue into two categories: quantity and content. Quantity of media use means the amount of time a young person spends in front of an electronic screen, whether it's TV, video games, phones, computers, or tablets. The average young person will spend ten thousand hours playing video games by the age of twenty-one. We also need to consider the amount of time an adolescent *doesn't* do something else, because screen time keeps going up. I already mentioned that the average young person in this country spends fifty-three hours a week with entertainment media, more than doubling in the last two decades. This increase is having two serious effects. It's contributing to epidemics of obesity and diabetes, and it is stealing away time that adolescents could use to do other things. With the incredible hyperrealism of video games, kids can explore worlds undreamed of a decade ago. But all too often, the wide world in their own backyards goes unexplored. While onscreen characters with washboard abs do midair somersaults, the kids in control are only working their thumbs.

We know now that there is a direct connection between heavy screen time and youth obesity. As the average American kid's weekly media diet increases, his weekly amount of physical activity plummets. A recent North Carolina study demonstrated that less physical activity leads to more body fat. It's simple logic. In addition, heavy media users see a lot of junk food commercials and tend to eat fewer fruits and vegetables. Tragically, many of these overweight youth aren't just having trouble fitting into their old pants; they're developing serious medical conditions, most notably diabetes, which in the United States has skyrocketed in the past decade, with the greatest rates of increase among the young.

Video games and other media are so simple to use it's easy to spend hour after hour in front of the screen. The immediate pay-off of electronic media—the hyperreal spectacle and multisensory barrage of excitement—can be too seductive to turn down. It's not that kids don't like being outside anymore; they probably figure they'll get around to it. But once they start in on their video games, they're hooked, and before they know it, the sun has set and it's too late to go out.

Video Game and Internet Addiction

Another problem on the rise for adolescents is video game addiction. It may sound like the latest fad diagnosis, but it's a serious problem for the young people who struggle with it. I am not talking about teens who simply enjoy playing video games and spend time doing it. The majority of these teens can balance their gaming with other activities like school, friendships, and extracurriculars. For video game addicts, on the other hand, gaming takes over their lives. Video game addicts exhibit all the same tendencies that people who are addicted to drugs or gambling do. They lie about how much they play. They eschew social contact in favor of their games. They play compulsively. Some even engage in dishonest behavior to support the habit. Recent research indicates that the prevalence of pathological gaming in the U.S. is around 9 percent, not dissimilar to that in other countries.

"This game is ruining my life. My friends are all online. If I'm not playing, I'm thinking about playing." These are the words of a high school student addicted to the online computer game *World of Warcraft*. There are 9.6 million *World of Warcraft* players worldwide and on average they spend twenty-four and a half hours a week immersed online.

"His grades are down the tubes, he skips meals, and he hardly spends any time with his friends." These are the words of a parent who phoned me desperate for help. I asked her to estimate how many hours a week her son spent playing games. "Forty-three," she immediately replied. "I kept track last week."

How will you know if your son or daughter is headed for trouble? You should be concerned if your child repeatedly breaks family rules about when and how much game playing is allowed, withdraws from friends and activities to spend time playing, sneaks and lies about game playing, neglects schoolwork and other responsibilities, or throws temper tantrums when limits are imposed.

Some parent-child arguments about video and computer games are part of twenty-first-century America, so don't panic if you have your share of those. On the other hand, don't ignore signs of a real problem with compulsive playing. Here are some tips to make sure computer and video game playing remain a positive part of your children's lives.

- Set clear ground rules about when, where, how much, and what kind of game playing is allowed.
- Put limits on game-playing time.
- Require that homework and other chores be completed first.
- Keep video and computer game consoles out of kids' bedrooms.
- Consistently enforce the rules.
- If your child refuses to cooperate, restrict access for a period of time. If nothing else works, go cold turkey. Get rid of the games, at least for a time.

Your teen doesn't have to be a video game addict to need your help deciding how much media is too much. The same advice applies. Whether it's TV, movies, the Internet, or video games, it all boils down to limiting the amount and monitoring the content. Media and technology can be great but too much of a good thing can be bad, and as we all know, not all media content is a good thing. You, as an adult, have to think of yourself as a stand-in prefrontal cortex or reasoning center for your adolescent.

This is not always easy. Two parents approached me at the conclusion of a seminar I presented on adolescents and media. They were very concerned about their sixteen-year-old son, Carl. "He is an Internet addict," they began. "We bought him a laptop for his birthday six months ago because he really wanted one and we thought it was a good idea. From the very beginning he spent hours and hours on the computer. We thought it was a phase that he would get over once the novelty wore off. But it kept getting worse. He's up till all hours of the night, has stopped doing things with other kids, and his teachers told us he's missing assignments. We've talked with him and threatened him, but nothing has changed."

"Let me ask you a couple of questions," I said. "First of all, do you have any limits on when and where he can use the laptop?"

"Kind of, but it is so hard to enforce them because he always claims he needs his laptop for homework" was the reply.

"It is really hard, no doubt. Next question: Do you know what he is doing on the Internet?"

The two parents looked nervously at each other. The mother's eyes filled with tears as she said, "I don't know how this happened. We're Christians and Carl has been raised a Christian and . . ." At this point she stopped talking and began to sob quietly.

I had a good idea what the next answer was going to be. "Is he spending a lot of his time at sex and porn sites?"

"Yes," came the father's barely audible reply. After a few seconds he continued. "We found out about three months ago that he was into porn. We were shocked. He was embarrassed when we confronted him, and he said he would stop. When he didn't, we brought him to talk to our minister. That didn't help either. Now he doesn't even promise to stop. He just tells us to mind our own business. We saw the notice in the paper about your seminar, and we told him we wanted him to come with us tonight, but he refused to come. We decided to come without him to find out what we can do."

"Have you laid out any consequences for him if he doesn't comply with your rules? For example, have you told him that you will disconnect the Internet access until he agrees to follow your rules?"

"I told him that very thing three weeks ago," the father said. "He swore and screamed at us and told us that we'd be sorry if we tried anything like that."

It was becoming clear that they were not only dealing with an Internet problem, but with a seriously defiant teen. "If I'm hearing you correctly, Carl is openly defying you. Has he ever done that before?"

This time Carl's mother answered, "He has always had a bad temper and we've had trouble getting him to do things before. But nothing has ever been this bad."

"Has he ever openly defied you in the past?" I asked again.

"Yes, but it was never anything this serious."

"I know that you realize that this is serious," I began. "You have to deal with two problems simultaneously. One is his Internet pornography problem and the other is his defiance. Dealing with outright defiance in teenagers is tough. This is what I would advise you to do. First of all, the two of you need to agree on a plan so you are prepared when you talk with Carl. Tell him calmly, clearly, and firmly that if he doesn't immediately follow your rules on computer use, he will lose the privilege of having his own laptop. Ask him if he understands that it is his choice as to whether he keeps his computer."

"Suppose he refuses to listen or starts to swear and scream again?" the mother asked.

"Immediately end the conversation," I said. "Tell him that you will talk to him only when he is ready to do so without screaming or swearing. Let him know that in the meantime you will immediately install parental controls so that you can check in and make sure he is respecting the new rules. He has to understand that you are in charge and that he cannot get his way by screaming and swearing. The key is that you have to be willing to carry through. Can you do that?"

"I don't know," Carl's mother said. "He gets so mad that I get afraid."

I have had this conversation with many parents of teens over the years and I have learned there are two parental fears when adolescents are defiant. The first is that their son or daughter will just not comply. The second is more serious. Some worry that their teen will get out of control and do something drastic like run away, hurt himself, or hurt them. This is the advice I gave Carl's parents: "If you're worried that Carl will just ignore your rules, you have to reassert your authority in the family by calmly enforcing whatever consequence you have laid out. Stay calm but firm. Instead of stating it like a threat, remind him that it is his choice. He needs to know that the two of you are in charge. If, on the other hand, you are worried about his or your own welfare, then that is a sign to bring in the reinforcements."

"What do you mean?" the father asked.

"That means that the situation is serious enough to get professional help. Ask Carl's school counselor or social worker for advice and recommendations. Now, things very seldom get to the point where they spiral out of control quickly, but if that does happen, don't be afraid to call 911 and get police assistance."

"You don't think it will get to that point, do you, Dr. Walsh?" the mother asked.

"No, I don't. In my experience that kind of a drastic step is rarely necessary. I just want you to know that you always have options. It will not do you or Carl any good if you don't address his defiance because you are afraid."

Carl's case was extreme because his parents were dealing with defiance on top of the Internet problems. Most parents will have enough challenge to provide guidance and limits that will lead their teens to make healthy decisions for themselves someday.

Three Ingredients Teens Need to Thrive in the Digital Age

DIGITAL PARTICIPATION

Confiscating all your teen's electronic gear until she's twenty-five might keep her from uploading inappropriate pictures to the Internet but it isn't going to help her practice the skills she needs in order to navigate the complex challenges of living in a connected world. As you consider your twenty-first-century parenting strategies, don't forget to honor the strengths associated with the teen brain and help your child across the digital divide. Young people are creative, energetic, and capable of incredible integrity and courage. Harness their passion and energy and direct it toward positive risk taking, honest conversations, and action-oriented projects. These are promising alternatives to the lockdown approach. We don't want to be hands-off but we also want to give our kids space to shine and help define what it means to be a good digital citizen for themselves and their peers. It is incredible practice just when they need it most.

DO

- ✓ Enjoy media together. Ask your teen questions about what they are interested in and where they hang out online, and what they like about it.
- ✓ Talk with your teen about the images, messages, and stories they are hearing online and in the media. Encourage them to think critically about media's impact on their thoughts, purchases, and behavior.
- ✓ Help bridge the new digital divide. Encourage your teenager to use new media for learning, for job or volunteer networking, and for participation in issues they care about.
- ✓ Connect your teens with community media organizations. Many have youth projects and youth TV shows where young people can build both digital skills and leadership.
- ✓ Find out if your adolescent's school is working on any school climate initiatives and see if they want to get involved. Youth-led campaigns that incorporate new media are exciting and impressive.
- ✓ Does your teen have strong opinions about a local issue around Internet safety? Encourage them to write an op-ed or a letter to the editor.

DON'T

- ✗ Don't talk about technology as if it is only a mindless waste of time.
- ✗ Don't overlook your teen's digital interests, skills, and strengths.
- ✗ Don't ignore the efforts at your teen's school around digital literacy and skill building.

DIGITAL CITIZENSHIP

Digital citizenship is a new term with an evolving definition. Some use it expansively to include the themes of participation, safety, and privacy. I like to think of digital citizenship as the habit of mind that guides the way that we treat one another online. It is the set of social emotional skills that enable us to be good to one another, including being caring, empathetic, responsible, and courageous. It is the emotional and moral compass that leads our kids to talk to an adult if they see something online that makes them feel uncomfortable or to take a stand against cyberbullying. Becoming a good digital citizen doesn't happen overnight. It happens over time as our kids experience minifailures and mistakes, as they reflect on the impact of their actions on others, and as they practice kindness in both the virtual and real worlds.

DO

✓ Start with a conversation. Talk about what good digital citizenship looks like. Reinforce the message that online bullying, cruelty, and teasing is out of bounds.

✓ Make sure that your child understands your expectations for online behavior and online respect.

✓ Tell your child that you will be installing parental controls and you will periodically check in on them. This is not a method to spy on them or catch them slipping up but to ensure that they are earning their digital privileges by demonstrating responsible behavior.

✓ Expect mistakes. Make sure that Internet "incidents" are an opportunity to communicate and reflect, not a platform for endless lectures.

✓ Make sure your child knows what to do if they are bullied online—tell them not to respond or retaliate but to tell a trusted adult.

✓ Remind your child that their "digital footprint" is public. Remind them to never say anything online that they wouldn't say face-to-face (or in front of parents!).

✓ Learn about and use the rating systems for different types of media.

✓ Talk to your teen about the digital stories he or she is seeing in the media.

✓ Recognize when your child is being an upstanding digital citizen. Hold a mirror up to their caring and respectful behavior.

DON'T

✗ Don't ignore cyberbullying.

✗ Don't use "cyber incidents" as a platform for endless lectures.

✗ Don't assume that your teen would not bully or harass another child.

✗ Don't underestimate the influence of violent media and video games.

DIGITAL DISCIPLINE

In addition to knowing how to use digital technologies to benefit themselves and their communities, teenagers need practice knowing when to turn off their devices. There has been a dramatic increase in parental and teacher concern about technology "overuse." As we've covered in this chapter, worries about focus and attention, multitasking, decline of real-world social skills, and "cyber-addiction" are growing and warranted. To be fair, it isn't only our kids who are having a hard time unplugging. A friend of mine's three-year-old staged an intervention on him a couple of years ago. She put her chubby little fingers over the top of his smartphone during dinner and said, "Daddy, please put that away, I'm trying to talk to you!" My friend knew he had a problem when he snuck into the bathroom ten minutes later to check his e-mail.

Digital discipline is the set of skills, behaviors, and practices that enable us to power down and unplug when we need to. I believe that this skill set is going to be of growing importance going forward. Twenty-first-century communities, be they business, academic, or family, are not only going to need digital innovators and digital citizens; they are going to need people who know when to put away their digital devices in order to focus, recharge, and connect.

DO

✓ Cut down on the multitasking and reduce digital distractions.

✓ Carve out screen-free times to connect. Mealtimes and short car rides might be a good time for this.

✓ Set a digital curfew at night and stick with it.

✓ Encourage your kids to work out conflict face-to-face. Start with siblings! Help coach them on the words they might use.

✓ Model good communication and don't duck the hard conversations. Texting is a great way to stay connected, but if something is important, make sure you follow up face-to-face.

✓ Support your school's cell phone and technology policies.

✓ Listen to your teen when he or she wants to talk. Put away your smartphone, close your laptop, and connect.

✓ Have clear rules about when, where, and how much technology is used.

✓ Have clear consequences for noncompliance. For example, "We agreed that you would keep your cell phone charging in the living room at night. If you choose to keep it overnight, you will lose your cell phone privileges for two days."

✓ Consistency is critical. Your teen needs to experience the negative effects of a poor decision. If you waffle, she will not learn this important lesson.

DON'T

✗ Don't ignore signs that your teen's Internet and technology use is out of balance.

✗ Don't let your teen avoid face-to-face communication by using technology.

✗ Don't assume that your teenager can resist the allure of tech distractions during homework or at night.

✗ Don't let time with technology crowd out your teen's exercise and sleep.

It's Not About Technology, It's About Us and Our Kids

At the end of the day, we know that technology skills are going to be key to our kids' twenty-first-century success. We also know that age-old skills like deep focus, concentration, quiet reflection, and good communication are also essential. This means that kids need more than access to technology. They also need to learn the discipline, ethics, and problem solving that will enable them to use digital tools in ways that are useful and meaningful to them and to the world.

The thing is, teenagers aren't going to develop these skills in a digital desert or afloat in a digital ocean without a rudder. They are looking to us to get beyond both the lockdown and the hands-off approaches. They are looking to us to help them become caring, resilient, and responsible. Our schools, communities, and conference rooms need more of them!

What do I want to continue?

_____

_____

_____

What do I want to change?

_____

_____

_____

ELEVEN

Food, Exercise, and the Story Behind Tired Teens

The group of high school juniors and seniors filed into the classroom where I was waiting as a guest of the school social worker to share the latest research on the effects of alcohol and drugs on the teen brain. The meeting had been offered as an optional "brown bagger," so I was pleasantly surprised to see the room quickly filling up. As the students began unpacking their lunch bags I couldn't help but notice the two girls in the front row opening cans of Monster energy drink.

"Do you really drink that stuff?" I asked with a trying-to-be-friendly tone.

"Sure, lots of kids do," came the reply from a girl who later introduced herself as Josie.

"Do you know how much caffeine is in that can?" I asked.

"A lot, I hope," joked her friend Brianna. "We won't make it through your talk if there isn't."

We both laughed, but I did decide on the spot to include some information on nutrition's impact on the teen brain. Here are some of the things I told them:

While everyone knows that good food builds strong bodies, brain scientists are helping us understand how important good nutrition is for brain health. Although our brains account for only about 2 percent of our bodies' mass, they burn up more than 20 percent of its energy. That's why the fuel we provide is so important for brain functioning. The average teen diet, however, is full of sugary, fatty foods that are not brain friendly. Just as a car won't run if you put sugar in the tank, brains can't function well without the right fuel. Eating healthy "brain food" improves how adolescents feel, think, and learn.

The Parent Survival Kit: Brain Food

Food marketers promote a lot of unhealthy brain foods to teens. Use the items in this survival kit to assess your understanding of the importance of brain-building foods.

PARENT SURVIVAL KIT

Brain Food

Yes No

☐ ☐ 1. The brain needs certain nutrients to function well.

☐ ☐ 2. My teenager eats a healthy breakfast.

☐ ☐ 3. I know that highly sugared and caffeinated soft drinks send the brain on an energy roller coaster.

☐ ☐ 4. I understand how important fruits and vegetables are for a steady energy supply to the brain.

☐ ☐ 5. My teen gets enough protein from meat and plant sources.

☐ ☐ 6. I know that what my teen eats affects how he or she feels.

☐ ☐ 7. I do what I can to steer my adolescent away from a lot of junk food.

☐ ☐ 8. Eating meals together as a family is important.

☐ ☐ 9. I have healthy snacks around to satisfy my teenager's appetite.

☐ ☐ 10. As a family we talk about and model healthy foods and healthy brains.

The more yeses you have in your survival kit, the more likely it is that your teenager's diet is brain-healthy.

Glucose, the Energy Food

Glucose (sugar) is the main energy source for the brain, and simple and complex carbohydrates supply it. As the names imply, the simple versions—refined and simple sugars—are broken down quickly, sending a mother lode of glucose to the brain for a quick jolt of energy. Unfortunately the brain doesn't function well with a "jolt." After the spike in energy, there is an even quicker drop, causing emotional slumps, tiredness, and concentration problems. Many teenagers, like Josie and Brianna, get into the habit of seeking out more simple carbohydrates and caffeine for a renewed burst of energy.

On the other hand, complex carbohydrates—found in fruits, vegetables, and whole grains—are broken down slowly, thereby supplying the brain with a constant level of glucose. This avoids the brain fuel feast-and-famine pattern caused by simple carbs and enables the brain's owner to maintain energy, attention, and emotional stability.

Proteins, the Brain's Building Blocks

The brain needs proteins to grow new brain cell connections. During digestion the body breaks down proteins into brain building blocks called amino acids. The brain uses these amino acids to create new neural pathways and to manufacture the neurotransmitters that are used to carry messages from one brain cell to another.

The body can manufacture some amino acids, but there are nine that we must include in our diet. Complete protein-rich foods are eggs, meat, fish, and dairy products such as milk, cheese, and yogurt. (Quinoa is the only plant source that is a complete protein food.) These foods contain all the essential amino acids the brain needs. Other plant sources of protein (grain products, beans, legumes, soy, and other vegetables) are incomplete proteins, and care must be taken to eat a variety of plant protein sources so that the brain gets all the amino acids it needs. A healthy diet includes a variety of protein sources, whether your teenager is a carnivore or a vegetarian.

Fats, the Brain's Insulators

You might be surprised to learn that our brains are mostly made of fat—over 60 percent. As we saw in chapter 2, billions of brain cells do their jobs by "talking" to one another, sending electrical signals down a long cable, or axon, that make the jump to another cell's axon with the help of neurotransmitters. Myelin, around 70 percent fat and 30 percent protein, is a protective covering that coats the outside of these cables and allows neurotransmitters to form "docking" spaces at the end of each cable. Myelination of neurons is important because it keeps the electrical signal intact as it moves down the cable, enabling that signal to move at lightning speed. Without this fatty insulator, brain cells would not be able to effectively process, remember, or think about the millions of bits of information coming into the brain every day.

The problem is that not all fats perform these essential services well. There are good and bad fats. Good fats help create brain cell membranes and myelin insulation for the axons that are flexible. Bad fats, however, stiffen the membranes, hampering that cell's ability to do its job.

So which are the good fats and which are the bad? Neuroscientists have found that the brain functions best when it's given long-chain polyunsaturated fats, especially the now famous omega-3s. These types of fats are found in milk and other dairy products, fish and fish oils, eggs, avocados, seeds, and nuts. The bad fats are saturated, or trans fats, which are found in partially hydrogenated vegetable oils and shortening. Processed foods, snacks, and sweets are loaded with them.

Vitamins, Minerals, and Other Micronutrients—the Brain's Guards

Vitamins are those small nutrients found in food with a long list of alphabet soup names like vitamins A, B complex, C, D, E, and K. Minerals include things like iron, phosphorus, sodium, magnesium, manganese, and calcium. We're urged to take them every day for a healthy body, but what do they do for the brain? If the brain handed out Academy Awards, vitamins and minerals would get the Oscars for best supporting actors. They are needed for neurotransmitter production, memory formation, energy production, immune system maintenance, cell damage protection, oxygen transport, and myelin production, to name a few. The brain needs thirty-eight of the forty-five nutrients the body requires for health. Luckily for us as well as our teenagers, the vitamins, minerals, and other nutrients our children need are found in abundance in a healthy, well-balanced diet.

Antioxidants—the Brain's Protectors

Oxidation is the process by which the brain converts glucose into energy. A by-product of this natural process is the release of substances called free radicals. Unfortunately, they start chemical reactions, which damage brain cells. The reason we humans have survived for all these millennia is that antioxidants come to the rescue by neutralizing free radicals. Fruits (especially blueberries), green leafy vegetables, fish, nuts, and oils are vitamins C and E–rich foods and are loaded with antioxidants, even more reason to give them prominent roles in our diets.

There's a teenagers' garden in our neighborhood. Each summer more than a dozen teens gather with a couple of adults and plant a large vegetable garden together. They plan, prepare the soil, plant the seeds, water, weed, and harvest. Every Friday, once the produce starts coming in, they run their own mini farmer's market outside a local café. They market the produce with posters around the neighborhood and make sure everyone going into the café knows they can buy some locally grown, great-looking veggies, and the price is right, too. The kids handle the sales and the profits are saved for a well-earned outing. When I watch these kids I realize that they are learning more than sales and marketing. They are making healthy food connections also, most importantly, where food comes from. I am sure that they are taking the next step: eating some of their harvest and loving it.

Strategies to Encourage Healthy Eating

Here are five suggestions to increase your teenager's brain food diet.

1. Eat a rainbow. A nutritionist friend of mine describes a brain-healthy diet with that easy-to-remember phrase. Brain-healthy foods come in a variety of colors, so think about a variety of vegetables, fruits, whole grains, dairy, and protein, and cook with olive or canola oil, and there you will find a rainbow of colors.
2. Don't skip breakfast. Virginia Tech University nutritionist Kiyah Duffey, among others, stresses that a healthy breakfast leads to all sorts of brain benefits, including better school performance.
3. Avoid food wars. Family meals can become battlegrounds if we're not careful. Most teenagers' food choices would not win any brain-nutrition awards. Many teens skip breakfast and think chips and pop are a balanced diet. It's a mistake, however, to constantly nag your adolescent about food. If you have healthy treats on hand, then your teenager is more apt to include them when he starts foraging.
4. Start small. Don't change your family's whole diet all at once. Just try making one change at a time. For instance, try whole-wheat spaghetti noodles instead of the familiar white ones.
5. Eat meals together as a family as frequently as possible. A University of Minnesota study found that teens who eat with their families do better in school and have fewer high-risk behaviors such as drug abuse, sexual activity, suicide attempts, violence, and academic issues.

Exercise and the Brain

Fourteen-year-old Barney's life was in danger of completely going off the rails. He couldn't read or write, had already been drinking for four years, and was in constant trouble in his Saskatoon, Canada, high school. "I could not get him to sit at his desk for ten minutes unless he was sleeping," recalls his teacher, Alison Cameron. She was at a loss as to what to do to help Barney when she learned about an innovative program in Naperville, Illinois, where all the high school students spend forty-five minutes every day in intense aerobic exercise. She was impressed enough by the reports of rising test scores and decreasing discipline problems that she asked her principal if she could use exercise equipment with her students. He agreed it was worth a try if she could raise the funds and find suitable space in the building. She found a local donor and negotiated with peers for space. Then she had to convince Barney and his friends to work out.

"This is really hokey" was Barney's initial reaction. "Why would I want to get on a treadmill?"

Alison eventually persuaded Barney and his classmates to try her exercise plan. Within months the students began every day with exercise without their teacher's encouragement. "Some students were actually coming to school in order to exercise," she recalls. More importantly, Alison had the proof to show that the program was making a big difference. In four months her students had jumped a full grade level in reading, writing, and math. "There's no way to explain what happened other than this exercise program," she states. While all the students benefited, Barney's transformation was the most impressive. His reading skills soared and his comprehension increased by an almost unbelievable 400 percent in four months. "I just noticed I was getting smarter," reported Barney. "I started paying attention more." Not surprisingly, Alison's program has been expanded throughout the entire school.

The Naperville project that Alison Cameron read about is called PE4Life and is based on the latest neuroscience linking exercise with brain development and function. It shouldn't surprise us that muscles and brains are connected. We are an animal species born to move, and though not the quickest, we run, walk, climb, jump, and swim quite well. Thousands of years ago quick moves kept us out of the tiger's jaws, but even better for our survival, fostered our ability to think and plan ahead for safety. Our survival depended on our muscles and our brains.

Animal research has been showing the movement/brain power connection for decades. In one experiment, scientists put some mice on running wheels, letting them exercise away while other mice had no wheels in their cages so they just sat around relaxing. The aerobic mice showed impressive brain growth, especially in the area of the brain related to memory and learning. Their lazy cousins got no such benefit. Now neuroscientists can study children's brains with MRIs, and they're finding brain changes as well. What they learned was that kids who exercised and played vigorously for twenty to forty minutes a day were better able to organize their schoolwork, learn math, and do class projects. The more active kids also showed more brain activity in the front part of their brains, the prefrontal cortex, where a lot of thinking occurs. Something happened between the muscles these kids moved and their brains.

The Parent Survival Kit: Exercise and Your Teen's Brain
Use these statements to see if your teenager is getting enough brain-healthy exercise.

PARENT SURVIVAL KIT

Exercise and Your Teen's Brain

Yes No

- ☐ ☐ 1. My teen is physically active every day.
- ☐ ☐ 2. I understand that moving muscles builds brains.
- ☐ ☐ 3. Aerobic exercise benefits the brain's memory center, the hippocampus.
- ☐ ☐ 4. I know that exercise releases important brain chemicals.
- ☐ ☐ 5. Exercise helps a teen do better in school and improves mood.
- ☐ ☐ 6. Teens benefit from a variety of exercise.
- ☐ ☐ 7. Screen time should be balanced with physical activity time.
- ☐ ☐ 8. Exercise builds the executive center of the brain and helps teens focus.
- ☐ ☐ 9. Exercising helps balance overall emotional health.

A sedentary lifestyle is not good for bodies or brains. Use this information to ensure that your teen is getting the exercise she needs.

What Happened to Barney's Brain

As Barney ran on the treadmill his muscles produced a protein (IGF-1), which quickly moved through his bloodstream right into his brain. Once there it got to work sparking the production of some very helpful chemicals, the star being BDNF. This acronym stands for brain-derived neurotrophic factor, what Dr. John Ratey, the author of *Spark: The Revolutionary New Science of Exercise and the Brain,* calls "Miracle-Gro for the brain." Like fertilizer in the garden, BDNF sprouted new dendrites on Barney's brain cells, especially in his brain's key memory and learning center, the hippocampus, that small structure in the center of the brain shaped like a seahorse. Although Barney couldn't feel it, the BDNF caused the neurons in his hippocampus to branch out and form new connections. Each one of those connections represented new learning. By increasing the neural connections, BDNF increased his brain's ability to take in and record new learning. As Barney said, "I just noticed I was getting smarter."

Besides benefiting the hippocampus, Barney's workout also caused more neural firing in his brain's prefrontal cortex (this seat of executive function includes working memory, inhibitory controls, and mental flexibility). This is why exercising students are better able to organize their schoolwork and complete projects. It's why Barney reported, "I started paying attention more."

Barney's reading comprehension took off because his "working memory" also benefited from his exercise. It enabled him to retain the information he read long enough to keep it all straight. Barney's behavior improved because another executive function skill—inhibitory control—made it easier for him to ignore distractions and manage his emotional and behavioral impulses. He also benefited from three neurotransmitters that exercise boosts: dopamine, serotonin, and norepinephrine. These work to regulate the overall thought and emotional balance of the brain. Dopamine, the "feel good" chemical, helped Barney feel motivated and helped focus his attention. Serotonin stabilized his mood. Norepinephrine helped him feel alert and energized.

What's true for the teens in Naperville and Saskatoon is true for all kids: exercise builds strong brains. Exercising changes the structure of the brain, increasing its ability to absorb new learning, manage the learning process, and retain information in memory. The evidence is clear that it translates into better school performance, mood stability, and emotional health.

Helping Teens Move

According to the CDC in its Youth Risk Behavior Survey, 71 percent of teens do not get recommended levels of physical activity. When kids get home from school, too many enter exercise-free zones. The number one activity choice for many teens these days is screen time: TVs, video games, iPads, and smartphones. The body that grew and craved activity during toddlerhood is the same body glued to a chair in front of a screen. Keep track of your teen's screen time. Add up the hours. Is he or she at risk for becoming a couch potato who misses out on the brain benefits that exercise brings?

Teens need daily exercise, so anything to get them moving is good. Encourage them to bike, walk, run, or skate either with friends or family. Some teens will exercise with dance or yoga. Many charities sponsor runs, bike rides, or walks to raise money. Involvement can be a great motivator to keep in shape. Pedometers can be great motivators, too. Buy an inexpensive model and encourage your teenager to keep track of steps every day. Health experts recommend 11,000 to 12,000 steps for girls, and 13,000 to 15,000 for boys.

Sleep and the Teen Brain

Every summer when our kids were growing up Monica and I planned some sort of family summer vacation, which would vary depending on our financial condition at the time. Many excursions involved camping. With our five-person tent we visited many beautiful places. The tent didn't, however, afford us much privacy or elbow room. It was big enough for us all to lie down and sleep secure in the thought that the nylon roof would keep us dry if it began to rain, but that was it. While cozy, our tight quarters did present us with a problem. Every morning at the crack of dawn the three kids woke up, but the Walsh family camping rule was that you couldn't get up till Mom or Dad was awake. So they would stare at us, waiting for the instant Monica or I became conscious. With the slightest hint of our being awake one of them would be ready to begin the day.

That all changed when our kids hit adolescence. In grade school my son Brian had been an early riser. Monica and I had made a pact when we first had children that we would not turn them over to the TV set on Saturday mornings or vacation days. So one of us always got up with the kids, fixed them breakfast, and then did something with them, no matter how early they woke up. Sometimes this involved getting them out of the house, so the other lucky parent got to sleep a couple more hours.

When Brian hit seventh grade, it became harder and harder to wake him up in the morning. If we were lucky, he'd mutter something like "C'mon, five more minutes, pleeeease!" or "Why are you making me get up so early?" as we struggled to get him out of bed. Usually he'd just murmur something indistinct and roll over. It got so we almost had to pull him physically out of bed. We thought the problem was that he was staying up too late. It was rare that he would even enter his bedroom before eleven o'clock.

We battled to convince him to go to bed earlier. We could make him go to his room, but he couldn't go to sleep. "I'm not tired. I just lie there," he'd tell us. He was nearly comatose in the morning when everyone else was starting the day, and full of energy at night when we were wiped out. We didn't know what to make of it or how to get Brian to be in sync with us, his parents. As we talked with friends who had teenagers, we realized we were not alone. These parents told us that on weekends their high school sons and daughters slept till noon, one, two, even three p.m., and it was impossible to get them to go to bed early. We were relieved to find out that Brian's new sleep pattern was common, but we still didn't understand why it had happened. This kid used to stare us into consciousness if we kept our eyes closed a moment past sunrise. How had he turned into such a night owl?

The Parent Survival Kit: Teens and Sleep

When parents are asked to list the most important issues facing adolescents, sleep isn't often one of the first things that come to mind. A proper amount of sleep is, however, an important component in the life of a healthy teen, and sleep can become a battleground for adolescents and their parents. Use this kit to determine if your parenting strategy is taking the importance of your adolescent's shut-eye into account.

PARENT SURVIVAL KIT

Teens and Sleep

Yes No

☐ ☐ 1. Changes in the teen brain change the sleep cycle for most kids.

☐ ☐ 2. Many teens get 25 to 33 percent less sleep than they need.

☐ ☐ 3. I encourage my teen to wind down late at night even if they can't fall asleep.

☐ ☐ 4. I discourage caffeine use in the evening.

☐ ☐ 5. I let my teens sleep later on the weekends so they can catch up.

☐ ☐ 6. My teen has a technology curfew each evening.

If you can answer yes to everything on this list, you can rest easy. Finding yourself answering no doesn't mean you should be up worrying at night, but it could suggest that you need to sit down with your teen and draw up a plan for bedtime.

Sleep and the Teen Brain

The explanation for how Brian turned into a night owl is, like so many other things, found in the teen brain. At puberty, two big changes affect sleep patterns. First, the way the brain regulates sleep and the amount of sleep needed begins to change. Second, the timing of the sleep/wake cycle shifts, so the times of day that adolescents get sleepy and feel fully alert and awake can be at odds with what we adults may think of as normal.

To understand the implications of these changes, it helps to have a sense of the importance and function of sleep. Some scientists think that sleep enables the brain to rebuild and replenish cells that have been working all day. Others think that sleep allows the brain to reinforce connections that were made during the previous day. One experiment that supported this hypothesis studied people who played the video game *Tetris*. In *Tetris*, the player arranges falling blocks of various shapes to make straight rows as the speed of falling blocks increases. It's difficult to master, and a player needs lots of practice to be able to react fast enough to handle the highest levels. In the experiment, the psychologists found that the people who played *Tetris* all day had dreams about playing *Tetris*. The researchers postulated that the dreams did the same work that practicing the game did, neurologically speaking. In both cases, repeating the skill established pathways in the brain for playing *Tetris* well.

If these scientists are correct, sleeping may be a way for the brain to get better at what it does when it is awake. Dreaming may be a practice for real life.

Besides being necessary for good health, the precise functions of sleep are not clear. Brain scans show the brain is actually very active during sleep, even though the rest of our bodies are quiet and still. This might seem to run contrary to common sense, but it's true: our brains are busy while we sleep.

Not getting enough sleep is hard on the body and the mind. Extreme sleep deprivation can lead to psychotic breaks. In some cases, people who have stayed awake for days on end have died. Although most adolescents are in no danger of the extreme consequences of being low on sleep, many of them are not getting enough. Anyone who does not get enough sleep has difficulty focusing, reasoning, driving safely, learning, and working.

How much sleep do teens need? Studies have long shown that adults need about eight hours each night, so it was assumed that adolescents, with their adultlike brains, needed eight hours, too. Some parents and psychologists even hypothesized that they needed less sleep than adults because they were wide awake well after their parents had gone to bed.

Well, it turns out that theory was a big mistake. Mary Carskadon of Brown University, a leading sleep researcher, has discovered that the adolescent brain needs about nine and half hours of sleep every night. So, even though they have a tendency to stay up late, adolescents need only a little less sleep than their younger brothers and sisters who generally need about ten. Unfortunately, most adolescents are not getting anywhere near enough sleep.

When I was a high school teacher, my eight a.m. homeroom was always full of sleepy freshmen. They would stagger into the classroom and fall asleep on their desks during the morning announcements. It seemed like they never knew what was going on in the school and they didn't: they hadn't heard the announcements! I often asked my students what time they had gone to bed. A common answer was midnight. They were getting six hours of sleep each night, seven at the most. That means they were 25 to 33 percent short on sleep every night! They were exhausted. Naturally they drooled onto the desks instead of organizing their schoolwork for the day. If only they had gone to sleep earlier, they wouldn't have been so tired, but because of the shift in the adolescent sleep/wake cycle, that was nearly impossible for them. Even if they had gone to bed earlier, they probably couldn't have gone to sleep.

For a healthy adult who works hard, sleep may seem as easy as rolling off a log, but it is actually very complicated. Scientists believe that as many as fifty different brain chemicals—hormones and neurotransmitters—are involved in sleeping. The chemicals need to be balanced to maintain our circadian rhythms—the cycle of changes that the body undergoes in a twenty-four-hour period. (The Latin word *circa* means "around." The second part of the word comes from the Latin *dies*, which means "day.") These rhythms affect when we get hungry, when we are most alert, and when we want social contact. Circadian rhythms also involve the sleep/wake cycle, which changes with puberty. We aren't exactly sure why it changes, but considering how many brain chemicals are needed for sleep, the cause probably lies in the dramatic changes taking place in the adolescent hormone system.

In a normal adult the circadian rhythms are in tune with the movement of the sun through the sky. During the day, the brain takes in the information that comes through the eyes and keeps track of the time of day. As light comes through the retina, it activates cells in the hypothalamus of the brain, which then sends a message to the pineal gland deep in the brain. The pineal gland secretes a hormone called melatonin.

If melatonin were one of the seven dwarves, it would be Sleepy. Supplemental melatonin in pill form is commonly recommended to manage jetlag. Sometimes it is called a "natural sleeping pill." Under a doctor's supervision, ingesting melatonin can help you fall asleep. If your circadian rhythms are working properly, however, you shouldn't need to buy a bottle of pills, because when it gets dark, the hypothalamus tells your pineal gland to increase its production of melatonin. As the level of melatonin in your body increases, you feel more and more sleepy. After you have gotten enough sleep, the brain tells your pineal gland to stop secreting melatonin, the level of the hormone drops, and you wake up.

Beginning at puberty that sleep/wake cycle changes. The melatonin surge occurs later and later, and the melatonin drop occurs later as well. This shift has been further exaggerated for twenty-first-century teens. The blue-spectrum light emitted by TV, computer, and personal device screens delays the sleep/wake cycle even more. The result is teens who are alert at eleven p.m. or midnight, when everyone else is tired, and teens who are dog-tired at eight a.m., when everyone else is getting in gear. So adolescents have two sleep problems: Because their brains are in the midst of so much development, they continue to need a lot of sleep—as I said, about nine and a half hours per night for the brain to regenerate and operate at peak efficiency. Because of the circadian shift, however, they get tired later than everyone else, yet they often have to get up earlier than everyone else. In the district where my kids attended high school, their first class started at 7:15 in the morning. To save money, the buses that dropped off the high school kids would head back out into the city and pick up the grade-schoolers. Nobody wanted first-graders to be standing alone at the bus stop in the pitch-black freezing cold at 6:30 on a winter morning, but if they'd planned the bus schedule around circadian rhythms, they would have taken the younger kids to school first. Our high school even had something called zero hour for kids who needed to squeeze one more class into the day. All three of my kids took zero-hour gym to keep time open later in the day for electives like language and art classes. As a result, they had to be dressed in their sweats at school by 6:15 in the morning. Many school sports teams have morning practices that start at similar times. Even if they don't tack an extra activity onto the beginning of the day, however, most adolescents are waking up far earlier than their bodies want them to on weekdays.

The result is a nation of sleep-deprived adolescents. They are short on sleep during the week and then they sleep until the afternoon on the weekends, throwing their sleep/wake cycle even further out of whack. Because they are averse to waking in the morning during the week and eager to sleep more on weekend days, adolescents are often accused of being lazy. The reality is that they're fighting a losing battle with their own bodies to stay awake, which puts them at risk of serious trouble.

Sleep deprivation is not a trivial problem. Brain imaging studies show that the prefrontal cortex is particularly vulnerable to sleep deprivation. The PFC, of course, is already under construction during adolescence and is the main brain center responsible for those all-important executive functions. For example, sleep deprivation impairs the working memory. Many kids probably aren't just irresponsible when they forget their books, assignments, and pencils. One student whom I taught in high school always had to ask to borrow a sheet of paper and a writing instrument. He also fell asleep in class a lot and didn't get the greatest grades. He would have done much better if he hadn't been exhausted all the time. Another teenager, who had French during first period for two years in a row, claims he learned nothing, but he remembers the teacher saying that he was always falling asleep.

Another side effect of sleep deprivation is an increase in the stress hormone, cortisol. A chronic increase in cortisol can compromise the immune system. My son had a friend, Thad, who began to get ill several times a semester starting in middle school. Although he was a good student he was always in danger of failing classes because of excessive absences. In Minnesota, high school students can take some or all of their classes at state colleges after their sophomore year if their grades are good enough. Starting first semester of his junior year, Thad took two evening classes at the university and avoided first and second hours at high school. His health improved almost immediately, most likely because he was getting more sleep and managed to lower his cortisol levels.

Lack of alertness is a side effect of sleep deprivation that may seem negligible, but when you consider all of the adolescents who have recently received a driver's license, it can be downright chilling. Many driving accidents occur because a teen driver was "not paying attention." I bet if all adolescents got enough sleep, there wouldn't be as many accidents.

Research also shows that sleep deprivation leads to an impaired ability to process glucose, which contributes to overweight and obesity. Perhaps lack of sleep is another of the many contributing factors to the childhood and youth obesity epidemic.

Mood disorders also coincide with chronic sleep deprivation. When you are deprived of sleep, your feelings are more intense and you have less ability to curb and control your emotions. Some of the slamming doors, sudden tears, and angry outbursts may be aggravated by sleep deprivation.

Some kids get stuck in a bad sleep pattern and develop a serious sleep disorder, "delayed sleep phase syndrome." This means their night and day are turned around. Probably a genetic disposition to this disorder kicks in at adolescence when the entire sleep/wake cycle changes.

Knowing this science of sleep and the teen brain, parents and other adults can help adolescents make an effort to get the sleep they need. One of the easiest ways to help them is to remove stimulation starting in the late evening and through the night. Limiting caffein-ated beverages, TV, video games, computer screens, and cell phones after nine or ten can help convince the adolescent brain that it's time for bed. Late-night stimulation such as hearing and answering the ping of a text message just makes the biological urge to stay awake more pronounced. Even though an adolescent may not be sleepy, it is important to help her wind down as the evening winds down. Quiet reading, quiet music, and other mellow activities are good ways to transition to sleep time. She still may not fall asleep till eleven, but that's a lot better than one a.m.

It's tempting to get kids up on the weekends so they don't waste the day in bed, but for their sake you should be tolerant of them catching up on weekends. On the other hand, you should make sure they don't get turned completely around. Sleeping until ten or eleven is probably just fine. Staying in bed until two or three in the after-noon may do them more harm than good.

Or, you can make a lot of noise like I used to do. My older son, Dan, and his friend Gaelen often "crashed" at each other's houses late on weekend nights. Monica and I encouraged the practice since they had to be home by a certain time and that way we knew where they were. Every Saturday morning there was a pretty good chance that when I woke up, Gaelen would be sleeping peacefully on Dan's floor in a sleeping bag. They were always up later than we were (some-times laughing loudly and waking us up), so I knew they needed to stay sleeping. I'd go downstairs, have breakfast, read the paper, and maybe even do a few chores. Eventually, around ten o'clock I'd get on the NordicTrack. It was the way I tried to stay in shape, and to get a good workout I had to ski pretty hard. It made quite a bit of noise. Enough noise to travel up through the ceiling to the floor where Gaelen was sleeping. After a half hour or so, Gaelen and Dan would wander downstairs bleary-eyed but fairly well rested. They never complained. It was ten thirty, after all. Time to get out of bed.

Some enlightened school districts are changing their start time based on the new adolescent sleep research. It's not clear yet if grades in these schools are up or not, but with improved attendance and less tardiness, both teachers and students report they are hap-pier and more alert. And if that's the case, those early-morning classes are more productive, too. It's a win-win situation. You may want to find out if your school administrators know about this information on the teen brain's need for sleep and encourage school districts to get more creative with bus schedules.

DO

✓ Talk with your teenagers about the connections between healthy brains and good nutrition, enough exercise, and adequate sleep.

✓ Encourage a "rainbow diet" and five daily servings of fruits and vegetables.

✓ Have family meals together as often as possible.

✓ Do what you can to get your teen moving and exercising.

✓ See if your teen will try wearing a pedometer to keep track of steps.

✓ Let your teens know that scientists have discovered they need at least nine hours of sleep every night.

✓ Encourage your adolescents to wind down at a reasonable hour even if they don't feel tired enough to sleep.

✓ Establish a technology curfew.

✓ Let your adolescent catch up on some sleep on weekends if possible.

DON'T

✗ Don't become the food police.

✗ Don't skip breakfast, lunch, dinner, or snacks.

✗ Don't let screen time crowd out exercise.

✗ Don't let your teens take any sleeping medications, including melatonin, unless recommended by a physician.

✗ Don't let your teens get in the habit of using a lot of caffeine or other stimulants to wake up in the morning.

✗ Don't let your teens accept jobs that will keep them up late at night.

✗ Don't let your adolescents watch TV, play video games, or use their cell phones or computers late at night.

What do I want to continue?

_____

_____

_____

What do I want to change?

_____

_____

_____

TWELVE

When Things Go Wrong in the Brain: Adolescent Mental Illness

After attending one of my workshops a few months earlier, Andrea was looking for some advice about her sixteen-year-old daughter, Emily. What Andrea had to tell me in our phone call was much more serious than she realized. "Dr. Walsh, something has come up with Emily. It might be nothing, but I just couldn't think of anyone else to call. For the past several months Emily has been wearing long-sleeve shirts every day. It seemed a little odd because, as you know, there have been some very hot days. When I asked her about it last week, she shrugged me off. She said she liked long sleeves. I didn't think much of it. You know how teenagers are with their fashions. Anyway, yesterday something else happened. I don't think she was expecting me to be in the hallway when she came out of the bathroom after a shower. Seeing me, she dashed to her bedroom like a scared deer. As she ran past me, I noticed red lines on her arm. When I asked her about them later she said that her friend's cat had scratched her. Something about that didn't sound right, so I asked to see her arms to make sure they weren't infected. She really resisted and almost burst into tears before she finally rolled up her sleeves. I was shocked by what I saw.

"I couldn't figure out what they were from, and it took a lot of prying. Finally, late last night she told me she has been cutting her arms with razor blades. I was horrified. But she said that all the kids were doing it and that it was no big deal. She said it was like piercing or tattoos. After Emily went to school this morning, I called my sister, who used to be a teacher. She said it didn't sound like a teenage fad to her. She thought it was serious. Is this cutting business part of what teenagers are doing these days?"

"Self-cutting is not normal. Your teen may know other kids who are doing it, and she may even think it's not a big deal, but it is. It's very different from piercing or tattooing," I said.

Andrea was quite anxious, worried that Emily might be trying to kill herself. According to health professionals, however, suicidal intention is not usually behind cutting. Teenagers who cut themselves, usually girls, are seeking relief from intense emotional pain caused by any of a number of things. Many kids who cut themselves find it difficult to express anger toward other people, so they turn it in on themselves. Sometimes it's related to underlying depression or an eating disorder. Sometimes girls who have been sexually abused start to cut themselves. To Andrea's knowledge, her daughter had not been abused.

I wanted to help Andrea and her daughter, but I knew that I wasn't the right person, so I referred her to another psychologist who specializes in working with girls like Emily.

I assured her that she was right to get Emily into therapy and that she should not be too hard on herself for overlooking her daughter's behavior for so long. The important thing is that she caught it. Sorting out the normal from the dangerous is not always easy with teenagers. I always tell parents that it never hurts to ask questions. Addressing problems early is crucial.

The Parent Survival Kit: Mental Illness

This kit can help you to be prepared to recognize signs of adolescent mental illness. In the event that you suspect that your child does show symptoms of mental illness, you must seek professional help.

Mental Illness

Yes No

☐ ☐ 1. Because many mental illnesses have a genetic component, I know the mental health histories of my teen's extended family.

☐ ☐ 2. I know that a pattern of symptoms that lasts for months is more indicative of a mental health problem than any one behavior.

☐ ☐ 3. I know the symptoms of the most common mental health problems of adolescents.

☐ ☐ 4. I know where to get good professional advice if I become worried that my son or daughter might have a serious emotional problem.

☐ ☐ 5. I know what my insurance benefits are for professional mental health services if I ever need them.

Mental illness can strike any family. Being prepared will not prevent a brain disease from striking, but it will enable you to intervene early to get your adolescent the help he or she needs.

Distinguishing the Normal from the Abnormal

Normal adolescence has its share of abnormal behavior. The point bears repeating because it gets at the essence of why adolescence can be so difficult for kids themselves and the people around them. After all, how do you deal with a "normally abnormal" time of life? There is no precise path, but life will be a lot easier if you recognize bumps in the road for what they are, a normal part of adolescence. One of the most important challenges for parents, therefore, is separating the normally abnormal bumps from warning signs that indicate much more serious problems.

As parents we can err in one of two directions. We can overreact to the normal ups and downs, thereby creating unnecessary pain and anguish for our kids, who already have a lot on their plates. Or we can miss telling signs of serious mental health issues, unwittingly depriving our adolescents of the help they may desperately need. The key to striking a balance between these two extremes is knowledge. In previous chapters we have already explored some serious issues like alcoholism and out-of-control violence. In this chapter, we explore some of the most common mental health problems that emerge during adolescence. It is beyond the scope of this book to cover every mental health issue in detail, so we will focus on the problems that parents are most likely to encounter, with information that can help you differentiate between normally abnormal and dangerous.

Reading warning signs is a matter of recognizing patterns. In the course of this chapter I will be listing symptoms to look for. Every parent of every teenager will find something on the list that will be true for his or her adolescent. Don't panic. It is not until you see *clusters* of behaviors that persist over time that you should be concerned that your son or daughter may be suffering from a mental illness. If you do become concerned that your son or daughter may be dealing with something more serious than the normal ups and downs of adolescence, you should share your concerns with someone who knows your teen and who knows something about teenage behavior. Andrea was right to call her sister, who convinced her to get help for Emily. In the midst of dealing with the challenges of parenting a teen, it is easy to lose perspective. Getting a second opinion can help you figure out the difference between experiencing normal adolescent problems and needing professional help. A good place to get that perspective is from the school that your son or daughter attends. Teachers and administrators see your kid every day and also deal with a wide range of other adolescents. If you have a relationship or regular contact with your teen's teachers and coaches, they will be more likely to key into your son or daughter. When it comes to helping adolescents through the most serious mental health challenges, parents usually need all the help they can get.

Attention Deficit Disorders
School staff helped alert Zack's parents to a serious problem. A brilliant fourteen-year-old who scored at the top of his ninth-grade

class on all the standardized tests, Zack was chronically late for class. He also frequently forgot assignments, talked out of turn, blurted out answers, repeatedly misplaced or lost his books and school supplies, and often slipped into conflicts with his teachers. While he had had these traits in elementary school, they had become more obvious and troublesome in the highly structured advanced baccalaureate program he entered as a ninth-grader. Several of his teachers told his parents about the problems he was having in class. Eventually, Zack and his parents discovered that he did not have an attitude problem, nor did he just need to "settle down and pay attention." A thorough evaluation led the family's pediatrician to diagnose Zack with attention deficit hyperactivity disorder, better known by its acronym, ADHD. That diagnosis did not solve Zack's problems, of course, but it did help him, his parents, and his teachers to figure out how best to help him learn in school.

Attention deficit without the pattern of agitation or hyperactivity is known as attention deficit disorder, or ADD. ADD and ADHD are the most common and most controversial mental health diagnoses for today's children and adolescents. They are not new disorders. Educational psychologists and researchers identified the pattern of symptoms more than a hundred years ago. About 5 percent of teens have the underlying brain disorder, and boys are six times as likely to be diagnosed with one of the types of ADD as girls. A normal brain focuses on one thing or activity and then shifts to another at an appropriate time. We call this capacity *attention*; it directs the brain's resources to focus on an idea or perform a task. Kids with ADD or ADHD either cannot make the shift to a new thing or activity or their attention is constantly shifting to whatever stimulus comes along. Scientists are not sure what causes some brains to have trouble measuring out appropriate attention, but the best research suggests that the disorders are linked to a problem with neurotransmitters. Their malfunction appears to have a genetic component, since parents with ADD and ADHD are five times more likely to have children with attention disorders than are parents who have normal attention spans.

Parents or teachers may consider the possibility of ADD or ADHD for a kid who displays the following pattern:

- has trouble paying attention,
- makes careless mistakes,
- is easily distracted,
- loses things frequently,
- tends to be impatient,
- fidgets or squirms,
- interrupts others,
- cannot sit quietly.

Every child (and every person) will exhibit these tendencies from time to time, so unless an adolescent shows these symptoms frequently, you should not suspect ADD or ADHD. If these symptoms are not leading to problems (frequent arguments, sloppy schoolwork, etc.), then you're probably not dealing with an attention disorder.

While the best research shows that 3 to 5 percent of teens have an attention disorder, in some parts of the country as many as one in five teens carries one of the two diagnoses. Because there is no definitive brain test to determine which teens are just being impulsive and which have ADD or ADHD, many adolescents are being diagnosed with a disorder that they do not have. Sometimes a physician will prescribe a medication just to see if it helps, without a thorough evaluation. As a result many adolescents who take medication for the disorder do not actually have it. You don't want your child to be taking powerful medications unnecessarily.

A thorough evaluation is the solution to the over-diagnosis epidemic. A teen should never be diagnosed or put on a drug without a comprehensive evaluation that includes a complete medical and family history; a physical examination; interviews with parents, teachers, and the teen; completion of specialized behavior rating scales; and observation of the teen. Parents who are concerned that their adolescent may have ADD or ADHD should seek the help of professionals who are trained and experienced in conducting these comprehensive examinations.

Medications have proven to be the most effective treatment for adolescents who really have ADD or ADHD. Drugs like Ritalin, Dexedrine, Cylert, and Adderall are stimulants that affect the brain's neurotransmitters. These medications help adolescents regulate attention and impulsivity and can make a profoundly positive impact in the lives of kids who suffer from an attention disorder. In the most successful cases, however, drugs are not the only means of treatment, and most experts agree that medication should never be the only treatment. Effective treatment should always include the following:

- Education for the teen and the family about attention disorders so everyone knows and understands the problem.
- Behavior management that increases the chances for success. For example, teens with ADD or ADHD respond best to predictable environments where expectations are clear and consistent, and consequences are known ahead of time. Breaking down instructions or directions into steps and strategies for keeping track of assignments and tasks helps a lot.
- Collaboration between home and school. Parents and teachers should work together to identify the specific attention skills that cause the most trouble. For example, some teens have trouble beginning a task because the directions are too complicated. Other kids have no trouble with directions, but have a terrible time making a transition from one activity to another. When everyone, including the adolescent, knows what skills need the most work, then progress is more likely.

Another type of treatment, "neurofeedback," is proving to be helpful with about half of the kids with ADD or ADHD. The teens are connected to a computer with painless sensors attached to their scalp and ears. The computer processes the teen's brain waves and converts them to images on a video game screen. Many teens are able to learn how to change and control their attention using this technology.

Parents have been worried by reports that children on ADD and ADHD medications are at greater risk for alcohol and drug abuse or addiction later in life. That concern was put to rest in 2013 when a very large study was published that provides evidence children and teens on stimulant medications are at no greater risk for later problems than other young people.

Adolescent Depression

Another common yet serious mental ailment for adolescents is depression. As with most mental illnesses, scientists have not determined the exact causes of depression. Many researchers believe the root is with the neurotransmitters; some others who scan the brains of depressed teens think they detect structural distinctions. Even kids who are happy-go-lucky when they are little can fall prey to overwhelming depression when they reach their adolescent years. That's what happened to Beth.

Beth, fifteen years old, was a popular girl with a gift for humor. She had a knack for telling stories and could get her friends laughing at her antics at the drop of a hat. Beginning at puberty Beth started to experience bouts of the blues that seemed unrelated either to her monthly cycle or external events. Beth agreed to let her mother come with her to a regular physical exam and talk to the doctor about her mood problems. The doctor barely paid any attention to their concerns. "That's common during adolescence," he said. "Stay active and don't dwell on problems. You'll be fine."

For the six months following that doctor's visit, Beth felt worse. She would confide to her mother late at night how bad she felt about herself. "The doctor said I'm fine, so it must be my fault," Beth told her mother with tears streaming down her face. "I've got nothing to feel bad about. I go to a good school, and I have a lot of friends who have worse problems than me. Why do I feel so bad? I just hate my life and I hate myself." After months of trying to help her daughter feel better, she brought Beth to see me.

Beth was clearly depressed. She constantly criticized herself as weak, so before we finished that first session, I wanted to make sure Beth knew that her depression was not her fault. "Beth, you need to know that you have a disease that is affecting your brain and it is not your fault that you are depressed. If your pancreas were acting up, would you consider that your fault?" Beth answered that of course she wouldn't. "Well, why are you blaming yourself that another organ, your brain, is acting up?" I asked. "We're going to put together a plan to help you get some relief from the disease you've got. But the first thing I want to ask you to do is to stop blaming yourself."

Because adolescent brains are subject to rapid changes and fluctuations, adolescent mood shifts and bouts of the blues, even sudden ones, are not unusual. But some teens, like Beth, have a sad or depressed mood that descends and never lifts. This is a sign of depression, a mental illness that usually makes its appearance during adolescence. Most of the depressed adults I have counseled over the years trace the beginnings of their disease to their teenage years. Beth's physician made the common mistake of chalking her depression up to normal teen moodiness. Beth's depression was actually easier to detect because she didn't display a lot of anger. Many depressed adolescents tend to be angrier than depressed adults. As a result expressions of anger tend to overshadow the more telltale symptoms of depression. Beginning in the midteens (usually fifteen to sixteen years old), the incidence of depression rises much more quickly for girls than it does for boys.

Among the telltale signs of teenage depression, one is very consistent: a tendency to focus on the negative. For depressed teens the glass is usually half empty when it comes to classroom performance, their prospects for romance, or their chances of success in the future. Depressed teens are often touchy or grumpy, and they become easily irritated. So far, you might be thinking that this sounds like the description of a normal teen. That's the problem. It's hard to distinguish depression from mood swings. If several of the following other symptoms appear in your child, however, he or she may be depressed:

- changes in appetite,
- unexplained weight loss or weight gain,
- sleeping too much or having trouble getting to sleep or staying asleep,
- low energy,
- feeling blue and discouraged for long stretches,
- feeling hopeless,
- vague physical complaints,
- recurring thoughts of death or suicide.

The increased risk for suicide is probably the most frightening aspect of teen depression. On the rise for American teens for more than fifty years, the high rate of suicide now makes it the third leading cause of death among teens.

Sue had been a student for three years in the high school where I taught, but barely anyone knew much about her. She got straight A's, so her teachers never needed to give her a lot of help, and she stayed out of trouble, so she was not well known in the office. When she wasn't in class she was studying in the library. Quiet and solitary, she came to school alone every day. As soon as her last class ended, she walked home without a companion. Between classes, she walked by herself next to the wall of the hallway. In retrospect it almost seemed like she was trying to be invisible.

When everyone returned from spring break the news arrived. Sue had killed herself with an overdose of sleeping pills the night before classes resumed. It wasn't until her mother had gone in to wake her to get ready for school that she discovered Sue's dead body. News like that travels like lightning through a high school. And as word spread, so did the most common and saddest question: "Who's Sue?" She had walked the halls of the high school every day for almost three years, and yet many students and teachers who had been in classes with her had to go to the yearbook to find out what she looked like. Sue had suffered her depression in silence and eventually died. I was a young teacher then, but I still get a sick feeling when I think that I passed by a girl with a terminal case of depression and never even noticed.

Sometimes teens commit suicide with no advance warning. More often they leave subtle clues. "Nothing matters." "What do I care? I won't be around forever." "I probably won't see you again." These kinds of statements may be hints that an adolescent is contemplating suicide. Suicidal teens may start to give away some of their possessions or become preoccupied with songs of sadness and despair. Other signals include neglecting their personal appearance, running away, using drugs or alcohol to deal with emotional pain, withdrawing from friends, and losing interest in pleasurable activities. Teens at risk for suicide often complain of being a bad person or feeling "rotten inside." Whether these signs indicate a real suicide risk or whether they are a call for help is not always immediately clear. In any case you should always take these symptoms seriously. Seek professional help if you have concerns about your child being depressed or suicidal. A variety of treatments, including psychotherapy, group therapy, structured programs, and of course medication, can offer teens the help they need.

Doctors commonly prescribe a group of antidepressant medications called selective serotonin reuptake inhibitors (SSRIs), which go by trade names such as Prozac, Luvox, Paxil, and Zoloft. They act on the neurotransmitter serotonin, which, as you now know, regulates mood. I would not rule out the use of antidepressants if a psychiatrist prescribes them, but I always recommend other treatments before turning to drugs. Even as a last resort, drugs should only be used if they are combined with counseling and a plan to monitor closely the effects and side effects of the drugs. The Federal Drug Administration has issued a warning that SSRIs may increase the risk for suicide among some adolescents. This advisory should make parents more vigilant. If any concerns do arise, they should be immediately shared with the prescribing physician.

Eating Disorders

I spent a day at an exclusive private high school in the Midwest, speaking to several classes and having informal discussions with groups of students. As I ate my lunch, I sat with a group of twelfth-graders engaged in a lively conversation about life as an adolescent. I told them that I was working on a book on the topic, and they were excited to suggest what I should include. One of them asked me if the book would have any information on eating disorders. I asked if she thought that was an important topic. "Are you kidding?" she responded. "Half the girls in this school have some kind of eating disorder." This eighteen-year-old girl was not reporting the results of a scientifically conducted survey, but she did have an accurate sense of the scope of the problem.

The prevalence of eating disorders in the United States is paradoxical. At a time when obesity is at epidemic levels, we have a parallel epidemic of anorexia nervosa, bulimia, and other eating disorders. These epidemics mirror our cultural confusion about food.

We deluge kids with supersized portions of high-calorie junk food as we simultaneously glorify unhealthy, unrealistic thinness. We entice kids to eat till they are stuffed and then tell them they are ugly if they're not supermodel thin. It's no wonder that so many Americans get stuck in one or the other extreme and so many teens, especially girls, suffer from eating disorders.

Anorexia nervosa is a serious disorder. It shows up in adolescence and most frequently afflicts girls, but teen boys also get caught up in it. A teen with anorexia has an intense fear of being fat and refuses to eat enough to maintain a healthy body weight. Adolescents suffering from anorexia have a distorted view of their own body, believing that they are overweight in spite of any evidence to the contrary. A teen with anorexia may be very irritable and moody and very nervous about food. She may exercise compulsively to work off the food she does eat. Physical symptoms can include an interruption of menstrual cycles, dry skin, and low blood pressure. Without treatment anorexia can become a chronic problem and lead to dehydration, heart damage, hormone imbalance, and even death.

An adolescent with bulimia usually appears to have completely normal eating habits. In reality a bulimic teen goes on eating binges and then, to prevent weight gain, purges the food by forced vomiting, laxative use, or enemas. Some teens fluctuate back and forth between anorexic and bulimic patterns. Untreated bulimia can result in cardiac damage, dental problems, rupture of the esophagus, seizures, and kidney damage.

Ann's story is all too common. She was a happy, healthy kid who never seemed concerned about her weight until she reached puberty. Then she started to think she was fat compared to the other girls in her class. During a visit to the family doctor, she said she needed to lose weight. The doctor, who was very sensitive to eating disorders, made it clear to Ann that her weight was perfectly healthy for her height and that she did not need a diet. Afterward, the doctor called Ann's mother, Nicole.

"Ann signed a release so I could report the results of her physical to you."

"Is anything the matter?" Nicole asked.

"She's very healthy. However, I was concerned with some of her comments about her weight. She told me she thinks she's overweight and wants to be on a diet."

"She's always saying that. You don't think she's fat, do you?"

"No, not at all. That's why I'm calling. A lot of girls are on diets who shouldn't be. If you see any signs of an eating disorder, please let me know. I don't want to worry you, but I watch my teen patients closely because eating disorders are such a problem at Ann's school.

"Keep your eyes and ears open, and call me if she has any symptoms."

The following lists are what Ann's doctor means by such symptoms:

SIGNS OF ANOREXIA
- Does your teen have irrational fears of being fat?
- Is he or she preoccupied with losing weight?
- Does your teen skip meals or not eat reasonable portions?
- Does he or she exercise compulsively?
- Does your daughter miss any periods now that she is well into puberty?
- Is your teen's skin exceptionally dry?

SIGNS OF BULIMIA
- Does your son or daughter eat a lot and purge the food by forcing themselves to vomit or using laxatives?
- Does he or she try to hide purging behaviors by running water while in the bathroom?
- Does your teen make frequent trips to the bathroom especially after meals?
- Does your teen hide stashes of food?
- Does your teen have puffy cheeks or neck with a very skinny body? (Vomiting irritates and swells the cheeks and glands in the neck.)

Weeks passed and Nicole's worries began to subside. Then one night at dinner, Ann announced she was going to start the Atkins diet. Nicole's stomach dropped, but she tried to remain calm.

"Ann, honey, you're already skinny. The doctor told you not to go on a diet."

"Oh, Mom, don't worry. I'm just going to try it out to lose ten pounds or so. It's no big deal."

Nicole could feel her anxiety rising. "Ann, I don't want you on any diet. I really mean it."

Tears welled up in Ann's eyes as she said, "You don't know what it's like to be fat!"

"Ann, you are not fat."

Ann broke down into sobs. "I am fat and I hate my body. I am so ugly."

Against Ann's protest the two of them met with the doctor later that week. Ann promised them that she would not diet. She said she understood what both her mother and the doctor were saying. Nicole felt relieved as they left the doctor's office, but she didn't know that Ann was about to take her mission to lose weight underground.

Monitoring Ann's eating became a cat-and-mouse game for almost a year. When she began to avoid meals by saying that she wasn't hungry or had just eaten at a friend's house, Nicole began to insist that she eat with the family. Family discussions about food became arguments that always ended with Ann pleading to be left alone.

Eventually Nicole received a call from the family dentist. "I just finished Ann's dental exam. I think you need to take her to a counselor."

Nicole's heart sank. "What are you talking about?"

"From the condition of Ann's teeth I'd say that she has been vomiting every day for months. I think Ann may be bulimic. I think she needs to see a professional right away."

The next day Nicole was back in the family doctor's office with Ann. The doctor came right to the point. "I'm referring you to an eating disorders program at the hospital for a full evaluation." Ann began to protest, but the doctor did not waver. She looked at Nicole. "We've been worried about this for over a year. Ann is at serious health risk and needs professional help."

Teens with anorexia or bulimia often become very secretive.

They may deny any problems they are having and can become very angry with anyone who tries to intervene; the patterns of denial are very similar to those that accompany alcoholism and drug addiction. The best possible way to help an anorexic or bulimic teen is with the aid of health professionals experienced in treating eating disorders. The most successful treatments involve a coordinated team that includes a physician, a nutritionist, and a counselor. Serious cases often require hospitalization. As is usually the case with any serious disorder, early identification and treatment leads to a better outcome.

Obsessive-Compulsive Disorder

The brain has an inborn mechanism that helps us shift attention from one thing to another, from one idea to the next. When everything is working as it should, we can disengage from the activity we have finished and focus our attention on something new. Scientists believe that the part of the brain that enables us to do this shifting, the anterior cingulate gyrus, is deep within the frontal lobes.

In the course of a normal life, everyone can have trouble focusing. Simple worrying about results of a test can make you distracted and unable to concentrate or sleep. But sometimes the brain's shifting mechanism gets stuck for no apparent reason, as was the case with fourteen-year-old Dennis. A quiet, polite boy from a devout Baptist family, he took his religion seriously from an early age and tried his best to live up to the ideals he learned in church and the religion class he attended on Wednesday evenings. His parents grew concerned when Dennis became overwhelmed with fears that he was a terrible sinner and was going to hell. They took Dennis to meet with their minister, and he referred them to me.

"I think Dennis's problem is psychological, not spiritual," he told them.

Within fifteen minutes of meeting the family, I agreed with the minister. Dennis was telling me about school and his teachers when he stopped in midsentence, looked away, and said, "Look at the sky, see the sky, that's the sky." I asked Dennis what he was thinking when he said that and what he meant by that phrase. "It doesn't mean anything," responded Dennis. "I say that to stop thinking about the devil. I keep having these thoughts about Satan. They happen all the time. If I say, 'Look at the sky, see the sky, that's the sky,' I picture the sky and that gets my mind off Satan."

I asked Dennis how often he thought about the devil and how often he would repeat this saying that he had invented. Reluctant to answer, he finally guessed that he said it hundreds of times in the course of a day. I asked him if he used his saying in school. He didn't say it verbally, he said, because the other kids would think he was crazy, but he did say it to himself in his head even though that didn't work as well as speaking the words out loud.

Dennis was suffering from a brain malfunction called obsessive-compulsive disorder, or OCD. Dennis's version was a bit unusual, but it had the two hallmarks of the disease: intrusive thoughts and a ritualistic behavior to deal with them. As many as 1 percent of adolescents suffer from OCD. Common forms include uncontrollable fears of disaster or germs coupled with obsessively habitual actions to cope with the worry. For example, a teen worried about germs may wash his hands repeatedly dozens of times a day until his skin is raw. Another OCD sufferer who is worried about fire may check the knobs on the stove dozens of times each day. Eventually, the fears and compulsive behaviors crowd out normal behaviors and interactions, interfering with normal living.

I explained to Dennis that the part of his brain responsible for shifting his attention, the anterior cingulate gyrus, wasn't doing its job for some reason. This explanation came as a great relief to Dennis because he, like many others with OCD, was terrified that he was going insane. His parents and I coordinated care with an adolescent psychiatrist who prescribed Zoloft, an SSRI drug that changes the level of serotonin and is quite effective in treating OCD. I counseled Dennis in ways he could recognize and overcome his obsessive behaviors. "Whenever you start to feel yourself becoming preoccupied, Dennis, the most important thing to do is relax. Remind yourself that there is a part of your brain that is stuck and that relaxing will help it get unstuck. Try not to get fooled into worrying about the devil. You need to trust your minister, your parents, and me that the devil is not the problem. The gear shift in your brain is the problem; it is getting stuck when you think about the devil." With the combination of a carefully monitored regimen of Zoloft and weekly counseling, Dennis improved dramatically and was able to lead a happy, healthy life.

Getting Help

What should you do if you decide your son or daughter might be suffering from one of the mental illnesses I have described or from some other problem that seems serious? To begin, ask around and get recommendations from the people you trust. School counselors, social workers, teachers, administrators, youth workers, and clergy make referrals all the time, so they get to know the competent professionals.

Be prepared to be assertive and involved. Although there are many caring professionals out there, the mental health services system for adolescents does not work smoothly or well. Getting quality care is not easy, especially when financial resources are very limited. Treating adolescents with serious mental health problems is challenging; it can be costly and take a lot of time.

With the passage of the Mental Health Parity and Addiction Equity Act of 2008 (MHPAEA) by the federal government, many insurance companies that offer mental health or substance abuse coverage are required to provide the same level of coverage that they do for other medical treatment.

The most common challenge from insurers or HMOs is the unofficial "denial of care," based on whether it is judged that the service is "medically necessary." Psychologists or psychiatrists who treat adolescents are often approved to provide only a small number of sessions, sometimes as few as three. I know from personal experience that it often takes more than three sessions just to establish enough trust so that a teen will begin to tell you what's really going on.

Some years ago I counseled Heather, a depressed fifteen-year-old girl. During the initial sessions I asked her all the standard screening questions, including whether she had ever been physically or sexually abused. She reported a normal childhood with an exceptionally loving and involved family. It wasn't until several months later that she trusted me enough to admit her father had been sexually abusing her on a regular basis for more than three years. In between sobs she told me her younger sister had revealed to Heather that she, too, was an incest victim. When the police investigation was concluded they discovered that still another sister, only nine years old, had also been victimized. I don't think Heather would have ever had the courage to reveal the real cause of her depression if we had had only three sessions to talk.

As the system now stands, after a session, a therapist has to prove to the payor or case manager that more care is required, medically necessary, *and* that improvement can be made. The therapist has to walk a thin line in these reviews and demonstrate that the problem is serious enough to warrant additional care while simultaneously showing that progress can be made very quickly so that the client is not judged to be "resistant." The reviews at insurance companies and HMOs are performed by "case managers" or "peer reviewers." In nearly every case that I have been involved in, these people have never met the adolescent I am treating.

This review system is in place to "improve the quality of care." In some instances that is a thinly veiled euphemism for saving the insurer money. Case reviewers are hired to keep costs down; if they approve too much care, they lose their jobs. I know professionals who did this day in and day out until they could no longer stand saying no for a living. I bumped into one at a mental health conference. Notoriously difficult to deal with, Randy was a mental health case manager for a managed care organization. He had denied my requests for additional sessions with teenage clients on more than one occasion. It is not wise for a psychologist to be identified as a "problem" within this large and powerful company that controls referrals and authorizations, but I had expressed frustration over his decisions, especially when they seemed unreasonable.

When I saw Randy that morning, he told me he had left his position. While explaining his decision, he also gave me a round-about apology. "My job was to say no. I was pretty good at it, as you remember. I could apply the standards and hold the line as well as anyone in the utilization review department. But that all changed when we discovered my daughter had become addicted to alcohol and pot. I knew how to manipulate the system to get her the help she needed. No one said no to us. And from then on it was harder to deny care for kids just like my daughter."

Gaining access to mental health care is not the only challenge you may face as a parent. For adolescents whose mental health problems cause them to act out, there is another danger. If their behavior gets them into legal trouble, then the responsibility to pay for mental health care shifts to the government, and the managed care company or insurance company is off the hook. I have had a few cases where an insurance company refused to pay for care, so the teen's behavior deteriorated till he got into legal trouble. At that point his care became the financial responsibility of the government. When the health care insurers duck their responsibility, they not only impose undue pain to the adolescent and his family but they also contribute to a trail of legal entanglements for the teen that may shadow him for years.

Another precarious scenario for troubled adolescents is a quick resort to medication. The present system forces many psychiatrists to become little more than medication dispensers without much time for psychotherapy. Medication can be an effective tool in helping a mentally ill adolescent, but it should never be used as a quick reaction to save money on therapy.

Because the mental health system is so frustrating and ineffective, many skilled and dedicated professionals have left the field. Good programs have closed because they did not have enough funding to provide safe, competent care for teens. In most areas of the country there is a serious shortage of services and long waiting lists. I am not explaining this to scare and discourage parents whose children are seriously ill, but to let you know how it works and why it's so crucial to be assertive and involved. You can get good care from the mental health system for your adolescent if you know how to avoid its various pitfalls. Here's how.

1. Read your insurance policy carefully to find out exactly what your mental health and chemical dependency benefits are. They may be described in a separate section of your policy.

2. Read your insurance policy or member handbook to determine the procedures for accessing care. The procedures may be different from the benefits. For example, your policy may state that you are entitled to thirty outpatient visits per year. The procedures, however, may state that all visits must be authorized in advance or reauthorized after every three visits.

3. Find out which providers are covered by your plan and what the financial penalties are if you see a professional outside the plan's network.

4. Find out the procedures for securing a second opinion and for getting a referral outside the plan in case one is needed.

5. Get recommendations for the best professionals you can use under your plan's benefits and procedures. Educators, clergy, and health care professionals can be helpful. Other parents can also be good sources for advice.

6. Once you begin to receive care don't be afraid to ask questions about treatment approaches, medications, referral options, and second opinions.

7. If you think you are not getting adequate care, contact the patient representative at the health plan. Share your concerns and find out your options.

8. I hope you never have to resort to them, but many states now have offices for health care complaints in either the department of health or the attorney general's office.

Serious brain problems aren't issues parents can handle on their own. Many parents of adolescents feel like they need outside help at some point. That's why it is important to pay attention. As parents we need to look out for the clues and seek help when we are in over our heads.

The disorders I have described in this chapter are some of the most common, but they are by no means the only mental health disorders that afflict adolescents. If you are concerned about the mental health of your teen, do not ignore what you are seeing, even if the patterns you are noticing do not fit onto any of the lists of symptoms in the previous pages. If you suspect something is seriously wrong, you may need help from a professional to figure out what your adolescent's problem is—or just to allay your fears.

DO

✓ Look for a pattern of symptoms that persist for a matter of months if you are concerned that your son or daughter has a mental health problem.

✓ If you're worried, seek advice from a teacher, counselor, coach, or other adult who knows your son or daughter.

✓ Get recommendations from people you can trust for the professionals or programs that are competent and caring.

✓ If you need professional help, find out exactly what your insurance policy covers and how the system works. Ask as many questions as you need to find out what your options and rights as a parent are.

✓ Get the best help possible for your son or daughter. If your health plan restricts you to a designated network, get recommendations about the professionals in the network. In addition, find out how to get approvals for care outside the network, even if you have to pay more.

✓ Be open to recommendations about medications, but make sure you learn about any side effects.

✓ Get help for yourself. There are often support groups for parents and siblings of mentally ill teens. They can provide information and emotional support to help you get through difficult times.

DON'T

✗ Don't ignore signs and symptoms of serious mental illness. Just like physical disease, diseases of the brain can strike any family.

✗ Don't panic. Tremendous strides have been made in recent years. I have seen adolescents so incapacitated by depression that they could not lift their heads return to a happy, productive life in a matter of months.

✗ Don't hesitate to ask professionals as many questions as are necessary to understand both the problem and the treatment.

✗ Don't accept care from a professional without appropriate credentials to work with adolescents.

✗ Don't accept care from a professional who seems rushed, appears unfamiliar with your child's case, doesn't address your concerns, or doesn't communicate well.

✗ Don't accept a prescription for medication without asking questions about side effects and effectiveness. Tinkering with the chemistry of the brain, always a serious step, is still as much an art as it is a science.

✗ Don't accept a medication-only treatment plan for an adolescent. The research is clear that medication with some form of counseling is far superior to medication alone. The medication may correct a chemical imbalance in the brain, but it does not teach teens coping skills or rewire the brain for new behaviors.

✗ Don't ever give up hope for a mentally ill adolescent.

What do I want to continue?

_____

_____

_____

What do I want to change?

_____

_____

_____

THIRTEEN

Friends, Peers, and Identity

Yvonne was worried about her only child, thirteen-year-old Jody. Her daughter's transformation into an adolescent was confusing and scary to Yvonne, partly because she lacked a frame of reference for understanding Jody. Yvonne had grown up as an only child and none of her friends had children as old as Jody. "I'm a single parent and I'm clueless about teenagers," Yvonne told me. "I don't know whether Jody is being normal or we're headed for trouble."

Jody was born when Yvonne was twenty and a sophomore in college. Yvonne never married Jody's father, and despite his assurances of support, he quickly disappeared from the scene. Her parents helped out financially and provided childcare so she could finish her degree in nursing. Yvonne and Jody had always been close. "My life revolved around my job at the hospital and Jody. She was a great kid. She was easygoing and never gave me any trouble. We spent hours and hours together and could talk about anything. She's always done well in school, has had a lot of friends, and has always been a pretty happy kid."

When I asked Yvonne if that was still the case, she told me that she had just been to teacher conferences and that Jody's teachers had raved about her. "Her grades are good, she's popular with her peers, and she's responsible." After a pause she asked the obvious question: "So you're probably wondering why I'm worried, right?" Before I could respond, Yvonne began to tell me.

"I can sense that Jody is pulling away. She's much moodier than ever, and when I ask her about her day, all I get are one-word answers. We hardly ever go out together anymore because she always wants to be with her friends. She used to ask for my advice, and now she rolls her eyes if I make a suggestion about anything." Yvonne went on to describe some pretty typical young adolescent behaviors, so when she finished, I told her that I wasn't hearing anything that signaled a serious problem and explained that physical changes in Jody's brain were leading to normal changes in her behavior. But Yvonne, still worried, said, "What's going on in her brain doesn't explain why she doesn't want to talk with me anymore." Yvonne paused, and when she spoke again, I saw there were tears in her eyes. "She told me last week that she was embarrassed by me. What does her brain have to do with that?"

Yvonne was right. Although the brain explains many of the changes during adolescence, it doesn't speak to all of the behavior typical of teens. Explaining adolescence solely in terms of neurons, hormones, and neurotransmitters is like describing the sun solely in the vocabulary of chemical reactions and thermonuclear events: it's accurate but incomplete. Stepping back from neuroscience, we need to understand the psychological and social dimensions of adolescence in order for you to better understand teens.

The Parent Survival Kit: Friends, Peers, and Identity

Brain development does not completely account for why teens act the way they do. Every parent needs to be aware of the larger context that influences teens' behavior. This kit helps you determine if you bear in mind the psychological and social hurdles that adolescents must leap over on their way to adulthood.

PARENT SURVIVAL KIT

Friends, Peers, and Identity

Yes No

☐ ☐ 1. I was self-conscious during my own teen years.

☐ ☐ 2. I look to other adults, not my kids, for emotional support.

☐ ☐ 3. My son or daughter has a circle of close friends.

☐ ☐   4. I let my kids question and challenge my values because I know that's how they shape and form their own.

☐ ☐   5. I know who my adolescent's friends are.

☐ ☐   6. My teenagers' school has a good bullying-prevention program.

☐ ☐   7. I talk to my teenager about peer pressure and the need for him to make his own decisions.

☐ ☐   8. In our family, teens are encouraged to express their opinions.

☐ ☐   9. I can say no to my teen on something I think is important even if "all the other kids are doing it."

☐ ☐ 10. I don't take it personally when my teenager seems embarrassed by me.

If you answered yes to the items in this kit, you are prepared to help your teen handle the complex psychological and social world he or she lives in.

Four Major Changes

There are at least four dramatic changes that take place during adolescence:

1. rapid physical changes such as growth spurts, voice changes, hair growth, skin problems, the development of sexual organs, and breast development in girls;
2. changes in both the intensity and volatility of emotions;
3. the shift of influence from parents to peers;
4. the search for identity—the need to answer the questions "Who am I?" and "Who do I want to be?"

While brain science can shed light on a lot of adolescent behavior, we need to consider a boy's or girl's reactions to these changes as well. In this chapter we will consider normal psychological reactions to these four changes.

Reactions to Physical Changes

During my years as a high school teacher and coach I was always amazed at the changes that would occur over the summer months for some of my younger students. I remember one boy who shot up five inches between his freshman and sophomore years. When I remarked on how much he had grown he seemed proud. He told me that he had to get all new clothes, and he bragged that he was now able to look down at the top of his mother's head for the first time in his life. The effects of a growth spurt on a teen's state of mind are powerful. While often proud of the changes, adolescents are also frequently preoccupied or embarrassed about them. So much rapid physical change leads to one of the common psychological traits of adolescents: they are very conscious of how they look. Physical appearance is a big deal, and kids who never combed their hair or cared a whit for what they wore when they were young will lock themselves in the bathroom to check themselves out for what seems like hours when they hit puberty. Typical adolescents can tell you at any one time exactly how many pimples they have. How do they know? They count them.

In my early years of teaching I had an eight a.m. homeroom for ninth-graders. During the early cold snaps of a Minnesota winter, when the bottoms of the thermometers would drop out, I watched in amazement as student after student came into the room with their heads encased in helmets of ice. They had gotten up, taken a shower, and then walked to school in twenty-degrees-below-zero weather.

I asked them, "Why don't you guys wear hats?"

They looked at me like I was from Mars. "What, are you nuts? That's not cool." What was most important was how they looked!

Adolescents' preoccupation with their physical appearance even shows up in the nicknames they give one another. I remember one morning my students filed in while I was reading something at my desk. As one entered, he yelled across the room to his friend, "Hey, Pinhead."

I thought to myself, "Who the heck is Pinhead?" As soon as I looked up, I immediately realized who Pinhead was. It was obvious.

There was a boy in the class whose head kind of came to a point. I had never noticed the shape of the boy's head before, but his classmates had. Hence the nickname. Another one of the students in that same class was nicknamed Flopper. The reason? His ears stuck out.

The pain that this emphasis on physical appearance causes for the seriously overweight adolescent, or the kid with severe acne, or the kid who enters puberty two years before her peers or two years after is acute. If this attention progresses to public humiliation or bullying, parents, teachers, and school administrators need to intervene. The adolescent preoccupation with physical appearance, while completely natural, can make life very difficult even for kids who, to adult eyes, look absolutely normal. Many schools have started anti-bullying programs, dealing with school climate and behavior expectations, and have established intervention procedures.

Robert was a student at the high school where I was a counselor. His physical development was years behind his peers'. All his classmates were well into their growth spurts by ninth or tenth grade, so while the other boys began to look more like men, Robert continued to look like a boy. Wisecracks about Robert's small size or his lack of development began to hurt. He didn't take showers after gym class to avoid jokes about his lack of sexual development. He became more sensitive as the physical gap between him and his peers widened. While his classmates might have considered their comments as kidding, Robert felt embarrassed and humiliated by their teasing. Eventually he began to lash out in response, but this only served to encourage some of the boys to have more fun at Robert's expense. Mocking Robert became a cruel sport for a group of six classmates. "Oh, look! Little Robert is going to get mad. We'd better watch out," they'd whine as they pushed him into lockers.

Robert dreaded going to school and faked feeling sick so he could stay home. When his parents were finally able to get him to tell them what was going on, he told them he couldn't stand school and hated the boys who took pleasure in making fun of him. He also told them he hated his body and wished he were dead. His parents contacted Robert's homeroom teacher, who suggested that they meet with me.

The four of us got together after school the next day, and Robert described what was happening. Within minutes Robert was crying, and his parents were livid that their son was being harassed. "I can understand why you're so upset," I said as I tried to comfort Robert and calm down his parents. "Being hassled like this is unfair and wrong. But I think I have some suggestions that might help." I asked Robert if he had any friends in his classes. He said that he did. Then I asked him how many kids were teasing him. "Probably about five or six do most of it," was Robert's answer.

"Robert, here's what I want you to do. Ignore the guys who are harassing you. Sometimes I recommend that people share their feelings with others, but not in this case. Bullies like these guys want to hurt your feelings. So if you let them see that you're upset, they'll know they're winning. Pretend you're not bothered. If you want to scream or cry, come down here and do it, but don't let them see that they're getting to you. It's not as much fun to tease someone who doesn't react. When you're not in class, stay with the kids who are your friends. Make plans to have lunch together. Try not to be alone when any of these guys are around."

Robert was doubtful this strategy was going to work. "These guys are such jerks. They won't stop."

"I don't know if they will or not, Robert, but it's worth a try. Check in with me twice a week for the next couple of weeks to see how things are going." Robert stopped by my office regularly and reported that he was doing what I suggested, but things were not improving. "Those idiots haven't let up at all," he told me. I told Robert it was time for Plan B. "What's Plan B?" he wanted to know.

"Robert, I want you to trust me to give me the names of the boys who are harassing you the most. I promise that I will not make things worse for you. You need to know that you are not alone in this." Robert gave me their names. That evening I made six phone calls. I talked to a parent of each boy on the list, and the conversation went like this: "Hello, this is Mr. Walsh, the counselor at the high school. I want to talk to you about your son to head off some trouble before it gets bigger. I know that your son has been involved in harassing and teasing a student named Robert. I don't want to get into all the details. I know it's happening and it needs to stop. I'd like you to talk to your son now and get him to stop. Otherwise I will have to get the administration involved and it will become a bigger deal." I got a variety of responses from those phone calls. Some appreciated the heads-up while others were defensive and wanted to know what evidence I had that their son was involved. This was my response to the second group: "I could get the assistant principal involved, but I'm trying to head this off before it gets even more serious. If you want to question all this, then we can schedule a meeting, but I will involve the assistant principal. I think the wiser thing to do is for you to tell your son that I called. Tell him that if he's not harassing Robert, then there's no problem. If he is, then he needs to stop." I have no idea what conversations took place in those homes that night, but I do know that I did not need to schedule any conferences with the assistant principal, and, more importantly, the harassment stopped. Robert and I met for several more weeks, but pretty soon he was on his way and a painful episode was starting to become history.

Sensitivity about physical appearance is not the only psychological reaction to the dramatic growth and changes taking place during adolescence. Another teen reaction is self-consciousness about behavior. There is no such thing as a subtle mistake in the world of adolescents. The poor student who stumbles and drops a lunch tray would probably like to crawl under a carpet somewhere, while the entire cafeteria erupts in shouts and laughter. Extremely conscious of how he is perceived by others, he suffers punishing attention from the other teens. When a teacher asks a question in class, the students have to decide two things before raising their hands. The first is "Do I know the answer?" The second, and much more important, is "What will the other kids in the class think?" Sometimes, teachers feel like they're going crazy. They know their students know the answers because they've been over the material before. The problem is that many adolescents don't raise their hands even when they know the answer because they are afraid they will lose face in front of the other students.

The Bullied Brain

Ezra, age fourteen, came home crying, shaking, and barely able to speak. "What happened?" his mother screamed. Between sobs he was finally able to tell his mother about the terrifying ordeal he had endured on the way home from school.

"Three kids jumped me and forced me into a Porta Potty at the park," he explained. "They wouldn't let me out, beat on the walls, and told me they were going to shove my head into the tank. I think they would have but they ran when a jogger came along."

"How long were you in there?" his mother asked.

"I don't know. Ten, fifteen minutes, maybe," Ezra replied.

"Do you know the boys?" she asked as she hugged her son.

"Yeah," he answered. "They're a year ahead of me in school and have been picking on me since school started in September. They never let up. They take my books, call me a faggot, and keep threatening me." He started to cry again as he added, "Today was the worst."

"Why haven't you told me or your father about this before?" she asked.

"I was afraid you'd call the school and that would make things worse. They'd really go after me if they knew I snitched on them."

While the teasing and harassment Robert endured was painful, Ezra's torture was a clear case of bullying. Incidents like Ezra's have been getting a lot of attention lately. And well they should. Even though bullying has been going on for many generations we are learning just how devastating its effects can be. Bullying has three ingredients, and Ezra experienced all three. First, bullying involves actions that are clearly intended to hurt. Second, the actions are repeated over time. Third, the bullies have a different "status." In Ezra's case the students were older, but popularity, socioeconomic class, or other factors can determine status as well.

Bullies usually target kids who are different in some way from dominant groups. Of course, there are many ways to be different. Ezra is gay. Other victims might be handicapped, belong to a minority racial or ethnic group, or practice a different religion. While

Ezra's tormentors physically attacked him, bullies can make life miserable in other ways as well. If they think that physical attacks might get them into trouble, they can resort to threats, insults, or ridicule. Their victims endure being ignored, excluded, insulted, and laughed at.

As we saw in chapter 10, Internet technology provides bullies with a new array of weapons. Many communities are battling an epidemic of cyberbullying, a word that wasn't even in my vocabulary when I wrote the first edition of this book. Instead of waiting by the door after school, cyberbullies do their damage via text messages, e-mails, and social media posts from a remote location. Cyberbullies send insults and threats electronically, often many of them. They circulate humiliating pictures or post demeaning descriptions on Web sites. Victims, often taunted on home computers or cell phones, feel there is no escape from their tormentors. Research shows that three times as many kids are cyberbullied as are bullied face-to-face.

Some bullying tragedies make national headlines. It turned out, for example, that Eric Harris and Dylan Klebold, the Columbine High School murderers, had suffered years of bullying before they turned to their murderous rampage. In 2010 Massachusetts teenager Phoebe Prince committed suicide after older students victimized her for months. Ezra's story, however, won't make cable news; nor will the bullying episodes that make 160,000 kids skip school every day. Brain science, however, is showing us how serious and long-term the damage can be. Studies reveal that there are long-lasting chemical and structural brain changes that account for the cognitive and emotional damage that can be as severe as the harm done by child abuse.

Canadian psychologist Tracy Vaillancourt, for example, reports that levels of the stress hormone cortisol are higher in bullied boys, meaning that their stress reaction system is in constant overdrive. Curiously, cortisol levels are below normal for bullied girls, perhaps meaning that their stress response systems are compromised.

Harvard scientist Martin Teicher scanned the brains of bullying victims and found significant shrinkage in the corpus callosum, the brain tissue connecting the left and right hemispheres. This makes it difficult for victims to process what is happening around them and to respond appropriately.

The amygdala is the brain's alarm center. When it is repeatedly activated the brain is in a constant state of arousal. It's as if the radar is finely tuned, always ready to pick up the slightest hint of a threat. It is very difficult to concentrate, remember, and learn when the brain is in survival mode, always scanning for danger.

These brain changes are the explanation for the symptoms bullying victims have: avoidance behaviors, anxiety, depression, appetite and sleep problems, feelings of helplessness, and suicidal thoughts. Bullying also causes cognitive problems including impaired memory, attention, and concentration. It's hard for the bullied brain to learn when it's always in a state of high alert, prepared for the next attack. Bullying victims and PTSD sufferers have a lot in common. The hypersensitivity makes it very hard to relax and enjoy activities.

The Power of Bystanders to Prevent Bullying

On a recent cold February evening I walked into Coon Rapids High School in suburban Minneapolis. I had accepted an invitation from a group of students and parents to talk about the "Bullied Brain." I didn't realize how much I would learn from these teenagers about bullying prevention before the night was over. Coon Rapids is one of five high schools in the Anoka Hennepin District, the second largest in Minnesota. Unfortunately the district had been in the news for the previous two years because of a rash of student suicides linked to bullying. While the district's administrators worked to implement prevention training and policies, students decided to take matters into their own hands. With social worker Donna McDonald as a mentor the teens combed through the bullying prevention research and discovered that empowered bystanders can create a safe school environment more effectively than teachers and principals. The event that evening was the kick-off for their "Obliviate the Hate" campaign. Their goal was to empower every student in their school with the knowledge and strategies to stop bullying dead in its tracks.

The students hung posters in school hallways about the bully-ing triad: the bully, the victim, and the bystanders. They wanted their peers to know that 85 percent of bullying happens with wit-nesses, 90 percent of whom never intervene. Some actually join in the bullying while others stay silent and keep out of the way. The joiners want to be part of the "in crowd," especially if the bully is popular. The quiet bystanders don't think their intervention will do any good or else they're afraid that they'll become the next targets if they speak up.

The "Obliviate the Hate" posters also promoted practical strate-gies that ranged from safe to courageous. On the safe end of the spectrum were suggestions like "Never egg on, laugh, or encourage the bully in any way," and "Walk away and make it clear that it's not cool." They also let students know it was okay to make an anony-mous report to a teacher or other adult. The courageous options included speaking up with "Knock it off," or "That's not funny."

A week later I was describing the student campaign to a friend who teaches at Cretin-Derham Hall High School in Saint Paul. He smiled and said, "I'm not surprised. We always thought our best bullying prevention program ever was Joe Mauer."

"What do you mean?" I asked. I knew that Joe Mauer, the future Hall of Fame catcher for the Minnesota Twins baseball team, had attended Cretin-Derham, but I couldn't figure out how he was con-nected to bullying prevention. My friend explained what he meant.

"Joe was a very popular guy in high school," my friend began. "The other students looked up to him because he was one of the most highly recruited athletes in the country. Although he chose baseball after being drafted by the Twins he also had football schol-arship offers from dozens of major college programs. When Joe would see some kids picking on others he'd walk up and calmly tell them to knock it off. When a six-foot-four superathlete told them to stop, they did."

"Joe Mauer, model bystander," I said.

Brain science lends even more urgency to confronting the scourge of bullying. There are studies suggesting that the brain changes are long-term and therefore can create emotional scars that last for a lifetime. Here are some things parents can do:

1. Let your children know that if they are victims, they should tell adults right away.
2. If your teen is a bullying victim, get involved by contacting the bully's parents, school, or, if needed, law enforcement.
3. Make sure your children and teens know any type of bullying is unacceptable behavior.
4. Check with your school to see if they have a bullying-prevention policy that they follow and enforce.
5. Encourage your school to provide bullying-prevention training for students, teachers, and staff.
6. Avoid peer mediation as a strategy to resolve bullying. While it is used in many schools, research now shows that it aggravates rather than prevents bullying.
7. Help your teens understand the power they have as "bystanders" to prevent bullying.

Reactions to Emotional Changes

Strong emotions are not exclusive to adolescents, of course. Children also experience all sorts of emotions, many of which are very raw. But because of the changes in the adolescent brain, new emotions like sexual desire, jealousy, and territoriality emerge. In addition familiar feelings like anger and sadness are more intense than ever. The result is emotional volatility and ambivalence. We discussed the volatility in earlier chapters but not the ambivalence. It is not unusual for an adolescent to have contradictory feelings at the same time, along these lines: "Mom, I want you to stop treating me like a kid, but please don't forget to tuck me in." Or "Get out of my life, but can you can give me money to go to a movie with my friends?"

Joan and Gary, who were having trouble getting along with their teenage children, told me about a painful scene one evening when their eighteen-year-old daughter had just returned from college for her first visit home at Thanksgiving. Complaining to her parents that she felt hemmed in by them after having so much freedom at college, she also made it clear that she couldn't wait to get back. In the same conversation, however, she was on the verge of tears about the pain she felt when she discovered that her mother had already moved a sewing machine into her bedroom. She seemed genuinely distraught. Her parents didn't know what to make of this. I told them not to expect consistency in adolescent emotions, even when that adolescent is in college.

The confusion caused by emotional ambivalence is often accompanied by dramatic fluctuations in feelings. An adolescent can be on top of the world at nine a.m., in the dumps at nine thirty, euphoric at ten a.m., and practically drowning at ten thirty—all depending on who did or did not say hello during passing time in the high school hallway. Once again, it is important to remember that these emotions are often as confusing for the adolescent as they are for those of us trying to make sense of the emotional fireworks on display.

Greg had always been what I call a "hot reactor." I use that term to describe someone who tends to react quickly and strongly. You never had to wonder if Greg was happy, sad, or angry. He would always let you know it in no uncertain terms. That natural tendency became exaggerated when Greg hit the seventh grade. Unfortunately, however, the range of emotions he displayed at home shrank. He saved happy and sad for his friends, while dispensing anger liberally with his parents and sisters. It seemed that the least little thing would set him off. Other family members all felt like they had to walk on eggshells whenever Greg was around. Greg's mother, Maria, was commiserating with her sister one day. A single parent, Ginger had kids who were a couple of years older; she had done some counseling with me when her son was about Greg's age and suggested that some brief counseling with me might be helpful.

I spent some time with Greg and his parents and then with Greg alone. My diagnosis after a couple of sessions was "early adolescence." There weren't any deep-seated issues between Greg and his parents, and he didn't have any serious underlying problem that I could detect. He was a hot reactor in the throes of puberty. When I asked him what he thought of his parents, he responded that they were "okay, but they just bug me." When I asked him why, he said that he didn't know. "I don't know why, they just do."

I told Greg and his parents about the changes in the adolescent brain, especially the part about the amygdala being so active in boys' brains. Greg said that this actually made a lot of sense to him. "I can get in a bad mood so quickly, and a lot of times, I don't even know why." He looked at his mother. "Sometimes when you start talking, I just want to tell you to be quiet."

Greg's mother looked hurt. "Why?" she asked.

I took Greg off the hook. "He doesn't know why, Maria. It's not something you're doing. It's his darn amygdala acting up. You're not a bad mom, and Greg's not a bad kid. It's part of growing up." Then I told them how to get through it. I told his parents to quit treating Greg with kid gloves. "Relax, but adjust your expectations. Give Greg some slack and don't expect him to be all happy around the family. Just consider this an extended period of grouchiness. This doesn't mean, however, that you should accept disrespect." Then I turned to Greg. "Being grumpy doesn't give you an excuse to treat your parents or sisters like dirt." I suggested that the three of them make a deal. I asked Greg's parents to let him be grumpy for a couple of years. Then I told Greg that his part of the deal was to treat the people in his family civilly, even when he felt grumpy. They all agreed. That was the last counseling session we had, but it wasn't the last time we talked. Since we shop at the same grocery store, about once a year we see one another and say a quick hello. Not too long ago Greg and his parents were all behind me in the checkout lane. Greg is now a senior in high school, and from the relaxed joking he was doing with his parents, I could see that they had all survived the emotional fireworks of early adolescence.

The Shift of Influence from Parents to Peers

Adolescents are keenly aware that they are no longer kids, and they don't want to be treated like children. Although they are still one big step away from adulthood, many of them feel as if they're already there. Two common reactions to this are withdrawal from parents and an emphasis on the importance of peers. Teenagers are frequently embarrassed by their parents. At the high school where I taught we had very good attendance at parent conferences, which were held in the evening, and the students were encouraged to come to the conferences with their parents. Together, they would go around and visit the teachers in their classrooms. As the families wandered the halls, many of the students would walk ten feet behind or ten feet in front of their parents. Their body language screamed, *I don't know who these people are. They just wandered in with me.*

When my daughter, Erin, was in high school, but before she got her driver's license, I often drove her and her friends to different events—hockey practice, school plays, stuff like that. Trying to be friendly, I often joined their conversations when I thought it appropriate. One evening Erin got very quiet after the last of her friends had been dropped off. Finally, she turned to me and said, "Dad, when you drive us somewhere, could you do me a favor?"

"What?"

"Please be quiet."

"Why, Erin?"

"Because you say such dumb things."

It stung, but I tried to bear in mind what was really going on. A typical adolescent, Erin was predictably embarrassed by her parent. No matter how respectful, friendly, or even cool I thought I was being, she would continue to be mortified if I opened my mouth.

Teenagers often don't want to go places or do things with their parents. When they're little, their parents decide so many things for them. They decide where they're going to live, what school to attend, what time they go to bed, and what they're going to eat for dinner. It's not surprising that as teens leave childhood, they need to put some distance between themselves and their parents. Part of growing up, after all, is starting to make some of one's own decisions. Pulling away from parents—even refusing to do what they want—is the way teens begin to exercise their own judgment.

As adolescents pull away from their parents, peers become more important. Consider this analogy. If by some trick of magic you were instantly transported to a distant village in a foreign country with a culture and customs very different from your own, what would you do? You don't know the customs—how to act, what's important and what's unremarkable. So you would have to take your cues on how to act from the villagers around you. That is essentially what adolescents are doing. As they enter puberty, they are transported to a new world and have to discover how they fit into it. They, along with their peers, are leaving the world of childhood. In unfamiliar terrain, they don't know exactly how to act. So what do they do? They look to the other people in this new territory with them—their peers.

There is, of course, irony in this. While adolescents will voice their desire for independence, they are often tightly controlled by the norms of their peer groups when it comes to dress, language, and customs. Teenagers place a tremendous amount of importance on fitting in. The landscape is new to them and they are unsure of themselves. All of us are a bit unsure of ourselves in a new situation. If you want proof of the importance of fitting in to adolescents, just watch any TV ad aimed at their age group. Every one of these ads suggests that by buying a certain product, teens will be liked by their peers. Madison Avenue knows that fitting in is psychologically crucial for adolescents. That's why they take dead aim for that nerve when targeting preteens and teenagers.

Adolescents will also take many more risks when they have an audience of peers. A Duke University psychologist and his team demonstrated this with a clever experiment. He recruited teenagers, college students, and young adults to take part in simulated car races while fMRI machines recorded their brain activity. Taking calculated risks, like racing through yellow traffic lights, was encouraged since the goal was to complete the racecourse as fast as possible. Taking foolish risks, on the other hand, caused accidents, which resulted in serious penalties. All three groups performed the same in the first round when they played alone. In the next round, however, the psychologists brought in the participants' friends to watch the action. While the college students and adults didn't alter their driving style, the teenagers raced through more yellow lights and took more ill-advised chances than they had in round one. They ended up in more crashes and were assessed more penalties. The fMRI scans also showed significant differences in the teen brains when their peers were watching. The reward centers of their brains, the ventral striatums, lit up in more brilliant colors when their peers were watching than when they played without an audience. Showing off for their friends gave them a bigger reward than winning the race.

While peer pressure is inevitable, it can also create some real dilemmas. I had a recent conversation with a mother and father about the pressure they were under to let their sixteen-year-old daughter go to Mexico over spring break without any adult supervision. "Kimberly is insisting that we let her go," they explained. "If you can believe it, Dr. Walsh, this has become a tradition at her school. All her friends are going."

"I'm not surprised at all," I told them. "I know that it is common for many high school kids to go in groups to sunny places over spring break. Do you want her to go?" I asked.

Their immediate response was an emphatic no.

"Then why are you even considering saying yes?" was my reply.

"All the kids are doing it. We're afraid that Kim will feel so left out if she's the only one who can't go. She's worked hard this year and we want to trust her."

I asked them if they wanted my unvarnished opinion about high school students going on unchaperoned trips. They said yes, so I told them. "I think this is nuts. I've talked with enough kids to know what happens on these trips: sex, drinking, and drugs. Parents who think otherwise have their heads in the sand. I know a lot of parents who have let their kids go, but I have yet to meet a single one who thought it was a good idea. I've got kids so I know how hard this can be for parents. Teens can really exert pressure. What's troubling is that parents are caving in to the peer pressure just like their teenagers are."

"So what do we do?" they asked.

"First of all, do you agree with what I just said?"

The mother spoke first. "Yes, I've been worried about this since last year when I heard about juniors going to Mexico alone. I was hoping Kimberly wouldn't want to go, but sure enough she started talking about it before Thanksgiving, for Pete's sake. I just wish the whole thing would go away."

"What do you think you *should* do?" I asked.

"Say no," they both said.

"Then here's what I think you should do. Call some of the other parents. I can almost guarantee you that they aren't comfortable with the plan either, even if they've already said yes. See if you can get some other parents to hold the line with you. You might even consider the possibility of arranging an alternative trip for the kids with adult supervision. Then tell Kimberly right away while spring break is still weeks away. If you wait until the last minute, it will be harder."

"I just dread this," Kimberly's father said as he shook his head slowly. "She is going to go ballistic."

"This is one of the toughest parts of parenting teenagers," I agreed. "You might want to say something like this: 'Kim, I don't expect you to agree with this, but we've decided that we are not going to let you go to Mexico over spring break. We've thought a lot about this. We know how hard you've worked and we'd like you to have some kind of reward. We'll work with you to come up with something that we can afford and agree with. But you can't go to Mexico.'"

Two weeks later I got a call from Kimberly's mom. She told me that I was right about the other parents. None of them was comfortable with the idea of their kid in Mexico without supervision. The night they told Kim she couldn't go was pretty rough. "There was a lot of crying and complaining," she said. "But it actually blew over more quickly than we expected. It helped when she found out some of her friends couldn't go either."

Peer pressure is inevitable and exerts a lot of force on teens. Parents need to make sure they don't become victims of peer pressure themselves.

The Search for Identity

Erik Erikson, the groundbreaking developmental psychologist, says that the main psychological task of adolescence is "identity formation." An adolescent's job is to figure out what kind of a person he or she wants to be.

When children are young, they will often echo the values and opinions of their parents. I remember one Sunday afternoon when my son Dan and I were watching a football game. The hometown team, the Vikings, was playing the rival Green Bay Packers. Dan, four years old, said that he wanted the Packers to win because he liked their uniforms. A second or two later he asked me whom I was rooting for. I told him I was rooting for the Vikings, the team in the white jerseys. After a couple of seconds of silence Dan said, "I'm for the Vikings, too." Typical for a young child, he wanted to be just like his dad.

When kids become adolescents, however, they need to begin to distinguish between their own values and the values of their parents. That means challenging, questioning, and reevaluating their family's values. A father complains about a certain type of music. His adolescent daughter is likely to think to herself, "Great. That's my favorite kind of music." A mother thinks a certain style of hair looks awful. Her adolescent son wonders, "How soon can I grow it to that length?"

Adolescents often make their own bodies testing grounds for controversy with hair, piercings, and tattoos. One summer evening when Monica and I were sitting on the couch in the family room reading, our then thirteen-year-old son Brian came in the back door. As he walked by the family room both of our jaws dropped when we saw his bright orange hair. It wasn't orange. It was *bright* orange. Luckily, we had the presence of mind to say nothing. We looked at each other and knew we were in agreement. This situation called for playing it very cool and casual. When Brian came into the room, we didn't say a word about his hair for a minute or so. We chatted about some other things. After a little while I said to Brian offhandedly, "Oh, Brian. I see you colored your hair. How do you like it?"

"I'm just trying it out."

I responded, "Oh, I think it looks cool."

Within twenty-four hours Brian's hair was back to its normal light blond shade. The orange washed out easily because Brian and his friends had colored his hair with Kool-Aid. I believe that if Monica and I had made a big deal out of it, it would have been bright orange for years.

Another way that adolescents form their identity is to experiment with different roles and different behaviors. Because the stakes in some situations can be high (for instance, with drugs, drinking, and sex), this experimentation can be very scary for parents.

Melanie was about fifteen when some of her friends started shoplifting. All through childhood and into adolescence she tried to follow the rules. She didn't like the idea of shoplifting—a cop had lectured her class in grade school that the cost of shoplifting gets passed on to everyone by the stores—but Melanie's friends kept insisting that she join them. One day half a dozen of them went to a shopping complex and drifted from store to store. They had planned their roles beforehand. Some of them would be lookouts while the others snatched up items. When they went into a little boutique selling fancy beads and other trinkets, it was Melanie's turn to steal. Making sure herself that the clerk's attention was elsewhere, she snatched up a ring made of a shimmering gray stone. Stuffing it into her pocket, she made a beeline for the door. When her friends met up with her a few moments later her, they scolded her for acting so suspiciously.

"You're going to get us caught. You've just got to act natural."

"How can I act naturally?" Melanie thought to herself. "I shouldn't be doing this." When she got home she sat in her room with the door closed for hours thinking about what she'd done, trying to sort through her emotions. When her mother called her down for dinner, she stayed in her room, saying she felt sick. She needed more time to think.

She knew she didn't like stealing, but she felt ashamed that it had scared her so much. It was, after all, just a stupid little ring. The store would probably never miss it. The other girls seemed to really get a kick out of shoplifting. Was she missing something? After turning it over in her head for a while, she decided that she would never shoplift again. She kept thinking about the little boutique with no other customers. She had probably helped it on its way to going out of business. It wasn't that she looked down on her friends for stealing from the store—they must have their reasons—but it just wasn't for her. She didn't want to be part of it.

When Melanie recounted this to me, I couldn't help feeling there was more to it.

"So you never shoplifted again?" I asked.

"Nope. Never. I really was glad I had tried it, though. To see what all the fuss was, I guess. But I knew it just wasn't for me."

"What about your friends?"

"Oh, they kept doing it. After a while, they got sick of beads and moved on to bigger items. They started selling stolen jeans out of the back of a car after school. Eventually they got caught. It was a pretty big deal. They had to do community service, I think. We weren't really very good friends by then, but I felt bad for them. It seemed like they'd never really stopped to think about what they were doing. They just thought it was so cool. I was just glad I'd had the sense to bow out when I did."

"Did you ever tell your parents?"

"My parents? No, I don't think I ever told them. Escaping that on my own seemed important, I suppose. I had that ring for years, though. It sat on a shelf in my room. Eventually it seemed shameful to keep it: whether it was because I felt bad about stealing or felt weak for feeling so bad, I don't know. Anyway, I gave it to a younger cousin of mine. She seemed very happy to have it, and that felt like a good ending to the whole thing."

Kids like Jody and Melanie are pretty normal teens; even normalcy is going to be hard for many parents because they still want to be as close to their children as they were when they were little. Yet teens need to get some distance. Letting teenagers find their own way can be scary, but they need space to become who they want to be. That's why it's important to think of new ways to maintain a connection. Not every teen dabbles in petty crime like Melanie on the passage through adolescence. However, every young person will go through growth and emotional change, departing from childhood in his or her own way. Some will sail through with only hints of a struggle with parents, peers, emotions, and experimentation. Others will wear their experiences on their sleeves. We adults need to help them through this journey to adulthood, whether the going is smooth or rough. How should you respond and parent in the most helpful ways? We'll see in the next chapter.

DO

✓ Expect your teenager to become sensitive to how he or she looks.

✓ Understand the importance of friends to your child.

✓ Be open to discussing values, even when your teens question yours or disagree. That challenging means they are starting to think for themselves, not that they are rejecting everything you think is important.

✓ Talk about peer pressure and how to manage it. Encourage your teen to make independent decisions.

✓ Explain to your teen the bystander power he or she has to prevent bullying.

DON'T

✗ Don't make derogatory remarks about your teenager's physical appearance.

✗ Don't be surprised if your adolescent becomes embarrassed by you. It's not you. She'll grow out of it.

✗ Don't put down your adolescent's friends. He will defend them. If you have worries about his peers, state them calmly.

✗ Don't base your parenting decisions on what every other teen is doing.

✗ Decide what you think is best.

✗ Don't sweat the small stuff. Save your relationship capital for the important issues.

What do I want to continue?

_____

_____

_____

What do I want to change?

_____

_____

_____

FOURTEEN

The Importance of Connection and Guidance

Close friends of ours, the godparents of our older son, gave us a plaque bearing this quotation: "There are two lasting bequests we can give our children. One is roots. The other is wings"—Anonymous.

Those words became etched in my mind over the years, and I thought of them many times as Monica and I raised our three children. The quotation applies to caring for a child of any age, but I think it takes on special significance for parents of adolescents. In a nutshell, it is the foundation for discerning how to be most helpful to our teenage children. Because they are leaving childhood, they are sprouting their wings and will soon make trial flights to leave the nest. They are not yet adults, though, so they still need help growing their own roots. Without the means to anchor themselves to the ground, they are in danger of being tossed around by whatever breeze life brings.

Maintaining the balance required to help adolescents grow wings *and* roots is more an art than a science. Every child is different, every family is different, and every situation is different. Even something that seems to apply to ninety-nine families may be wrong for the hundredth.

We are learning more and more every year about what is going on in kids' heads during adolescence, but knowledge is only power if we know what to do with it. One of the greatest benefits of the new adolescent brain research is the perspective it provides us adults. The challenges of adolescent moodiness, angry outbursts, messy rooms, impulsiveness, withdrawal, and defiance take on different meanings when we realize that they are all a normal part of necessary brain development. Knowing what's going on in there doesn't mean you should just roll over and wait until they turn twenty to correct and guide them, however. In fact the implications of adolescent brain research suggest that you need to stay more involved than many parents have been. At the same time, insights about the adolescent brain can help you avoid some of the traps that are so easy to fall into, the no-win arguments that can typify so many adult-adolescent interactions.

The Parent Survival Kit: Connection and Guidance

Staying connected with your teen while still maintaining the authority to guide him to responsible, healthy choices is an ongoing task that can feel like a high-wire balancing act. This kit focuses on what you need to maintain your balance.

PARENT SURVIVAL KIT

Connection and Guidance

Yes No

☐ ☐ 1. I know who my teen's teachers are.

☐ ☐ 2. Our family does things together.

☐ ☐ 3. I spend time with my kids every day and talk to them about how things are going.

☐ ☐ 4. I offer to help my kids with their homework when appropriate.

☐ ☐ 5. My adolescent son or daughter shares family chores and responsibilities.

☐ ☐ 6. Important family traditions are maintained.

☐ ☐ 7. We take family vacations.

☐ ☐ 8. My teen has other caring adults involved in his or her life.

☐ ☐ 9. I recognize and encourage my teen's strengths.

☐ ☐ 10. I have reasonable rules for my teen that I consistently enforce.

If you can agree with the statements in this kit, you are equipped to provide the crucial connection and guidance your teen needs. If you answer no to any, examine your priorities and look for ways to stay involved in your teen's life.

Connection

As a first-year teacher, I had a group of hard-to-handle fifteen-year-old boys in my English class. One day I was trying to get the class involved in a discussion, and because it wasn't going very well, I was getting very frustrated. One boy, Matt, had already tested my authority a couple of times, and I could feel my anger starting to rise as he sat there sneering at me. When he said something under his breath to his friend seated beside him, I reacted.

"What was that, Matt?"

"Nothing," he muttered.

"Don't tell me 'nothing'!" The volume and pitch of my voice were already rising. "I want to know what you said." By now I was standing next to his desk.

"I said this class stinks," Matt said as he looked up at me.

The battle was on. I was going to show this fifteen-year-old who was in charge.

"Then why don't you just get out of this class?" By now I was almost yelling.

Matt didn't move.

"Now!" I shouted.

He still didn't move. The whole class, with breath held, sat waiting to see who would win the power struggle. As Matt got up and sauntered out of the class at a glacier's pace I gave him a parting shot: "And you're not getting back in here until you apologize in front of the class."

This is a perfect example of how *not* to deal with a teenager. Matt was the student and I was the teacher, but when it came to dealing with a difficult adolescent, I got an F. In less than forty-five seconds I had fallen into more traps than I could keep track of. I lost my temper with a defiant adolescent. I escalated the situation instead of defusing it. I had been drawn into a power struggle, and worse still, tried to win in the open field: I challenged and embarrassed the boy in front of his peers.

Fortunately for me, I learned some lessons the hard way over the years while I taught, counseled, coached, and parented. A few years later I would have handled the situation with Matt differently. By then I had learned that a good teacher spots a kid like Matt early and sets about creating an alliance. I would have gotten to know Matt outside of class. Brief conversations in the hallway or after class can build a personal bond. That connection pays dividends in the classroom when things get rocky. If I had recruited Matt as an ally, then he would have been less likely to sabotage the class or openly defy my authority. If Matt had still been disruptive in the class, I would have talked to him afterward and used humor to bring him around. I might have said something like this: "Matt, what's the big idea of giving me a hard time in class? Do I have to send my buddies out to do a number on your kneecaps or something?" In my experience, once you get them laughing, it is then much easier to deliver the real message. "So, Matt, cut me some slack in class. Tomorrow I want you and your buddies to take the lead in the discussion. If you think it's dumb, let me know afterward, but during class at least pretend to look interested. Okay?"

Helping teens learn to fly with their feet firmly planted on the earth requires more than knowledge; it requires strategy. If adolescents are to survive and thrive, adults need to supply large amounts of three ingredients—connection, guidance, and love.

On some level, it seems intuitive that we humans enjoy connecting with one another. When I walk into the office, I feel better if someone greets me. Connection obviously feels good. This is true for kids, teens, and adults alike.

Brain science helps us understand that connection is essential. More than just making us feel good, connecting is something we are born hardwired with. As Dr. Bruce Perry says in his book *Born for Love*, "Connections are written into the architecture of our nervous system." As you may recall from chapter 6, babies are born with a very limited repertoire of coping mechanisms. When they experience stress and duress they cry and wait for caregivers to help calm them down. They automatically look to other people to regulate their emotional lives. Interactions with caregivers who are present, attentive, attuned, and responsive form the foundation of a healthy stress response system. Children and adults alike continue to rely on human connection as the primary way to manage stress and to achieve feelings of calm and security. Even an eighty-year-old will experience lowered blood pressure if a spouse, partner, or friend is there to hold his hand. As our children grow up, their maturing executive functions will enable them to calm themselves down, gain perspective, and adopt other strategies to cope with stress.

Adolescence is a sensitive window where connections are especially potent. The executive functions that enable adolescents to handle stress are under construction just as their lives become more complicated and they take on greater levels of responsibility. During this time of great psychological and biological change, the connections that young people have with friends, adults, schools, and communities are key determinants of their health and well-being. For a long time, scientists studied what went *wrong* during adolescence. The picture they painted of teens was downright scary, focused solely on the risky behaviors of adolescents. Since the mid-nineties the focus has turned to what goes *right* in the lives of adolescents. What are the internal and external strengths that enable some teens to hit the inevitable bumps and bruises of adolescence but come out thriving? What makes young people resilient? When we look at the teens who are okay, sometimes against all odds, a powerful variable continuously bubbles to the top of the list: connectedness.

It turns out that relationships are a powerful protective factor that shields youth from risk and allows them to build on their strengths. In fact, when it comes to reducing risk-taking behaviors, we couldn't concoct a better antidote if we tried. Adolescents who feel connected to their family are more likely to delay sexual initiation, report lower levels of substance use, and are less likely to engage in violence. Young people who feel connected to adults in their schools are more likely to stay in school, attend class, and get higher grades and test scores—and show lower levels of risky behaviors. This makes a lot of sense when we consider what is going on in their brains. Secure connections enable teens' brains to manage stress and relax, unleashing the power of the cortex for learning and healthy decision making. And the good news keeps coming. Connection is a universal, cross-cutting protective factor. This means that a network of positive connections with adults is good *for all* adolescents, across gender, racial, ethnic, and social class groups, not just groups of teens labeled "at risk." It is clear that far from just feeling good, connection is a core ingredient of healthy adolescent development.

Meaningful connection involves seeing and honoring your teen's strengths and giving them spaces to express them. It means encouraging their passions, their potential, and what the late Peter Benson of Search Institute calls their "sparks." Dr. Benson said that a spark is exactly what it sounds like: something that lights up a teen inside and gives purpose to his or her life. His research showed that kids who thrive have two important qualities. They know what their sparks are and have adults who support them. Most kids have no problem naming their sparks. Several studies show that creative arts, athletics, and learning are on the top of the kids' list of sparks. Unfortunately, too few teens have the relationships with adults needed to fuel them. Search Institute's recent *Teen Voice* survey uncovered a relational deficit among teens in this country. They found that only about one in five young people has a strong web of positive, sustained, and meaningful relationships with adults. Likewise, the Commission on Children at Risk, a group of prominent doctors, research scientists, and youth-serving professionals, named a lack of connectedness as a major contributor to deteriorating behavioral and mental health among youth in the United States.

Just because we know that connection is important for teens doesn't mean that it is easy to cultivate it. Though teens tell researchers that they want close relationships with their parents and rely on them for support, this comes as a great surprise to many of their parents. It is normal for an adolescent to ask for a divorce from the family. They are reluctant to go places or do things with their families. They complain that they don't have enough time with their friends. But even though they're asking, sometimes even screaming, for a divorce, don't give it to them.

One of our family's more ambitious excursions was a two-week road trip to the mountains. Monica and I were very excited that summer. We both love the mountains and were looking forward to sharing a wonderful experience with Dan, fifteen, Brian, twelve, and Erin, just turned eleven. We packed on Friday evening so we could start the next morning before the crack of dawn. Brian was hanging out with some of his friends in the neighborhood as we began to load the car. Our requests for help were completely ignored. As I pressed Brian to do his part, ignoring my requests turned to hostile resistance.

"Why can't you load the car?"

"I don't even want to go on this stupid vacation, so why should I load the car?"

"Come on, Brian," I said in a forced-friendly voice.

After a lot of back-and-forth, negotiations, and threats, two trying-to-be-happy parents and three sullen teenagers finally loaded up the car. The next morning as we tried to get them going, all three complained that we were leaving too early. Erin suggested leaving about noon. We explained once again that we wanted to reach the Black Hills by nightfall to camp, and since it was at least a ten-hour drive from Minneapolis, we needed to get going. Erin and Dan climbed into the car complaining about how ridiculous it was to leave before dawn. Brian continued with his theme of not wanting to go in the first place. "Family vacations are so stupid" was the last thing I heard him say as he settled into an hours-long, stony, cold silence. Given the alternative he was offering, I was thankful that he gave us the silent treatment well into South Dakota. When the sun did begin to make its way above the horizon, I felt like it had already been a long day. Unbeknownst to me, the day was just getting started.

South Dakota allows the sale of fireworks. As soon as we crossed the border, Dan started in. "When are we going to stop so I can buy some fireworks?"

"Remember what I said, Dan?" I answered. "We haven't decided if we are going to buy fireworks. I only said we will check into it."

"What do you mean? I've got money. I'm getting fireworks."

We finally stopped at a small town for a break. Monica and I gave each other a look when we realized there was a large fireworks warehouse beside the gas station where we parked to fill the tank. It was unavoidable: we had to at least have a look. When we stepped into the building, Dan's eyes lit up. He had never seen so many fireworks. And these were the big ones, the kind you can never find in Minnesota. As Dan ran off down the aisles in giddy amazement, I asked the guy selling them how all of this worked in the eyes of the law.

"Well, it's a hundred percent legal to buy all of these different classes of fireworks in South Dakota. But you can only set them off on private property."

This law probably makes sense in South Dakota, because there are a lot of wide-open spaces and large ranches. We Walshes, however, did not live in a wide-open space and did not own a ranch. By the time I caught up with Dan he had his arms filled with monster fireworks—not little bottle rockets and sparklers, but the kind that you can see from the next county.

"Dan, I'm sorry, but it's illegal to get those."

"What are you talking about? They're selling them."

"Yes, but you can only set them off on private property."

"Oh, come on, Dad."

"You can get some little ones and some bottle rockets, but you'll have to put the mortar shells and the heavy artillery back."

Dan threw a fit. I got an earful about how unfair this was, how we never let him do anything he really wanted to do. Then he explained how boring our family was and what a horrible vacation this was going to be, and he told us about laws that matter and others that do not. Somehow I got the rockets out of his arms and his body back in the car. We were once again on the road; the summer sun beat down, but the atmosphere was decidedly chilly in the car. Brian still wouldn't talk because he wanted to be home with his friends. Dan wouldn't talk because he was steamed about the fireworks. Two down, one to go.

Within an hour Erin was complaining about the heat. We didn't have air conditioning and the South Dakota prairie was hot. Soon Erin's complaints escalated to wailing about the heat and the fact that she hated this trip.

Three for three.

Monica and I looked at each other. One thought played repeatedly in my head like a broken record, and I found out later that she was thinking the same thing. Why were we doing this? Why were we torturing ourselves? Why didn't we disown them, sell them, or drown them and hide the bodies? Then the two of us could go on a vacation that we could enjoy.

One Christmas many years later, all three of our kids were home from their far-flung lives. One night at dinner, with the five of us around the table, we started to reminisce about old times. The topic of vacations came up. We started to tell stories about different vacations. Eventually Dan, Brian, and Erin tried to decide which was the best vacation we'd taken. They all agreed that one of the best ever was that trip to the mountains.

We make a huge mistake as parents if we grant the divorce our kids request. Monica and I wanted to scream many times during that mountain vacation, but we are both very glad we went. For all of the unpleasantness we endured, there were great times on that trip too, of course, and it was something we did as a family when our lives were beginning to head in different directions. Years later, we still share the experiences, part of an important connection between parents and children.

As parents we need to strategize ways to stay connected, because even though our adolescents don't think they need us anymore, they do. Research consistently shows that the most protective factor for teens is parent connection and involvement. Parents who know where their kids are, who they are with, what they're doing, how they're doing in school, who their friends are, and what their sparks are, keep their children out of trouble just by being a big part of their lives.

Maintaining family rituals and vacations is a great way to stay connected. It's reasonable to make allowances as the kids get older; they want and need some freedom; but it is sad that so many families just give up because vacations and traditions become such a hassle. Teens need to know that they are still part of a family. They may not be happy about that fact at the time, but it's still important to hang on to the particular things that make your family unique.

Today, when activities and responsibilities send family members in a thousand different directions, it's even more important to plan for connection time. If you don't, it won't happen.

Another important factor in staying connected is keeping other adults involved with your adolescents. Sometimes adolescents cannot or do not want to talk with their parents; their parents are just too close. At these times it is important for adolescents to have some other adults they trust—a teacher, a coach, an aunt or uncle, or a family friend. The key is to involve other adults in your kids' lives early on so that the relationship is there when they hit adolescence. When we asked close friends to be godparents to our three kids, it was a serious conversation. We asked them to be involved and stay involved with our kids. All three couples did and all three of our kids still stay close to the adults that we invited into their lives. It isn't necessary to make the relationship as formal as a traditional godparent role, but it is important that the adults who are there to help your children understand how important they are.

We had a particularly tense time with Brian when he was sixteen. We had discovered a problem, and our conversations about it were not getting anywhere. I called two men who are my close friends and who are also close to Brian. "Will you guys take Brian out to breakfast? I don't need to know what you say, but I need you to talk with him. Right now I can't get through." The three of them spent hours together that Saturday. I never asked Brian or my friends what was said. When Brian was in his early twenties I asked him if he remembered that Saturday.

"I remember it clearly," he said.

"Was it helpful?" I asked.

"You know, it actually was," said Brian thoughtfully. He added, "I still carry something in my wallet that Bob"—Brian's godfather—"gave me that day." I still don't know what Brian has in his wallet, and I don't need to know. But I am grateful that there were other caring adults who could be there for Brian at that tough spot.

Staying connected means remembering you're family, even if your adolescent isn't willing to reciprocate. Never make personal attacks. When the hormones are flowing and their reasoning center in the prefrontal cortex is asleep, adolescents can really push our buttons. Exasperation can lead to heated exchanges. It is during those heated exchanges that there is danger that we will say some devastating things—names, insults, or barbed criticism—that will only make the situation worse. A personal attack is never productive, and it's probably the best way to sever your all-important connection.

When I was a school counselor, I was called into a situation where a seventeen-year-old boy had written something very sexually explicit about a young female teacher. Somehow she had gotten her hands on it. When she read it, she became understandably upset and shaken, so she marched with the student right down to my office. They came in and closed the door and she handed me the piece of paper. Then she started to cry and left my office. There I was standing with this student in front of me. I was so upset about the effect of this writing on the teacher that I turned to the student and blurted out, "This is sick!" That happened more than thirty years ago, but I can remember it as if it were yesterday. Any chance I had of helping that boy was destroyed the moment I personally attacked him.

I would have been much more helpful to both the student and the teacher if I had pursued a different tack. The words "This is sick" immediately cast me in the role of adversary. Instead, I should have tried to establish enough trust with the student that he would have seen me as an ally. After the teacher ran out, I could have done something like this: I could have looked at the student and said, "Do you think this is going to turn into a big deal?" The student would undoubtedly say yes. "I agree. I think this is a big deal. Do you want me to help you through this?" With those words I would be forming an alliance, and a teen in big trouble would welcome the help. Then I could proceed along these lines: "What do you think you should do next? My advice would be to be proactive and immediately apologize to the teacher, tell her it will never happen again, and tell her that you are willing to accept any punishment that she and the assistant principal decide. I can guarantee that if you fight it or if they think that you don't understand what you've done, it will be much worse for you because they will want to teach you a lesson and make you pay." Of course, I wouldn't stop here, because I haven't done anything yet to help him understand how mean and abusive his note was. I would never get to that level, however, unless I could first get him to trust me and to act respectfully. If I could accomplish that, then I could do the important work of helping him change his attitudes and behavior with a discussion like this: "Why do you think she was so offended? How would you feel if someone said something really insulting or hurtful to you or to your mother?" I would also encourage him to write a letter of apology, because I have found that writing something increases a student's responsibility and ownership.

Staying connected depends on the adult remembering that someone needs to act reasonably even when an adolescent can't. Don't escalate. Brain-based communication problems (like those we discussed in chapter 5) sometimes cause adolescents to react quickly and emotionally. Situations can escalate, and it is an adult's responsibility to try to prevent that. The adolescent brain does not equip the adolescent for a job with the bomb squad. Escalating arguments, rather than defusing them, is their specialty. Brain changes can sometimes send the adolescent on an emotional roller coaster. Caring adults need to empathize with their teens but not join them for the ride.

Staying connected means staying open to different possibilities. A good rule of thumb for all of us is to spend twice as much time and half as much money as we can afford with our teens. The statistics on the little amount of time that parents spend in one-to-one communication with our adolescents are frightening. On average, adolescents in the United States spend seventy times more time in front of TV, video games, and computer screens than they do in one-to-one communication with their dads. The situation with their mothers isn't much better. Ongoing conversations with our kids about the tough topics like tobacco, alcohol, drugs, and sex are essential to helping them make the right choices. But connection does more than just keep adolescents out of danger; it also makes them happier and healthier, and it helps them stay close to you even when they've grown up. Researchers at Search Institute asked teens about what defines adults who "get" them and heard very consistent answers from young people across the country: "They listen and pay attention, are honest and dependable, and seem to enjoy spending time with us." If that is what teens are telling us, it seems that we should do everything we can to deliver.

Find new ways to be with your adolescents, and take advantage of opportunities that arise. As teens start to pull away, a lot of the occasions to do things together disappear. When my kids were young they would want to go outside and play catch after dinner. Sometimes, when I was tired, all I wanted to do was to sit quietly and read the newspaper, but then I would remember that there were only so many more years that they would want to play catch. When they got older, they wouldn't want to do anything with me. Those thoughts were what motivated me to put down the paper and pick up the baseball glove.

When my kids started to reach adolescence, I had to invent new ways to be a part of their lives. Dan enjoyed skiing. For a time we would go out to try cross-country skiing as well as some of the local hills for downhill. When Brian was into collecting baseball cards in middle school, I would volunteer to take him to card shows on weekends because I knew it would be something he wanted to do. When Erin got excited about hockey, Monica and I took her and her friends to see games.

You have to engineer good conversations. While my kids were teenagers, I went out to breakfast with one of them every Friday morning. Those early Friday mornings were sacred; I never scheduled a meeting for Friday breakfast if I could help it. Each of the kids took turns, and they got to choose the restaurant. (I can name all the good breakfast places in Minneapolis and Saint Paul.) It was nice because it was early in the morning. Nothing had happened yet, so we could have some calm talks about good things. Don't get me wrong: some of those breakfasts were very quiet, but it was still a way to be in touch. Erin now has a child of her own and last week she commented, "I wonder when I can start that breakfast tradition with Miles. Remember that, Pops? Is two years old too young?"

Monica always amazed me with her strategies for staying connected. When the kids were adolescents and they asked her what she wanted for her birthday, she would often ask them to make her a CD of their favorite music. Not music that they thought she would like, but *their* favorite songs. It was a way she could keep in tune with their tastes and thoughts. She had many good conversations with the kids that got started with those mixes, and she still has the CDs.

Monica also had a wonderful idea for how I could connect with our three adolescents. We ended up calling it the "sixteen-year-old adventure." Each of the three kids got to choose a trip that the two of us would take during the spring break of the year they turned sixteen. I'd use one of my vacation weeks and we'd head off—just the two of us. Dan and I skied in British Columbia. Brian and I went to Manhattan for some sightseeing and went skiing in Vermont. Erin and I visited Ireland. It wasn't cheap, and sometimes my schedule was a nightmare in the weeks surrounding the vacation, but those trips were worth the sacrifice.

Connecting with your teenager doesn't need to involve spending a lot of money on trips or meals. There are lots of ways to stay connected. I've picked up suggestions from friends and other counselors, including putting notes in teen lunch bags, offering to chaperone your teen and her friends so they could go to a concert, making popcorn without being asked, going to the movie he wants to see, taking the kids on camping trips, giving a small present for no reason, and many others. Ask your teen about their sparks. Nurture them and give them fuel. Sometimes that means getting out of their way to let them figure it out and shine. Teenagers need adults not just to keep them out of trouble; they need adults who care about them enough to help them thrive.

We can bend over backward to forge strong relationships with our teens, but that doesn't go very far if they sense that we don't value their voices or take their ideas and opinions seriously. The prefrontal cortex might be under construction, but that does not mean that teens aren't capable of incredibly wise and thoughtful contributions. Brain science can be misused to justify treating teens like they are "broken" or depict them as loose cannons that need to be monitored and contained until adulthood. No doubt it can feel like that sometimes, but that isn't the whole story. The teen brain can also be a strength. The flip side of risky behavior is their energy and commitment to action. Rather than sending teens to their rooms for ten years while we wait for their PFC to mature, we could be harnessing the strengths of the teen brain and funneling teens' energy into positive risk taking and opportunities to practice the skills of leadership, participation, organizing, and problem solving.

Years of youth development research tell us that young people need experiences where they can achieve a sense of success, competency, and personal power. Young people want to feel like they have influence over issues that matter to them, both in their homes and in their communities. Rather than fear their participation, we should start encouraging it. This is exactly what brain science begs us to do. Whatever the brain does a lot of is what the brain gets good at. Young people who have opportunities to exercise their prefrontal cortex practice key skills that serve them well into their adult lives. If your teen shows interest in getting involved in projects, clubs, or groups in the community or at school, support their participation. We all benefit from having young people at the table.

Guidance

Connecting with your teens isn't the same as being their friend. Respecting their opinions isn't the same as saying "anything goes." They have plenty of friends. They need you to be the parent. No matter what teens may tell us, they still need guidance and limits. Since an adolescent's rational, prefrontal cortex is still developing, we parents, teachers, coaches, and other adults need to serve as surrogate PFCs.

When Dan was about fifteen years old, he announced to Monica and me that he no longer needed a curfew on weekends.

"Oh, really," I replied. "And why exactly is that?"

"Well, look," he reasoned calmly. "I'm really mature now. I don't get in any big trouble. I get good grades. None of my friends has a curfew. And how will I learn to exercise good judgment if you don't give me the freedom? You know, it's time you stopped treating me like a kid."

As I recall, the best I could come up with that night was "Because I said so," but now, my answer would be a little bit different: "You know, Dan, you may think that you are completely mature, but the latest brain research says otherwise. There are still some important circuits in your brain that have to get wired together. And until that is finished, you've got a curfew. Don't blame me. Blame science."

Limits like curfews provide the structural support for good decision making. Sure, kids can get in trouble at nine p.m., but the odds go up dramatically when there are no limits, they feel no accountability, and they're out on the streets past midnight.

Setting limits will often bring up the issue of trust. A common teen complaint is "What's the matter? Don't you trust me?" Kids will often speak of the word *trust* as if it means only one thing. Trust is not one-dimensional: I trust my kids in many ways, but I don't necessarily trust their ability to withstand overwhelming pressure. *Temptation,* an old-fashioned word that is not used much anymore, is important to keep in mind when considering adolescent brain development. Temptation occurs when the pressure to do something strains the psychological resources to resist. Since impulse control is a skill of executive function, which has not yet matured, adolescents are often unable to resist impulses in situations where they are overwhelmed.

Guidance comes in many shapes and sizes. Talking about values and attitudes like respect, cooperation, honesty, service, and compassion with our kids can be as important as giving clear-cut rules. Even more important is modeling the behaviors that reflect those values. Adolescents hate sermons, so conversations about values should be dialogues. Discussions prompted by YouTube videos, movies, TV programs, and news stories are excellent ways to strike up these conversations. For instance, in English class kids learn about the ancient Greek concept of the tragic flaw. What is it about a character that causes him or her to make the mistakes that lead to tragedy? It's a great way to explore some of the world's great stories, but it can be interesting to apply the idea to adolescents' own lives. No wonder there are so many Shakespeare film adaptations set in modern teenage situations. Many kids devote a lot of thought to these fictional characters. Talking about them with your teenagers can be a good way to get a dialogue about values rolling.

Guidance also means setting clear expectations about behaviors. You have to pick and choose your battles carefully, though. There are many important issues to worry about during adolescence, so it makes sense to save your energy and emotional capital for those. Does it really make sense to argue about a messy room when you can close the door? How many arguments have there been about hairstyles when there are much more important things to deal with? Think of your attention and energy as units of which you have a limited supply, and invest them in the areas that really matter. The key is to set limits and consequences clearly for your kids. By setting limits and enforcing consequences ahead of time, you can avoid power struggles and ugly confrontations later on.

My colleague Gwen and her husband, Jon, had two teenage daughters. They found a clever way to avoid the never-ending arguments about chores. Bobbie and Jessie both received allowances, but they didn't collect them until they turned in their "work cards." Gwen explained how it worked. "We printed up cards with the list of chores that each of the girls is responsible for. When they finished the job, they initialed that spot on the card, and then when it passed inspection, Jon or I signed off in our space. When the card was completed, they got their allowance." I asked if there was any partial payment for partial completion. "Nope. It was all or nothing. It was Jon's idea and it worked like a charm. The power struggles about chores vanished. It was as good as the 'bad word jar.'" Naturally, I had to ask her what that was. "Well, that was my idea. The girls started to use some of the foul language they heard at school or in the media. I got tired of fighting with them about it, so I instituted the 'bad word jar.' Whenever Bobbie or Jessie used foul language they had to put a quarter in the jar. At the end of the month we used the money for a family treat or gave it to a charity. It worked great. In fact, when my forty-six-year-old brother was visiting and used a swear word, Bobbie brought over the jar and made him put a quarter in. When my brother said he couldn't afford to swear in our house, Bobbie smiled and told him that was the idea."

As I mentioned, Monica and I had curfew arguments and struggles with Dan when he was about sixteen. He thought our curfews were too early. On his way out one Saturday night I reminded him that his curfew was eleven p.m. He got angry and insisted that eleven p.m. was an idiotic time to come home. I said that I didn't expect him to agree, but I did expect him to observe the curfew. He rose to the occasion.

"There's no way I'm coming home at eleven p.m. I'm just not."

The temptation was to have the showdown right then and there. I could feel my own anger beginning to percolate. Instead, I bit my tongue and calmly said, "If you don't come home by eleven, then for every minute you're late, that amount times four will be subtracted from your curfew for the next month."

He was really testing me, so he said, "Big deal, I just won't pay attention to those curfews either."

Trying to conceal my rising anxiety and worry, I pulled out my ace. "Dan, if you can't handle a curfew, you can say good-bye to the car for a long time."

"Who cares?" was his parting shot as he went out the door. Were Monica and I worried that night? Of course we were. We couldn't be sure what Dan would do. It wasn't until 10:55, when the car pulled into the driveway, that we knew he'd decided to obey our rules. Apparently once he'd escaped the heat of the moment, he'd taken the time to think about the consequences. Life without the car was too horrible a prospect.

As adolescents get older, you have fewer levers to use to guide them. Use of the car is a big one. Think very long and hard before you let your teen own a car. Even though it can be a major pain to constantly haggle with teens over using the family car, having some control over where and when they go is a powerful bargaining chip. Don't give it up lightly.

When I was a teacher, I used to organize classroom discussions on topics like curfews and rules—touchy topics among teens. First I divided the class into pairs. One student could speak for him- or herself and their peers, but the other person had to take the role of parent. After a period of time they switched roles. Everything had to be written. No talking. So one student would write what he or she thought and would then push the paper across the desk for the other to respond in writing. I did this exercise many times with many students because the results were always enlightening. It was amazing to read the responses of these teenagers when they were in the role of parent. They would really express an understanding of the care and concern that parents must have about their adolescent children.

There were two interesting things about this exercise that I stumbled into. First, by taking on the role of parent, my students had to think through the issues in a reflective way. Second, in writing their responses, they had to slow down their reply, so their words were carefully considered rather than emotionally reactive. What was happening, without my realizing it, was that this exercise forced the adolescents to use the reflective CEO of the brain, the executive function in the prefrontal cortex. When they did engage their PFCs, they not only understood their parents better but they also often expressed appreciation for what their parents did. They also seemed to understand what they frequently put their parents through.

It is not your teen's job to say what connections and guidance he or she needs. Teens often seem to be asking for no connection and no guidance at all. But that's not what they really need or want. During adolescence they want the wings. We need to let them try out their wings, but we need to also make sure that they have roots.

Love

What makes this difficult balancing act possible—and worth all the work? That's the third ingredient: love. We parents love our children, even though at times we'd like to brain them. Communicating this love to teenagers is vital to helping them through adolescence, even if they act like they want to disown us. You don't need to get mushy in a social situation that will embarrass them in front of their peers. You do need to communicate that the reason you are so intent on maintaining connections, setting limits, and guiding them is that you love them. They may not seem to hear you, or seem to want to hear you, but in those slow, quiet moments when they give their brains' prefrontal cortexes a chance to think things over, they'll know that even if you're making them miserable in the moment, you're doing it because you love them. Loving them is the first, and last, step in giving adolescents their roots and wings. In the next, and final, chapter we'll explore what loving a teenager means.

DO

✓ Search for ways to connect with your teenager.
✓ Spend time together as a family.
✓ Involve other adults in your teenagers' lives.
✓ Maintain family traditions even when teens complain about them.
✓ Have a curfew that you enforce.
✓ Insist that your teen share in family chores and responsibilities.

DON'T

✗ Don't lecture. If lectures worked, you wouldn't need to keep repeating them.
✗ Don't grant the divorce from the family that your teen may seem to request. He doesn't really mean it.
✗ Don't stop going to school activities.

What do I want to continue?

_____

_____

_____

What do I want to change?

_____

_____

_____

FIFTEEN

In Conclusion

Oh, the places you'll go! There is fun to be done!
There are points to be scored. There are games to be won.

—DR. SEUSS

I have been fortunate enough to be invited to lead a class for the day by a teacher at the high school my three kids attended. Each year I generate a wide-ranging discussion with a class of seniors shortly before they graduate. The teacher has students call to extend the invitation, and they usually begin with an apology. "We know how busy you are, but do you think you might have time—"

I always interrupt them. "Yes, of course I have time. Let's find a date that works." The truth is that I look forward to that visit every year. I'd be disappointed if the call didn't come. Thanks to my one-day teaching gig, every spring I get to walk down the halls of Minneapolis South High School, where I am struck by how different the world of today's adolescent is from the world I grew up in: different languages are spoken in the hallway; there are kids of every race and ethnic background in every class. The music, the dress, and the slang vary from year to year.

As different as today's adolescents are, I am also struck each spring by the similarities that transcend generations. Seniors are still excited but worried about the future. Ninth-graders are still loud and boisterous. Sophomores are still trying to figure out if and how they will fit in. Juniors are still complaining about parents and teachers. It's all so familiar, as is the idealism, the loyalty, and the importance of friendship. Today's adolescents do live in a different, faster, technology-driven world of constant change. But their brains face the same developmental challenges that all adolescents have always had. And the adolescent brain explains much of the adolescent experience.

It seems that every generation of parents repeats the same question posed in the musical *Bye Bye Birdie:* "What's the matter with kids today?" There is nothing the matter with kids today. The fact of the matter is that the revolution at work in the adolescent brain results in some pretty confusing, scary, and challenging behavior. All too often, the behavior caused by the adolescent brainstorms scares or angers us adults.

A young woman of twenty-eight told me once that she never wanted to have children. The reason was not because she didn't like babies or because her life plans just didn't allow for taking on the responsibility of raising children. "I don't think I could stand dealing with them when they were teenagers," she told me. These were the words of a woman who, nine years earlier, had been a teenager herself.

Though adolescents sometimes seem to be asking us to get out of their lives while they figure these things out, they don't really mean it. Research that I cited earlier has consistently shown that the common characteristic for kids who thrive in adolescence is that they have adults in their lives who care about them, pay attention to them, and love them. In the last chapter we discussed the need for adolescents to have connection and guidance with caring adults as their brains finish the developmental processes. The third essential ingredient that every adolescent needs is, of course, love.

It's easy to say, like the Beatles, that love is the answer. It's quite another prospect to express love to adolescents who sometime seem determined to keep you at bay. It's not easy to love an adolescent who tells you that you're ruining his life, screams that she can't stand being in this family, criticizes everything you say, wants to debate every little issue, or answers your every question with a monosyllable.

I recently had a conversation with a mother whose oldest daughter had just turned thirteen. "She criticizes me for everything I say. And then if I don't say anything, she gets mad because she thinks I'm ignoring her. I can't win."

Loving an adolescent is not always easy, but that's the challenge before us, and it's a challenge to which adults have risen for countless generations. First of all, we have to get our expectations in line. Brain science gives us the perspective we need, at least in part, to not be surprised when our kids act impulsively, or misinterpret what we say, or experiment in ways that scare the living daylights out of us. It's not really personal, though it sure can seem that way sometimes.

One way to meet the challenge with love is to accentuate the positives so we don't fall into the trap of only responding to negatives. We need to catch our adolescents being good. Be careful not to overdo it because adolescents are smart. They will start to think it's phony if we go overboard. As long as we don't fall over ourselves to congratulate our adolescent every time she wipes her feet on the mat, a well-placed and consistent thank-you, a compliment, or a sign of appreciation can go a long way. The message comes through loud and clear that we notice and we care.

Another important way to express our love is to admit when we are wrong. We should apologize when we've made a mistake. Try as we may to be perfect, we will blow it sometimes. We may overreact or say something we wish we hadn't. If an apology is called for, we should give it. Most importantly, an apology can repair a frayed, loving relationship. It also provides a model for an adolescent to follow.

We should tell our teens that we love them even when they don't respond. Whether or not they act embarrassed, we can't assume that they know how we feel. Somewhere down the line they'll appreciate that we said it out loud. When Brian was an adolescent he seemed to ignore us every time Monica or I told him that we loved him. It was almost as if he hadn't heard us. I've noticed that now that Brian is an adult, he finishes every phone conversation with "I love you, Dad."

Try to establish an emotional connection at the end of the day. Monica and I always tried to have a "chat" with each of our three kids in the evening. Sometimes the chats were very short, a matter of seconds. Other times they would turn into marathons. We never knew which was in store. But those long important conversations would never have happened if we hadn't created the opportunity for them.

When we make a habit of putting twice as much energy into listening as we put into talking, adolescents will eventually take advantage. Really listening to our kids lets them know that we are interested and that we respect their thoughts and opinions. We don't have to agree with everything they say, but if we truly listen, even disagreements will be more productive. As teens attempt to form their adult personalities, they need to try new thoughts and feelings out loud. Listening to them with an open mind is a sign of profound respect.

A sense of humor can also go a long way toward keeping the bonds of affection tight. We don't want to laugh at our teens, but when the timing is right, laughing with them and laughing at ourselves is a great lubricant for parent-teen relations. In the midst of taking the whole world extremely seriously, adolescents sometimes need the release of a good laugh.

Many years ago someone told me a parable about a mother eagle and her babies. I think it has a lot to say about raising adolescents. A mother eagle lived in the remote north woods with her three baby eagles. After weeks of keeping them safe in their lofty forest home, the day finally came to help them begin life on their own. She picked the first eaglet up in her talons and began the short flight. Just before she let her child go in midair she asked the eaglet a question: "Tell me, how will you treat me when you are grown?" The young eaglet immediately responded that he would dedicate himself to taking care of his mother. "I will attend to your every need and make sure that you want for nothing."

The mother eagle looked sad as she kept hold of the eaglet and returned to the aerie. "Perhaps we will try your flight another day, but you are not ready yet. I still have important things to teach you."

Returning her baby to the nest, she gingerly picked up the second eaglet in her powerful talons. When they were a good distance from the nest, she repeated the question: "Tell me, how will you treat me when you are grown?" The second eaglet responded that he would be completely obedient as he got older. "I will follow your every directive. You will never have any trouble from me."

The mother eagle once again looked sad as she held her grip and wheeled through the air in an arc back toward the nest. She said, "You have a great deal to learn about life, and you, too, are not yet ready to fly away."

She gripped the third and last of her young. Once again, as they flew high up over the forest canopy, the mother eagle asked, "Tell me, how will you treat me when you are grown?"

The last eaglet looked up and said, "I don't know how I will treat you when I am grown. I only know that I will treat my children with the care and love with which you have treated me." The mother eagle smiled and said, "You have learned the most important thing about love. You are ready to fly." And with that she let the fledgling go. He dropped through the air, like a stone, tumbling head over tail . . . and then he spread his small wings and shakily began to fly. The mother eagle smiled. She knew in her heart her eaglet had learned his lessons and was ready to begin life on his own.

The real test in parenting an adolescent is loving while expecting little in return and being willing to carry our kids from one precarious position to the next. In the end, if we've succeeded, the connection between parent and child will remain a part of their adult relationship. Raising an adolescent is an investment. It has its share of satisfactions and rewards—eventually. Waiting for a happy ending can be difficult. At times it seems there is little reward. That's when we just have to hope and trust that our kids will come out okay at the other end. It is at those times that we need to remember that the connecting, guiding, and loving we provide is an investment on a future return. As with all investments, there are risks. And as with all investments, the real payoff is a long way off.

But whenever we spend our time with our child when we would rather be doing something else—whenever we invest our energy when we are exhausted; bite our tongue when we want to lash out; take a deep breath and count to ten when we want to scream; hold the line on a family rule when it would be much easier to give in;

have the courage to talk about difficult topics, like sex and alcohol; tell our adolescents that we love them and that nothing can ever change that; tell our adolescents that although we may get frustrated, we will never give up on them; swallow our pride and apologize to our adolescents when they deserve it; go out of our way to meet their friends; stay connected with their school; deal with problems head-on instead of slipping into willful denial; put a note of encouragement in their lunch bag or backpack; talk about our values; ask them about their favorite music or video; set and enforce limits; show up at their activities; share a good laugh; and do the million other things we can to connect with, guide, and love our adolescent children and students—every time we do any of these things, we are increasing the value of our investments.

We need not worry about the return. It will come when we realize that we have helped our teens survive and thrive in one of the most important stages of life. We will have helped them through the perilous journey from childhood to adulthood. Along the way, there will be hazards and detours. No matter what we do, our kids will make mistakes during adolescence. The goal of parenting is not to help them avoid all mistakes. Persevering through difficulty, reflecting on a bad decision, and knowing what it feels like to make the wrong choice are vital parts of growing up. Rather than sheltering adolescents from life, we need to help them learn to deal with it. When kids' lives are too tightly controlled, they never get a chance to test their wings. I've heard countless stories from college dorm advisors about college freshmen who go wild when they get to campus. More often than not they are the ones whose adolescence was too tightly controlled.

Control is not the key. Connection is. If we have a connection with our kids, then we can help them learn from their mistakes. If we are disconnected from them, how will they know what to make of their painful missteps? The interactions between caring adult and growing adolescent are much like the connections forming in an adolescent brain. The more an adolescent has a diversity of positive experiences, the greater number of strong connections form in the neural pathways of her brain. The brain isn't just the sum of its parts, a collection of cells; the brain is most amazing because of the

292 WHY DO THEY ACT THAT WAY?

way it is connected. The more connections it has, the more that brain will be able to do, withstand, and create. The connections between adolescents and adults who love them work the same way. The more we make, reinforce, and re-create connections between our adolescents and the parents, teachers, and other caring adults in their lives, the greater chance they will have to sprout their wings and fly.

Adolescence is not a problem to be solved. It is an experience to be lived. At the end of the adventure, when your adolescent is an adult, you'll be able to answer the question of whodunit: you and your kid, together. From there, to paraphrase Dr. Seuss, they'll have places to go and fun to be done. Thanks to your help, the game can be won.

NOTES

Chapter One: Making Sense of Adolescence

17 *Research shows that adolescence is getting longer* Laurence Steinberg, *You and Your Adolescent: The Essential Guide for Ages 10–25* (New York: Simon & Schuster, 2011), pages 69–74.

19 *Swiss psychologist Jean Piaget* Dorothy Singer and Tracey Revenson, *A Piaget Primer: How a Child Thinks* (New York: New American Library, 1978), page 24.

19 *Even though the teen brain does not alter in size or shape* Lise Eliot, *What's Going On in There?* (New York: Bantam, 1999), page 392.

20 *With these powerful machines, scientists can* B. J. Casey, Rebecca M. Jones, and Todd A. Hare, "The Adolescent Brain," in *The Year in Cognitive Neuroscience,* Annals of the New York Academy of Sciences (2008), pages 111–126.

Chapter Two: A Guided Tour of Their Brains

29 *A baby arrives in the world* Marian Diamond and Janet Hopson, *Magic Trees of the Mind* (New York: Plume, 1999), page 37.

30 *Francis Crick, the co-discoverer of the DNA molecule* Francis Crick, *Astonishing Hypothesis: Scientific Search for the Soul* (New York: Scribner: 1994), pages 91–105.

30 *When a baby is born, only about 17 percent of his neurons are linked* J. Dobbing and J. Sands, "Quantitative Growth and Development in the Human Brain," *Archives of Disease in Childhood* 48 (1973), pages 757–767.

30 *. . . in nearly all cases nature and nurture* Lise Eliot, *What's Going On in There? How the Brain and Mind Develop in the First Five Years of Life* (New York: Bantam, 1999), page 9.

30 *The crucial role of experience* Robert Ornstein and Richard Thompson, *The Amazing Brain* (Boston: Houghton Mifflin, 1984), page 80.

31 *For every one neuron there are about ten glial cells* Robert Sylwester, *A Celebration of Neurons* (Alexandria, VA: Association for Supervision and Curriculum Development, 1995), page 29.

31 *Neuroscientist Paul MacLean describes the human brain* Paul MacLean, *The Triune Brain in Evolution: Role in Paleocerebral Functions* (New York: Plenum, 1990).

32   . . . is governed by the amygdala Joseph LeDoux, The Emotional Brain
        (New York: Simon & Schuster, 1996), pages 169–174.

32   The hippocampus (named after the Greek word for "seahorse" Daniel
        Schacter, Searching for Memory (New York: Basic Books, 1996), page 55.

32   The hypothalamus is the master control Robert Ornstein and Richard
        Thompson, The Amazing Brain (Boston: Houghton Mifflin, 1984),
        page 28.

33   It plays the role of the brain's executive Daniel Amen, Images of Human
        Behavior (Newport Beach, CA: MindWorks Press, 2001), pages 3–4.

33   We'll talk more about the prefrontal cortex for two reasons Jane Bernstein
        and Deborah Waber, "Executive Capacities from a Developmental
        Perspective," in Executive Function in Education, Lynn Meltzer, ed.
        (New York: Guilford Press, 2007), page 39.

34   . . . both the left and right sides Robert Ornstein and Richard Thompson,
        The Amazing Brain (Boston: Houghton Mifflin, 1984), pages 151–163.

34   . . . the corpus callosum: Robert Ornstein and Richard Thompson, The
        Amazing Brain (Boston: Houghton Mifflin, 1984), page 34.

36   . . . David Hubel and Torsten Wiesel David Hubel and Torsten Wiesel
        wrote a series of papers that earned them the Nobel Prize in 1981:
        Journal of Physiology 160 (1962), pages 106–154; Journal of
        Neurophysiology 26 (1963), pages 994–1002; Journal of Neurophysiology
        28 (1965), pages 1041–1059; Journal of Comparative Neurology 146
        (1972), pages 421–450.

37   Neuroscientist Marian Diamond Marian Diamond and Janet Hopson,
        Magic Trees of the Mind (New York: Plume, 1999), pages 9–306.

38   . . . in the first three years of life D. Walker et al., "Prediction of School
        Outcomes Based on Early Language Production and Socioeconomic
        Factors," Child Development 65 (1994), pages 606–621.

38   . . . The ability to differentiate sounds Lise Eliot, What's Going On in
        There? How the Brain and Mind Develop in the First Five Years of Life
        (New York: Bantam, 1999), pages 370–385.

39   . . . people who are abused as children M. Teicher, "Scars That Won't
        Heal: The Neurobiology of Child Abuse," Scientific American (March
        2002), pages 68–75.

40   . . . key brain areas undergo their blossoming and pruning J. N. Giedd,
        J. Blumenthal, N. Jeffries, et al., "Brain Development During
        Childhood and Adolescence: A Longitudinal MRI study," Nature
        Neuroscience 2 (1999), pages 861–863.

40   . . . major construction from childhood into adolescence P. Thompson,
        J. Giedd, R. Woods, et al., "Growth Patterns in the Developing Brain
        Detected by Using Continuum Mechanical Tensor Maps," Nature 404
        (2000), pages 190–193.

Chapter Three: Why Adolescents Are Impulsive

44 *Phineas Gage wasn't a scientist* Antonio Damasio, *Descartes' Error* (New York: Avon, 1995), pages 3–17.

46 *Dr. Jay Giedd, a neuroscientist at the National Institutes of Health* J. Giedd, J. Blumenthal, N. Jeffries, et al., "Brain Development During Childhood and Adolescence: A Longitudinal MRI Study," *Nature Neuroscience* 2 (1999), pages 861–863.

Chapter Four: Risky Business: Helping Teens Put on the Brakes

61 *For an explanation of these phenomena* C. Buchanan, J. Eccles, and J. Becker, "Are Adolescents the Victims of Raging Hormones?: Evidence for Activational Effects of Hormones on Moods and Behavior at Adolescence," *Psychological Bulletin* III no. 1 (1992), pages 62–107.

62 *Hormones actually are behind a wide range of erratic adolescent behaviors* Debra Niehoff, *The Biology of Violence* (New York: Free Press, 1999), pages 150–153.

63 *Part of the brain, the hypothalamus* Robert Ornstein and Richard Thompson, *The Amazing Brain* (Boston: Houghton Mifflin, 1984), page 28.

63 *By the end of adolescence* Michael Gurian, *A Fine Young Man* (Los Angeles: Tarcher/Putnam, 1999), page 32.

63 *The amygdala also has receptors for testosterone* J. N. Giedd et al., "Quantitative MRI of the Temporal Lobe, Amygdala, and Hippocampus in Normal Human Development: Ages 4–18 Years," *Journal of Comparative Neurology* 366 (1996), pages 223–230.

64 *. . . it is also likely to trigger surges of anger, aggression* Debra Niehoff, *The Biology of Violence* (New York: Free Press, 1999), pages 158–161.

64 *For girls, there are two important growth hormones* Michael Gurian, *The Wonder of Girls* (New York: Pocket Books, 2002), pages 78–80.

64 *. . . it's the hippocampus—the memory center* J. N. Giedd et al., "Quantitative MRI of the Temporal Lobe, Amygdala, and Hippocampus in Normal Human Development: Ages 4–18 Years," *Journal of Comparative Neurology* 366 (1996), pages 223–230.

64 *. . . estrogen and progesterone also have* Michael Gurian, *The Wonder of Girls* (New York: Pocket Books, 2002), pages 79–82.

Chapter Five: What We Have Here Is a Failure to Communicate

78 *Deborah Yurgelun-Todd, a researcher* "Inside the teenage brain. One reason teens respond differently to the world: immature brain circuitry." Found at http://www.pbs.org/wgbh/pages/frontline/shows/teenbrain/work/onereason.html (accessed October 17, 2013).

79 *. . . they often misinterpret the cues as anger or aggression* Jennifer Pfeifer et al., "Entering Adolescence: Resistance to Peer Influence, Risky Behavior, and Neural Changes in Emotion Reactivity," *Neuron* 69 (2011), pages 1029–1036.

Chapter Six: Stress and the Teen Brain

92   . . . Dr. Bruce Perry shares in his book Bruce Perry, Born for Love: Why Empathy Is Essential and Endangered (New York: William Morrow Paperbacks, reprint edition, 2011), page 38.

94   In his book Why Zebras Don't Get Ulcers Robert Sapolsky, Why Zebras Don't Get Ulcers (San Francisco: W. H. Freeman, 1998), pages 6–19.

95   In addition, the brain produces less "brain-derived neurotrophic factor," or BDNF J. Licinio and M-L Wong, "Brain Derived Neurotrophic Factor (BDNF) in Stress and Affective Disorders," Molecular Psychiatry 7 no. 6 (2002), pages 515–519.

95   As we'll see in chapter 11 BDNF is considered "Miracle-Gro" for the brain John J. Ratey, Spark: The Revolutionary New Science of Exercise and the Brain (New York: Little, Brown, 2008), pages 38–40.

97   That said, in the absence of close, caring relationships Bruce Perry, Born for Love: Why Empathy Is Essential and Endangered (New York: William Morrow Paperbacks, reprint edition, 2011), page 39.

100   Psychologist Carol Dweck and her team at Stanford Carol Dweck, Mindset: The New Psychology of Success (New York: Ballantine Books, reprint edition, 2007), pages 3–39.

103   The late Peter Benson of Search Institute reviewed the research Found at http://www.search-institute.org/developmental-assets/lists (accessed October 17, 2013).

103   Bonnie Bernard, one of America's leading researchers on resilience Bonnie Bernard, Resiliency: What We Have Learned (San Francisco: WestEd, 2004).

107   Resilient kids focus on strengths rather than weaknesses G. C. Patton, M. M. Tollit, N. Romaniuk, et al., "A Prospective Study of the Effects of Optimism on Adolescent Health Risks," Pediatrics 127 (2011), pages 308–316.

Chapter Seven: Understanding Male and Female Brains

112   Girls' brains seem to be equipped J. Harasty, K. L. Double, G. M. Halliday, et al.,"Language-Associated Cortical Regions Are Proportionally Larger in the Female Brain," Archives of Neurology 54 (1997), pages 171–176.

112   . . . the supposed male math superiority J. S. Hyde, E. Fennema, and S. J. Lamon, "Gender Differences in Mathematics Performance: A Meta-analysis," Psychology Bulletin 107 (1990), pages 139–155.

112   . . . boys and girls are equally intelligent Arthur Jensen, The g Factor (Westport, CT: Praeger, 1998), pages 531–544.

113   . . . the left hemisphere develops before Susan Gilbert, A Field Guide to Boys and Girls (New York: HarperCollins, 2000), page 8.

114   The corpus callosum, the bridge of nerve fibers Ibid.

114   . . . the INAH-3 becomes larger in boys' D. F. Swaab, L. J. G. Gooren, and

M. A. Hofman, "The Human Hypothalamus in Relation to Gender and Sexual Orientation," *Progress in Brain Research* 93 (1992).

114 *Hormones play a big part* Lise Eliot, *What's Going On in There? How the Brain and Mind Develop in the First Five Years of Life* (New York: Bantam, 2000), pages 434–435.

115 *For every 100 boys earning their bachelor's degrees, 132 girls are getting theirs* "Fast Facts: Degrees Conferred by Sex and Race," National Center for Educational Statistics (2010) at http://nces.ed.gov/fastfacts /display.asp?id=72 (accessed August 27, 2013).

115 *Seven out of ten kids in special education classes are male* "Educating Boys for Success," National Education Association (2013) http://www.nea .org/home/44609.htm (accessed August 27, 2013).

116 *The Common Core State Standards, adopted by almost all states* "What Are Common Core State Standards?" Carolyn Thompson via ABC News (August 27, 2013) http://abcnews.go.com/Politics/wireStory/common -core-state-standards-20072017 (accessed August 27, 2013).

119 *Estrogen and progesterone spikes* Michael Gurian, *The Wonder of Girls* (New York: Pocket Books, 2002), pages 79–80.

121 *For example, when a boy asks for help on a science experiment* "Back to School: Five Myths about Girls and Science." A press release from the National Science Foundation, www.nsf.gov/news/news_summ .jsp?cntn_id=109939 (accessed August 27, 2013).

Chapter Eight: Love, Sex, and the Adolescent Brain

128 *Around the age of ten* M. McClintock and G. Herdt, "Rethinking Puberty: The Development of Sexual Attraction," *Human Development* 5 (1996).

128 *The combination of the maturing INAH-3 module in the hypothalamus* Michael Gurian, *A Fine Young Man* (Los Angeles: Tarcher/Putnam, 1999), pages 90–96.

128 *The sex drive in boys and girls* Helen Fisher, *The Anatomy of Love* (New York: Ballantine, 1994), page 53.

129 *Andreas Bartels and Semir Zeki* A. Bartels and S. Zeki, "The Neural Basis of Romantic Love," *NeuroReport* 11 (2000), pages 3829–3834.

130 *. . . as Dr. Stanton Peele wrote in his book* Stanton Peele, *Love and Addiction* (New York: Signet, 1981).

130 *Dr. Helen Fisher, an anthropologist* "The Science of Love," found at www.bbc.co.uk/print/science/hottopics/love/print.shtml (accessed October 17, 2013).

132 *For girls the hormone associated with a warm* T. R. Insel, "Oxytocin: A Neuropeptide for Affiliation: Evidence from Behavioral, Receptor, Autoradiographic, and Comparative Studies," *Psychoneuroendocrinology* 17 (1992), pages 3–35.

132 *For boys, the attachment hormone* Barbara Strauch, *The Primal Teen* (New York: Doubleday, 2003), page 147.

136 *Fortunately, teen pregnancy rates in the United States have started to decline* Data found at U.S. Department of Health and Human Services Web site, Trends in Teen Pregnancy and Child Bearing, http://www.hhs .gov/ash/oah/adolescent-health-topics/reproductive-health/teen -pregnancy/trends.html (accessed December 17, 2013).

136 *Nevertheless they are by far the highest* Melissa S. Kearney and Phillip B. Levine, "Why Is the Teen Birth Rate in the United States So High and Why Does It Matter?" *Journal of Economic Perspectives, American Economic Association,* 26 (2012), pages 141–163.

137 *In addition, the United States has the highest rates of sexually transmitted diseases* "Sexually Transmitted Diseases," Children's Hospital of Wisconsin, http://www.chw.org/display/PPF/DocID/22764/router.aspn (accessed July, 30, 2013).

137 *Chlamydia, known as the silent STD* Data found at Centers for Disease Control and Prevention Web site, Sexually Transmitted Disease Surveillance, 2011, http://www.cdc.gov/std/chlamydia/STDFact -chlamydia-detailed.htm (accessed August 20, 2013).

138 *Another disease that is extremely easy to spread is genital HPV infection* Data found at Centers for Disease Control and Prevention Web site, http://www.cdc.gov/media/releases/2013/p0619-hpv-vaccinations .html (accessed August 20, 2013).

138 *In 2006 an effective vaccine was introduced* Lauri Markowitz et al., "Reduction in Human Papillomavirus (HPV) Prevalence Among Young Women Following HPV Vaccine Introduction in the United States, National Health and Nutrition Examination Surveys, 2003–2010," *Journal of Infectious Diseases* 208 no. 3 (2013), pages 385–393.

138 *There were 2,200 new cases of teen HIV/AIDS in 2009* Data found at Centers for Disease Control and Prevention Web site, http://www.cdc .gov/hiv/risk/age/youth/index.html (accessed August 1, 2013).

139 *According to the Centers for Disease Control and Prevention, 47 percent* "Prevalence and Timing of Oral Sex With Opposite-Sex Partners Among Females and Males Aged 15–24 Years: United States," National Health Statistics Report Number 56, August 16, 2012.

140 *A large national study showed that teaching about contraception* Pamela Kohler, Lisa Manhart, and William Lafferty, "Abstinence-Only and Comprehensive Sex Education and the Initiation of Sexual Activity and Teen Pregnancy," *Journal of Adolescent Health* 42 (2008), pages 344–351.

144 *Studies suggest that one third* "Alcohol, Drug Abuse, and Mental Health Administration: Department of Health and Human Services," Report of the Secretary's Task Force on Youth Suicide, DHHS Publication No. ADM 89-1623 (Washington, DC: U.S. Government Printing Office, 1989).

144   *Anthropologists have shown* Deborah Blum, *Sex on the Brain: The Biological Differences between Men and Women* (New York: Viking, 1997), page 131.

144   *Scientists have observed* A. Perkins and J. A. Fitzgerald, "Luteinizing Hormone, Testosterone, and Behavioral Response of Male-Oriented Rams to Estrous Ewes and Rams," *Journal of Animal Science* 70 (1992), pages 1787–1794.

145   *Twin studies and other genetic research* J. M. Bailey and R. C. Pillard, "A Genetic Study of Male Sexual Orientation," *Archives of General Psychiatry* 48 (1991), pages 1089–1096.

145   *A combination of the genetic, hormonal* J. Foreman "What Biology Says About Homosexuality," *StarTribune*, December 7, 2003.

Chapter Nine: Monkey Wrenches in the Brain: Alcohol, Tobacco, and Other Drugs

150   *In a recent study, 24 percent of high school seniors qualified as heavy drinkers* Janet Hopson, "Bad Mix for the Teen Brain," *Scientific American Mind* (July-August 2013), pages 68–71.

156   *Tragically, alcohol-related causes claim the lives* "College Drinking," National Institute on Alcohol Abuse and Alcoholism, 2012, http://pubs.niaaa.nih.gov/publications/CollegeFactSheet /CollegeFactSheet.pdf (accessed August 23, 2013).

156   *Most of the damage done by alcohol* H. S. Swartzwelder, W. A. Wilson, and M. I. Tayyeb, "Age-Dependent Inhibition of Long-term Potentiation by Ethanol in Immature vs. Mature Hippocampus," *Alcohol Clinical Experimental Research* 1 (1995), pages 1480–1485.

156   *Heavy alcohol use also interferes* A. M. White, P. E. Simson, and P. J. Best, "Comparison Between the Effects of Ethanol and Diazepam on Spatial Working Memory in the Rat," *Psychopharmacology* 133 (1997), pages 256–261.

157   *Thus, adolescents who drink a lot of alcohol* L. M. Squeglia, A. D. Spadoni, M. A. Infante, et al., "Initiating Moderate to Heavy Alcohol Use Predicts Changes in Neuropsychological Functioning for Adolescent Girls and Boys," *Psychology of Addictive Behaviors* 23 (2009), pages 715–722.

157   *Adolescents are oversensitive* M. M. Silveri and L. P. Spear, "Decreased Sensitivity to the Hypnotic Effects of Ethanol Early in Ontogeny," *Alcohol Clinical Experimental Research* 22 (1998), pages 670–676.

158   *There's one more piece of bad news* P. Rohde et al., "Natural Course of Alcohol Use Disorders from Adolescents to Young Adulthood," *Journal of the American Academy of Child and Adolescent Psychiatry* 40 (2001), pages 83–90.

159   *In 2010 22 percent of teen drivers in fatal crashes* National Highway

Traffic Safety Administration (NHTSA), Dept. of Transportation (US) (Washington DC: NHTSA, May 2012, cited May 29, 2013).

159　*In a 2011 study 24 percent of teenagers reported* Centers for Disease Control and Prevention, Youth Risk Behavior Surveillance—United States, 2011, MMWR Surveillance Summary 61(2012) (No. SS-4), pages 1–162.

160　*Nicotine's potent effect on the brain* T. Slotkin, "Nicotine and the Adolescent Brain: Insights from an Animal Model," *Neurotoxicology and Teratology* 24 (2002), pages 369–384.

160　*Nicotine has a triple whammy* H. D. Mansvelder, J. R. Keath, and D. S. McGehee, "Synaptic Mechanisms Underlie Nicotine-Induced Excitability of Brain Reward Areas," *Neuron* 27 (2002), pages 349–357.

161　*The percentage of high school students who smoke* Centers for Disease Control and Prevention, "Current Tobacco Use among Middle and High School Students—United States, 2011," *Morbidity and Mortality Weekly Report* 61 no. 31 (2012), pages 581–585 (accessed August 23, 2013).

161　*Unfortunately a threat to this downward trend* Centers for Disease Control and Prevention 2013 National Youth Tobacco Survey (NYTS), http://www.cdc.gov/tobacco/data_statistics/surveys/nyts/ (accessed October 15, 2013).

162　*In 2012, 28 percent of tenth-graders and 36 percent of* 2012 Data from In-School Surveys of 8th-, 10th-, and 12th-Grade Students, www.monitoringthefuture.org/data/12data.html#2012data-drugs (accessed May 29, 2013).

162　*In addition, the evidence is growing that marijuana use impairs working memory* Jing Han, Philip Kesner, et al., "Acute Cannabinoids Impair Working Memory through Astroglial CB1 Receptor Modulation of Hippocampal LTD," *Cell* (2012). doi:10.1016.

162　*The brain networks affected by marijuana* M. T. Kucewicz, M. D. Tricklebank, R. Bogacz, et al., "Dysfunctional Prefrontal Cortical Network Activity and Interactions Following Cannabinoid Receptor Activation," *Journal of Neuroscience* 31 no. 43 (2011), pages 15560–15568.

163　*The circuits there are directly involved with enjoyment* M. Bloomfield et al., "Dopaminergic Function in Cannabis Users and Its Relationship to Cannabis-Induced Psychotic Symptoms," *Biological Psychiatry* (2013), http://dx.doi.org/10.1016/j.biopsych.2013.05.027 (accessed August 23, 2013).

163　*Cocaine is physically and psychologically dangerous* S. Stocker, "Cocaine's Pleasurable Effects May Affect Multiple Chemical Sites," *NIDA* 14 no. 1 (1999).

164　*Between 2008 and 2013 there was a 33 percent increase in prescription drug abuse* "Teen Abuse of Prescription Drugs Up 33 Percent, Includes Ritalin, Adderall" at www.naturalnews.com/040146_prescription _drug_abuse_ADHD_teenagers.html (accessed May 30, 2013).

166 *The research is very clear* A. Mann, "Relationships Matter: Impact of Parental, Peer Factors on Teen, Young Adult Substance Abuse," *NIDA* 18 (2003), pages 11–13.

166 *The study found that a teenager with "hands-on" parents is four times less likely* "National Survey of American Attitudes on Substance Abuse XVII," a report from the National Center on Addiction and Substance Abuse at Columbia University (2012), http://www.casacolumbia.org /templates/ChairmanStatements.aspx?articleid=691&zoneid=31 (accessed August 31, 2013).

Chapter Ten: iTeens: Media and Technology

174 *Young people ages eight to eighteen* "Generation M: Media in the Lives of 8–18 Year Olds," report from the Kaiser Family Foundation, January 20, 2010, http://kaiserfamilyfoundation.files.wordpress. com/2013/04/8010.pdf (accessed June 4, 2013).

174 *Seventy-eight percent of twelve- to seventeen-year-olds* "Teens and Technology 2013," Pew Internet and American Life Project, March 13, 2013, http://www.pewinternet.org/~/media//Files/Reports/2013/PIP _TeensandTechnology2013.pdf (accessed June 4, 2013).

174 *. . . exchange an average of 167 texts per day* "Teens, Smartphones & Texting," Pew Internet and American Life Project, March 19, 2012, http://www.pewinternet.org/~/media//Files/Reports/2012/PIP_Teens _Smartphones_and_Texting.pdf (accessed June 4, 2013).

175 *. . . almost a third of young people* "Teens and Online Video," Pew Internet and American Life Project, May 3, 2012, http://www .pewinternet.org/Reports/2012/Teens-and-online-video.aspx (accessed June 4, 2013).

178 *The headline read* A. Boyle, "15-Year-Old Astronaut Abby Fuels Her Outreach Mission With Social Media," *NBC News,* May 8, 2013, http:// www.nbcnews.com/science/15-year-old-astronaut-abby-fuels-her- outreach-mission-social-1C9847623.

179 *Sixty-nine percent say that their peers are "mostly kind"* "Teens, Kindness, and Cruelty on Social Network Sites," Pew Internet and American Life Project, November 9, 2011, http://pewinternet.org/Reports/2011 /Teens-and-social-media/Summary/Majority-of-teens.aspx (accessed June 4, 2013).

179 *Researchers with the University of California's Digital Youth Project* M. Ito et al., "Hanging Out, Messing Around, and Geeking Out: Kids Living and Learning With New Media" (2010), http://mitpress.mit.edu/sites /default/files/titles/free_download/9780262013369%20_Hanging_Out .pdf (accessed June 4, 2013).

179   *Researchers with the Connected Learning Research Network* M. Ito et al.,
       "Connected Learning: An Agenda for Research and Design," January
       2013, http://dmlhub.net/sites/default/files/ConnectedLearning_report
       .pdf (accessed June 4, 2013).

181   *Researchers with the MacArthur Research Network on Youth and
       Participatory Politics* C. Cohen and J. Kahne, "Participatory Politics:
       New Media and Youth Political Participation," June 2012, http://ypp
       .dmlcentral.net/sites/all/files/publications/YPP_Survey_Report_FULL
       .pdf (accessed June 4, 2013).

181   *One of the most powerful Internet safety videos* http://thedigitalcitizen.ca
       /portfolio/the-digital-citizen/ (accessed July 20, 2013).

181   *A group of high school students in Tulsa, Oklahoma, created a campaign*
       http://www.projectunmask.com/ (accessed July 22, 2013).

181   *The University of California's Mimi Ito describes the new digital divide*
       M. Ito et al., "Connected Learning: An Agenda for Research and
       Design," January 2013, http://dmlhub.net/sites/default/files
       /ConnectedLearning_report.pdf (accessed June 4, 2013).

182   *Senior researcher at Microsoft Dana Boyd reminds us* Matt Richtel,
       "Wasting Time Is New Divide in Digital Era," *New York Times*, May 29,
       2012.

182   *Nearly a third of the time adolescents use media* "Generation M: Media in
       the Lives of 8–18 Year Olds," report from the Kaiser Family
       Foundation, January 20, 2010, http://kaiserfamilyfoundation.files
       .wordpress.com/2013/04/8010.pdf (accessed June 4, 2013).

182   *For example, a researcher in the United Kingdom* G. Small and G. Vorgan,
       iBrain: Surviving the Technological Alteration of the Modern Mind (New
       York: HarperCollins, 2008), page 21.

182   *A couple of researchers at Cornell proved this* H. Hembroke and G. Gay,
       "The Laptop and the Lecture: The Effects of Multitasking in Learning
       Environments," *Journal of Computing in Higher Education* 15 (2003),
       pages 46–64.

183   *As Nass puts it, heavy media multitaskers are "suckers for irrelevancy"*
       A. Gorlick, "Media Multitaskers Pay Mental Price, Stanford Study
       Shows," *Stanford News*, August 24, 2009, http://news.stanford.edu
       /news/2009/august24/multitask-research-study-082409.html
       (accessed June 4, 2013).

184   *For starters, neuroscientist Jaak Panksepp at Washington State University*
       J. Panksepp, "Affective Neuroscience: The Foundations of Human and
       Animal Emotions" (New York: Oxford University Press, 1998), pages
       144–163.

184   *University of Virginia's Daniel Willingham adds* A lecture by Daniel
       Willingham at Learning and the Brain Conference, Arlington,
       Virginia, spring 2013.

185   *A recent study found that drivers were more likely to engage in risky driving*

C. Holland and V. Rathod, "Influence of Personal Mobile Phone Ringing and Usual Intention to Answer on Driver Error," *Accident Analysis and Prevention* 50 (2013).

186 *Emerging research shows it does and underlines the need to balance* C. Nass et al., "Media Use, Face-to-Face Communication, Media Multitasking, and Social Well-Being Among 8–12 Year Old Girls," *Developmental Psychology* 48 (2012).

188 *Depending upon the study* Pew Internet and American Life, "Teens and Sexting," December 15, 2009, and National Campaign to Prevent Teen Pregnancy, "Sex and Tech," December 2, 2008.

189 *Believe it or not, young people still spend an average of thirty hours* "Generation M: Media in the Lives of 8–18 Year Olds," report from the Kaiser Family Foundation, January 20, 2010, http://kaiserfamilyfoundation.files.wordpress.com/2013 /04/8010.pdf (accessed June 4, 2013).

189 *For example, a RAND Corporation study* Rebecca L. Collins et al., "Watching Sex on Television Predicts Adolescent Initiation of Sexual Behavior," *Pediatrics* 114 (2004), pages 280–289.

190 *Pro-social video games encourage helpful behavior in our kids* D. Gentile, et al., "The Effects of Prosocial Video Games on Prosocial Behaviors: International Evidence from Correlational, Longitudinal, and Experimental Studies," *Personality and Social Psychology Bulletin* 35 (2009), pages 752–763.

190 *Hyperviolent games tend to do the opposite* V. Strasburger and E. Donnerstein, "The New Media of Violent Video Games: Yet Same Old Media Problems," *Clinical Pediatrics,* August 22, 2013 (e-published before print).

190 *Media violence is a risk factor* D. Gentile and B. Bushman, "Reassessing Media Violence Effects Using a Risk and Resilience Approach to Understanding Aggression," *Psychology of Popular Media Culture* 1 (July 2012).

191 *The average young person will spend* Jane McGonical, "We spend 3 billion hours a week as a planet playing videogames. Is it worth it? How could it be MORE worth it?" TED Conversations, http://www.ted .com/conversations/44/we_spend_3_billion_hours_a_wee.html.

191 *We know now that there is a direct connection between heavy screen time* J. Boone, P. Gordon-Larson, L. Adair, et al., "Screen Time and Physical Activity During Adolescence: Longitudinal Effects of Obesity in Young Adulthood," *International Journal of Behavioral Nutrition and Physical Activity* 4 (2007).

192 *Recent research indicates that the prevalence of pathological gaming* D. Gentile et al., "Pathological Video Game Use Among Youths: A Two-Year Longitudinal Study," *Pediatrics* 127 (2011), pages 319–329.

Chapter Eleven: Food, Exercise, and the Story Behind Tired Teens

202 *Although our brains account for only about 2 percent of our bodies' mass* John Medina, *Brain Rules* (Seattle: Pear Press, 2008), page 39.

205 *You might be surprised to learn that our brains are mostly made of fat* Nicola Graimes, *Brain Foods for Kids: Over a Hundred Recipes to Boost Your Child's Intelligence* (Illinois: Delta, 2005), pages 12–15.

205 *Neuroscientists have found that the brain functions* Fernando Gómez-Pinilla, "Brain Foods: The Effects of Nutrients on Brain Function," *Nature Reviews Neuroscience* 9 (July 2008), http://www.nature.com /nrn/journal/v9/n7/abs/nrn2421.html (accessed February 9, 2009).

206 *The brain needs thirty-eight of the forty-five nutrients* Lise Eliot, PhD, *What's Going On in There? How the Brain and Mind Develop in the First Five Years of Life* (New York: Bantam Books, 1999), page 446.

206 *. . . antioxidants come to the rescue by neutralizing free radicals* Larry McCleary, MD, *The Brain Trust Program* (New York: Penguin, 2007), page 83.

207 *Virginia Tech University nutritionist Kiyah Duffey* Kiyah Duffey, "Rise, Shine and Eat: Why Breakfast Boosts Your Child's Brain Power," http://drdavewalsh.com/posts/159 (accessed July 12, 2013).

207 *A University of Minnesota study found that teens who eat with their families* Gary Small and Gigi Vorgan, *iBrain: Surviving the Technological Alteration of the Modern Mind* (New York: HarperCollins, 2008), pages 92–95.

208 *While all the students benefited, Barney's transformation* Interview conducted by CBC News at http://www.johnratey.com (accessed July 16, 2013).

209 *The aerobic mice showed impressive brain growth* Henriette van Praag, Brian R. Christie, Terrence J. Sejnowski, et al., "Running Enhances Neurogenesis, Learning, and Long-term Potentiation in Mice," *Proceedings of the National Academy of Science* 96, (1999), pages 13427–13431.

209 *Now neuroscientists can study children's brains with MRIs* Michelle Ploughman, "Exercise Is Brain Food: The Effects of Physical Activity on Cognitive Function," *Developmental Neurorehabilitation* 11 (July 2008), pages 236–240.

210 *This acronym stands for brain-derived neurotrophic factor* John J. Ratey, *Spark: The Revolutionary New Science of Exercise and the Brain* (New York: Little, Brown, 2008), page 40.

210 *Like fertilizer in the garden, BDNF sprouted new dendrites* Ibid, pages 38–39.

210 *Besides benefiting the hippocampus, Barney's workout* Charles Hillman et al., "Aerobic Fitness and Cognitive Development: Event-Related Brain Potential and Task Performance Indices of Executive Control in

Preadolescent Children," *Developmental Psychology* 45 (January 2009), pages 114–129.

211 *The evidence is clear that it translates into better school performance* John Ratey in a speech at the Learning and the Brain Conference, Arlington, Virginia, May 4, 2013.

214 *At puberty, two big changes affect sleep patterns* M. H. Hagenauer, J. I. Perryman, T. M. Lee, et al., "Adolescent Changes in the Homeostatic and Circadian Regulation of Sleep," *Developmental Neuroscience* 31 (2009), pages 276–284.

215 *Scientists believe that as many as fifty* H. Heimer, "Who's in Charge Here? Orchestrating Sleep and Waking in the Brain," *BrainWork* (July-August 2003), pages 6–7.

216 *This shift has been further exaggerated for twenty-first-century teens* M. A. Carskadon, "Sleep in Adolescents: The Perfect Storm," *Pediatric Clinics of North America* 58 (2011), pages 637–647.

217 *Sleep deprivation is not a trivial problem* W. D. Kilgore, "Effects of Sleep Deprivation on Cognition," *Progress in Brain Research* 185 (2010), pages 105–129.

219 *It's not clear yet if grades in these schools are up or not* Kyla Wahlstrom, "Changing Times: Findings from the First Longitudinal Study of Later High School Start Times," *NASSP Bulletin* 86, no. 633 (December 2002), pages 3–21.

Chapter Twelve: When Things Go Wrong in the Brain: Adolescent Mental Illness

223 *Teenagers who cut themselves* Steven Levenkron, *Cutting: Understanding and Overcoming Self-Mutilation* (New York: W. W. Norton, 1999), page 19.

226 *ADD and ADHD are the most common* L. Eugene Arnold, *Contemporary Diagnosis and Management of Attention Deficit/Hyperactivity Disorder* (Longboat Key, FL: Handbooks in Healthcare, 2002).

228 *That concern was put to rest in 2013 when a very large study* K. L. Humphreys, T. Eng, and S. S. Lee, "Meta-analysis of the Longitudinal Association of Stimulant Medication Teatment for ADHD and Substance Use and Abuse/Dependence," *JAMA: Psychiatry* (2013), page 1273.

230 *Among the telltale signs of teenage depression; Diagnostic Criteria from DSM-IV* (Arlington, VA: American Psychiatric Association, 1994).

231 *On the rise for American teens for more than fifty years* "Suicide: Facts at a Glance, 2012," Centers for Disease Control and Prevention, www.cdc.gov/violenceprevention/pdf/Suicide-DataSheet-a.pdf (accessed August 1, 2013).

232 *Doctors commonly prescribe a group* Z. Moldenhauer and B. Mazurek Melnyk, "Use of Antidepressants in the Treatment of Child and Adolescent Depression: Are They Effective?" *Pediatric Nursing* 25 (1999), pages 643–644.

233 *Anorexia nervosa is a serious disorder* A. Cotter, *Anorexia and Bulimia: Diseases and Disorders* (Farmington Hills, MI: Lucent Books, 2001).

237 *. . . the part of his brain responsible for shifting* Daniel Amen, *Healing the Hardware of the Soul* (New York: Free Press, 2002), page 54.

238 *With the passage of the Mental Health Parity and Addiction Equity Act* "Mental Health Parity and Addiction Equity," http://beta.samhsa.gov /health-reform/parity (accessed August 31, 2013).

Chapter Thirteen: Friends, Peers, and Identity

252 *Canadian psychologist Tracy Vaillancourt, for example, reports* T. Vaillancourt, E. Duku, D. Decantanzaro, et al., "Variation in Hypothalamic–Pituitary–Adrenal Axis Activity among Bullied and Non-bullied Children," *Aggressive Behavior* 34 (2008), pages 294–305.

252 *Harvard scientist Martin Teicher scanned the brains of bullying victims* M. H. Teicher, J. A. Samson, Y. S. Sheu, et al., "Hurtful Words: Exposure to Peer Verbal Aggression Is Associated with Elevated Psychiatric Symptom Scores and Corpus Callosum Abnormalities," *American Journal of Psychiatry* 167 (2010), pages 1464–1471.

255 *Avoid peer mediation as a strategy to resolve bullying* David Farrington and Maria Ttofi, "School-Based Programs to Reduce Bullying and Victimization," *Campbell Systematic Reviews* 6 (December 2009), pages 1–148.

259 *A Duke University psychologist and his team* J. Chein, D. Albert, L. O'Brien, et al., "Peers Increase Adolescent Risk Taking by Enhancing Activity in the Brain's Reward Circuitry," *Developmental Science* 14 (2011), pages F1–F10.

Chapter Fourteen: The Importance of Connection and Guidance

269 *Brain science helps us understand that connection is essential* Paul Tough, *How Children Succeed: Grit, Curiosity and the Hidden Power of Character* (New York: Mariner Books, 2013), pages 33–40.

270 *Adolescents who feel connected to their family are more likely to delay* I. Borowsky, M. Ireland, and M. Resnick, "Violence Risk and Protective Factors Among Youth in School," *Ambulatory Pediatrics* 2 (2002), pages 475–484.

270 *Young people who feel connected to adults in their schools are more* "School Connectedness: Strategies for Increasing Protective Factors Among Youth," report from the Centers for Disease Control and Prevention,2009, http://www.cdc.gov/healthyyouth/adolescenthealth /pdf/connectedness.pdf (accessed July 7, 2013).

271 *This means that a network of positive connections* M. Resnick, "Healthy Youth Development: Getting Our Priorities Right," *Medical Journal of Australia* 183 (2005), pages 398–400.

271 *Dr. Benson said that a spark is exactly what it sounds like* Peter Benson,

Sparks: How Parents Can Help Ignite the Hidden Strengths of Teenagers (San Francisco: Jossey-Bass, 2008).

271   *Several studies show that creative arts, athletics* "Finding the Student Spark: Missed Opportunities in School Engagement," an *Insights and Evidence Report from Search Institute* 5 no. 1 (November 2010).

271   *Likewise, the Commission on Children at Risk* "Hardwired to Connect: The New Scientific Case for Authoritative Communities," a report of the Commission on Children at Risk (New York: Institute for American Values, 2003), http://www.americanvalues.org/ExSumm -print.pdf (accessed August 25, 2013).

271   *Though teens tell researchers that they want close relationships* M. Ungar, "The Importance of Parents and Other Caregivers to the Resilience of High-Risk Adolescents," *Family Process* 43 (2004), pages 23–41.

277   *Researchers at Search Institute asked teens* "Teen Voice 2010: Relationships That Matter to Teenagers," a publication of Search Institute and Best Buy Children's Foundation, 2010, http://www .search-institute.org/sites/default/files/a/TeenVoice2010.pdf (accessed August 24, 2013).

ACKNOWLEDGMENTS

I have been putting the thoughts together for this book for many years. My first debt of gratitude, therefore, goes to the thousands of adolescents whom I have had the privilege and pleasure of teaching, coaching, and counseling during the past four decades. Some of their stories are included in these pages with names and identifying details changed. All of the adolescents I have met over the years taught me much more than any books or research papers ever could. Thank you.

I learned the most about adolescence from my own three children. Dan, Brian, and Erin are all parents themselves now, having survived whatever mistakes Monica and I made along the way. Many of their stories are also in these pages, but all their identifying facts are still intact.

It is important for caring adults to be involved in adolescents' lives. All three of our kids were fortunate to have an extended family who stayed closely connected with them. Dale and Karen Panton, and Cathy Seward and Tom Peichel were always there for Dan, Brian, and Erin to count on. Bob and Josie Donnelly were as well, and one of our great losses was Josie's death since the first edition of this book appeared.

As for the book, I'm indebted to many others who helped me bring it to this form. My literary agent, Marly Rusoff, has been a source of expert guidance and constant encouragement. My Atria editors, Leslie Meredith and Donna Loffredo, combined an enthusiasm for the project with suggestions that were always an improvement. Field experts, also known as parents of adolescents, have provided helpful feedback, especially in the past decade as the first edition circulated to so many.

The actual writing has been a wonderful partnership. I continue to appreciate the contributions of my friend and writer, Nat Bennett, who was so helpful in the first edition. It has been particularly gratifying to me to have my daughter, Erin, do so much of the heavy lifting—both research and writing—in this updated version.

Finally, my wife, Monica, has been my partner in every aspect of this project. Just as she did ten years ago, she has left her imprint on every page in this edition. More than anything else, however, I am grateful to her for marrying me more than forty-three years ago and for teaching me so much about being a parent.

INDEX

ABOUT THE AUTHORS

DAVID WALSH, PhD, has emerged as one of the country's leading authorities on adolescents, parenting, and family life. He spent ten years teaching and coaching high school students before joining Fairview Health Services in Minneapolis to develop and direct innovative counseling programs for youth and families. He founded and led the internationally renowned National Institute on Media and the Family for twelve years before founding Mind Positive Parenting. He is also on the faculty at the University of Minnesota. As a psychologist he has counseled thousands of individuals and families.

Dr. Walsh is a highly sought-after speaker and has presented workshops to parents, educators, and other professionals throughout the world. A consultant to the World Health Organization and the Ministries of Education of Japan, South Korea, and Singapore, he has testified before congressional committees on numerous occasions. He gives workshops that blend humor, warmth, scientific substance, and practical advice. Dr. Walsh's books have been translated into eight languages. He has written scores of articles for professional and popular publications.

Dr. Walsh is a frequent guest on national radio and television. He has appeared on NBC's *Today Show, Good Morning America, The CBS Morning Show, The News Hour with Jim Lehrer, Dateline NBC,* ABC's *20/20,* National Public Radio's *All Things Considered* and *Morning Edition,* and has been featured on three nationally broadcast PBS specials. He has been the recipient of numerous awards, including the Council on Family Relations' Friend of the Family Award.

He received his BA degree from Mount Carmel College, his MA degree from the University of St. Thomas in Saint Paul, and his PhD in educational psychology from the University of Minnesota. He and his wife, Monica, have three adult children and a growing number of grandchildren. They live in Minneapolis, Minnesota.

ERIN WALSH, MA, is an in-demand speaker and trainer throughout North America on parenting, the role of technology in youth development, and raising resilient teenagers in the Digital Age. She is a co-founder of Mind Positive Parenting. In addition, Erin teaches at the University of Minnesota and the Higher Education Consortium for Urban Affairs (HECUA) and provides training for Youth Frontiers. In her work with HECUA she is the program director of a program for college students called Making Media, Making Change.

Erin has worked with youth and teens for more than a decade and serves as the board chair for YMCA Camp Widjiwagan, a wilderness-based youth-development program. She has written extensively on youth development and parenting. She lives in Minneapolis with her partner and two children.